MAKING A DIFFERENCE SCHOLARSHIPS
FOR A BETTER WORLD

Third Edition

MIRIAM WEINSTEIN

SAGEWORKS PRESS
SAN ANSELMO CA

Publisher's Cataloging-in-Publication
(Provided by Quality Books, Inc.)

Weinstein, Miriam (Miriam H.)
  Making a difference : scholarships for a better world
/ Miriam Weinstein. -- 3rd ed.
  p. cm.
  Includes index.
  ISBN 0-9634618-7-7

  1. Scholarships--United States-- Directories.
2. Social Action--Scholarships, fellowships, etc.--
Directories. 3. Environmentalism--Scholarships,
fellowships, etc.--Directories. 4. Universities and
colleges--Moral and ethical aspects--United States--
Directories.   I.Title.

LB2338.W39 2003   378.3'4'0973
                           QBI03-200056

Thanks to Radha Blackman for all her work in preparing the third edition.

Cover design by Miriam Weinstein
Published by SageWorks Press
            P.O. Box 441
            Fairfax, CA 94978
            1. 800. 218.4242
            www.sageworks.net
            info@sageworks.net

Please contact SageWorks for bulk discount pricing for non-profits, youth, social change, environmental, service and other similar organizations.

Also by Miriam Weinstein: Making A Difference College & Graduate Guide: Education to Help you Shape the World Anew

Making a Difference
Scholarships
For a Better World

Dear Friends,

If you are reading this book, I assume you are one of the wonderful, remarkable young people who are working to make a better world. While collecting the scholarship and award information to print in this book, I have had the absolute privilege of reading about many of your peers who have already received awards for their work. I don't know if I can adequately express the range of feelings I experienced: admiration, awe, excitement, and hope.

This introduction is primarily written for students preparing to go to college, but there is lots of good information in it for graduate students as well. Graduate students should be sure to read the additional introduction on fellowships from Who Cares Magazine.

There is so much meaningful community work being done by teens today, an age which most adults and the media in our society relegate to a wasteland of slackers, drugs, graffiti and violence. You are truly inspirational. You are the hope of the future. I wish there were hundreds and thousands more scholarships and awards for you. Even without them you clearly find reward enough in the volunteer work you are doing, or you wouldn't be doing it. This is heartening.

There are several different sections in this book. There are scholarships from colleges to their own entering and continuing students who do community service. There are scholarships for students majoring or interested in areas of importance for making a difference - health, environment, peace and more. Then there are awards and fellowships for young people actively engaged in working for a better world. Many of these sponsors also give generously to organizations you have started, are starting or for which you are working. And, lastly, a good number of these awards are just that - awards or project funds, not scholarships. This means you are eligible even if you aren't college bound or, alternatively, have already graduated from college or grad school.

Please be especially careful about not applying for awards or scholarships for which you are not eligible. In particular, the scholarships listed by individual colleges are either awarded automatically as part of your application to the college (sometimes through applying for financial aid) or are for students already in attendance. Do not contact these colleges for information regarding these scholarships unless you are applying/attending there. The information is primarily included to encourage you to consider applying to these colleges, and to acknowledge those colleges that are truly supportive of students working to make a better world.

To heighten you chances of success:

• Start your search early in your junior year, or even at the end of your sophomore year. There are a good number of major awards that are limited to high school juniors (hey, it takes time to read 100,000 essays).

• Get organized. Keep track of your community service hours and organizations, and of any awards or honors you may have received. Keep copies of recommendations, newspaper clippings, photos.

• Be aware that the availability, criteria for, and size of scholarships are always subject to change. By the time you read this book, some of these awards may be out of date or no longer in effect, while others will have become available. Phone numbers and area codes change, etc. Always double-check.

• Be timely, apply early. The "Apply by" dates should be read as "received by" this date. So if it says "Apply by January 15" assume your application needs to be there by January 15. In other words, allowing for holidays, snow, etc., mail your application January 1. Although some listings say "postmarked by" such and such a date - play it safe, act as if your application should be there by that date. Remember, Federal Express and UPS will not deliver mail addressed to a post office box, and therefore should not be used if a post office box is given. If you are mailing to a post office box and running late, use Express Mail from the Postal Service. One organization told me some local schools were closed for two weeks because of a snow storm. Students couldn't get to the guidance office to get the application forms. Their late applications were not accepted, even though it wasn't the students fault.

• Double-check dates again. The dates in this guide have often been changed to "mid- March or mid-April" - when you see an inexact date call, write, email, check with the appropriate person at your school or college, or visit the web site and get the exact date. Assume your materials need to be there by that date not just postmarked.

• Be neat and thorough. Type your responses, or do them on your computer. When an organization receives thousands and thousands of essays, they might not bother with yours if it is hard to read.

• If your application requires letters of recommendation, give the person plenty of time. If you need three references, maybe there are five people you could ask - just to be safe. Don't ask your teacher or organization leader at the last minute. Not only are they busy, but you also want to give them time to write a thoughtful recommendation. Give them a stamped addressed envelope so they can mail it back to you.

• Keep accurate records of all community service or civic/peace/environmental actions with which you have been involved. Is there a newspaper article in which you are mentioned? Save it. Something on the web? Download it. Colleges tell us they want students engaged in working for a better world more than ever, but some are starting to check to see if you have actually done what you say you have.

• Follow instructions. If the directions say to send a stamped, self-addressed envelope, be sure to do so. Use a #10 size envelope (that's the long one). And don't wait until 10 days before your application is due to send in your request. If the listing says for instance "call only to get a list of coordinators", please limit your calls to the stated purpose. Apply to the right place! If it says apply through your guidance counselor, check with them before calling the organization.

• Use the web. Scholarship/fellowship information often changes, and this is the best way to make sure that the information is up-to-date. Many of the scholarship/fellowship sources allow you to download applications directly from their web sites and, in some cases to apply on-line. If you decide to apply on-line ,download the materials first, take your time, and do a careful job of going through them; when you are completely ready, go back and do the on-line application.

• The eligibility criteria and application information listed in the guide are generally abbreviated. Double-check to see if you need an application form, if you meet all the criteria, and if you have all the materials requested. If the scholarship says it is limited to high school juniors, do not apply if you are a senior.

• Once again, if the scholarship or award is college-based, do not contact the college unless you are applying or already in attendance there.

• Applications are often available (even on web sites) for only a month or so prior to the deadline. If you look on a web site and don't find information, check back closer to the "apply by" date.

There are also many organizations in your own city or county which may offer scholarships and awards to local students involved in community service. Check with your local Rotary, Circle K, and other similar groups. Perhaps you have a local community foundation which has scholarships available. Of course, there are hundreds and hundreds of other scholarships than those listed here - and you shouldn't limit yourself to the ones in this book; but these scholarships and awards are directed to you, the very special young people working to make a better community, nation and world.

About College...

Apply to all the colleges you are interested in, and get your financial aid applications in early. Your background of consistent community service or activism will make you extra attractive to most colleges and graduate schools. Never count yourself out of a private college because of finances. Depending on your family income, you can often get a better financial aid offer from an expensive private college than from a state school. This means it won't cost any more to attend a college that costs $25,000 a year than one that costs $5,000 a year. Tell your parents to read this sentence 10 times!

You and your parents need to be aware of the financial aid policy regarding scholarships at the college you choose to attend. While some colleges will credit you the whole scholarship you receive, other colleges will decrease their own institutional grant aid correspondingly - from 25% to even 100%. Work to get an agreement with them that they will not penalize you more than 25% of the award. Make sure they will honor the agreement as long as your are in attendance. Get it in writing. And I'm sorry to say this but, depending upon the size of the award, in conjunction with your financial aid, you could be looking at taxes.

You might want to consider AmeriCorps as an option for getting some great experience and extra money for college. By the way, that money is also taxable.

Does your college counselor, school, public library, or local bookstore have a copy of Making A Difference College & Graduate Guide, Education To Help You Shape The World Anew? If not, recommend it to them! One way or another, get your hands on a copy. The colleges in it are looking for people like you. You'll find the Guide a fascinating introduction to higher education - much of it engaged, hands-on, and community based. I guarantee there are many distinctive colleges in it that you've never heard of, that aren't listed in other college guides, and that your guidance/college counselor will probably never recommend - but that you'll be very enthused to learn about.

A college counselor who works with AmeriCorps in Rhode Island sent 300 students in 3 years to colleges that she learned of from Making A Difference College & Graduate Guide! She said the book is a lifesaver for students who want to make a difference. So, go find yourself a college which is a good fit for you -- not just academically and financially, but also spiritually, politically, and ethically.

The Making A Difference College & Graduate Guide also has information about Peace Corps Masters Internationalist and Peace Corps Fellows Programs which offer special financial benefits to students.

For students who are about to graduate college, or are recent graduates but not planning on graduate school, please read both the first Kitchen Sink section and the graduate section. Both have fellowships offered by community organizations apart from academia.

Once again, good luck on finding a scholarship and sincere appreciation to you for being a caring, involved, contributing human being. I am truly moved by your efforts, and because of you, the world is a better place. Please remember to vote, it's crucial.

Miriam Weinstein
www.making-a-difference.com
mw@sageworks.net

The Kitchen Sink

◇ ◇ ◇

Incredibly Great Awards

for

High School

College

Graduate School Students

including

Community - Based

Fellowships

AAJA - Asian American Journalist Association

Offers scholarships to outstanding high school seniors and undergraduate and graduate students. Students are selected based on the following criteria: commitment to the field of journalism; sensitivity to Asian American issues as demonstrated by community involvement; journalistic ability; financial need.

National AAJA General Scholarship Awards

For students pursuing careers in print, broadcast or photo journalism.

Award: up to $2,000

AAJA S.I. Newhouse National Scholarship And Internship Awards

For college students pursuing careers in print journalism. While the scholarship is open to all students, AAJA especially encourages applicants from historically underrepresented Asian Pacific American groups, including Vietnamese, Cambodians, Hmong and other Southeast Asians, South Asians and Pacific Islanders. S.I. Newhouse Scholarship winners will be eligible for Summer Internships with a Newhouse publication.

Award: up to $5,000

Minoru Yasui Memorial Scholarship Award

Awarded to a promising Asian American male broadcaster. A civil rights advocate and attorney, Minoru Yasui was one of three Nisei who challenged the internment of Japanese Americans during World War II.

Award: $1,500

Mary Moy Quan Ing Memorial Scholarship

For a graduating high school senior who is enrolling in college and pursuing a journalism career.

Award: $1,500

AAJA Local Competitions

Many AAJA chapters offer local scholarships or internship competitions. Students residing near or attending school in an area served by an AAJA chapter may be eligible to apply. Call the Asian American Journalists Association's national office for information on availability of local scholarships.

For more information:

programs@aaja.org   (415) 346-2051

www.aaja.org/html/programs_html/programs_scholarships.html

Alston/Bannerman Fellowship For Minority Activists

Honors outstanding activists of color and gives them an opportunity for reflection and renewal. Fellows receive stipends of $15,000 for sabbaticals of three months or more. The Bannerman Program recognizes that working for social change usually means long hours at low pay, with few tangible rewards and few escapes from the day-to-day pressures. Without time to stop and reflect, the pressures can prove overwhelming; but without resources, it is impossible to take the time. Therefore, the Fellowship gives long-time activists of color the financial support and freedom to take a break and recharge.

The Bannerman Program also seeks applicants who have helped to build community organizations or institutions that have a clearly defined and involved constituency, address significant social and economic issues, have had tangible success and acknowledge the cultural values of the community; have demonstrated a strong commitment to grassroots leadership development; and have contributed to building a movement for social change —-for example, by defining new strategies or issues, by organizing new constituencies, or by developing networks, alliances or coalitions to advance a progressive agenda. In addition, preference will be given to applicants who have a special need for a sabbatical; have more than ten years of experience; are working with low-income people; and are working at the grassroots level.

Fellows work on a broad range of issues from environmental justice to fair wages, from immigrant rights to native sovereignty, from political empowerment to economic revitalization and have been community and labor organizers, volunteer leaders, and cultural workers and community developers. Fellows use their sabbaticals however they think will best re-energize them for the work ahead.

Eligibility: person of color; at least ten years experience as a community activist; resident of the US or its territories.

Stipend: $15,000

Given: 10

Apply by: December 1

For more information:

Bannerman Fellowship Program
1627 Lancaster Street
Baltimore, MD 21231

(410) 327-6220
info@Alston/Bannerman.org
www.bannermanfellowship.org

AmeriCorps Promise Fellows

The AmeriCorps Promise Fellows Program is an opportunity for people who have demonstrated leadership skills and a commitment to service in their communities. Fellows serve for one year as leaders with national, state, and local nonprofit organizations - coordinating activities intended to support children and youth. For example, Fellows may: Develop a youth service program at a Volunteer Center; replicate a successful after-school program across the school district; train volunteers to enlist low-income families in health insurance programs; create a job-shadowing program for high school students; or establish a statewide database of effective practices for mentoring programs.

In addition, AmeriCorps Promise Fellows gain valuable experience and skills that can be personally rewarding and open up new professional opportunities. Fellows are recruited directly by local and national nonprofit organizations. List is available at the web site below.

Organizations employing AmeriCorps Promise Fellows include the I Have A Dream Foundation; State Commissions for Community Service; Camp Fire Boys and Girls; City Year; Communities in Schools; National Association of Community Health Centers; National Jewish Partnership for Social Justice; Notre Dame Mission Volunteer Program; Oglala Sioux Tribe; Points of Light

Foundation; and the Youth Volunteer Corps of America

Eligibility: Qualifications vary, but many positions require a bachelor's degree and/or professional experience in a particular field. Appropriate backgrounds include recent graduates, part-time students, advance degree candidates in public policy, social work, public health, and business schools; professionals in nonprofits, corporations, other private sector organizations, education; and alumni of AmeriCorps, Peace Corps, the military, and other service organizations.

Award: $13,000 living allowance + benefits, $4,725 education award.

Given: 550 - 1,000

For more information:

Corporation for National Service	1-800-942-2677
promise@cns.gov	www.americorps.org/promise/index.html

ASHOKA FELLOWSHIP

Ashoka is a global not-for-profit organization that finds and supports outstanding individuals with ideas for far-reaching social change. The men and women who become Ashoka Fellows share a strong entrepreneurial character as well as their passion for social causes. Social entrepreneurs are people whose creativity and drive open up major new possibilities in education, health, the environment, and other areas of human need. Just as business entrepreneurs lead innovation in commerce, social entrepreneurs drive social change.

The strength of the Fellowship depends on its electing only the highest quality social entrepreneurs with the most powerful ideas. Ashoka seeks creative, ethical, entrepreneurial people with truly new and practical ideas for solving a public need. Nominators, who are usually from the same country and work in the same field as the candidate, seek out nominees and screen their qualifications.

For more information:

Ashoka headquarters	(703) 527-8300
1700 North Moore St., 2000	info@ashoka.org
Arlington, VA 22209	www.ashoka.org

GLORIA BARRON PRIZE FOR YOUNG HEROES

The Barron Prize recognizes young people from diverse backgrounds who have shown extraordinary leadership in making our world better — whether by protecting the environment, helping people, halting violence, or leading other important service work. Past winners have organized a rodeo for disabled kids; led the effort to conserve a local river; and created a scholarship fund for African girls.

Eligibility: residents of the U.S.A. or Canada, aged 8-18, must be nominated by responsible adults — teachers, librarians, civic or religious leaders, or others — who have solid knowledge of a young person's heroic activities, and who are not related to the nominee.

Award: $2,000	# Given: 10
Nominate by: May 31	

For more information:

The Barron Prize

P.O. Box 17
Boulder, CO 80306-0017

ba_richman@barronprize.org
www.barronprize.org

BROWER ENVIRONMENTAL AWARD FOR YOUTH LEADERSHIP

Every year, youth across the country lead projects to conserve, preserve and restore the earth. Earth Island Institute acknowledges these leaders these environmental heroes. Recipients are chosen for their outstanding and innovative environmental achievements.

Award: $3000   # Given: 6

For more information:

www.earthisland.org/bya/

CANON NATIONAL ENVIROTHON

The National Envirothon is an annual competition for high school students throughout North America. The best teams from over 50 states and provinces compete with one another in five subjects: Wildlife, Forestry, Soil, Aquatics, and Current Environmental Issues. The first, second, and third place team members win scholarships for college or trade school.

The Envirothon Extra Mile Award is given to the team demonstrating the most spirit, cooperation, leadership, and friendship. Winners are recognized at the awards banquet, and the team receives $100 cash and a trophy.

Team Awards: 1st Place $3,000 per student

2nd Place $2,000 per student

3rd Place $1,000 per student

Competition dates vary from state to state.

For more information:

Kay Asher, Program Coordinator

Nat'l. Association. of Conservation Districts

P.O. Box 855, League City

Texas 77574-0855

800-825-5547 extension 16

envirothon@nacdnet.org

www.envirothon.org

fax (281)332-5259

CANON NATIONAL PARKS SCIENCE SCHOLARS

The Science Scholars Program aims to support research on critical problems facing the region's national parks, encourage the use of national parks as laboratories for science, and develop world leaders in science and conservation, by encouraging the best graduate students in the Americas to conduct research critical for conserving national parks throughout the region. For this program, the Americas include Canada, the United States, Mexico, the countries of Central and South America, and the countries of the Caribbean.

The program awards scholarships to support student research in the national parks. Discipline areas are biological sciences (such as botany or ecology), physical sciences (such as geology, hydrology and atmospheric sciences), social/cultural sciences (such as economics, sociology, anthropology and archeology), and technology innovation in support of conservation science (in such fields as informatics, remote sensing, photomonitoring, and radiotelemetry).

Eligibility: Enrolled in a doctoral program in the Americas, have (or will soon have) completed their coursework, prepared approved dissertation.

Award: $25,000   # Given: 2 per topic (8) renewable

$2,000   # Given: 4

Apply by: July 1

For more information:

Dr. Gary E. Machlis, Program Coordinator   (208) 885.7054

Canon National Parks Science Scholars Program   gmachlis@uidaho.edu

University of Idaho, College of Natural Resources, Room 16

PO Box 441133, Sixth and Line Streets

Moscow, ID 83844-1133   www.nature.nps.gov/canonscholarships/

CAPTAIN PLANET

The Captain Planet Foundation seeks to facilitate and support hands-on environmental projects for children and youth. The objective is to encourage innovative programs that empower children around the world to work individually and collectively to solve environmental problems in their neighborhoods and communities. Through environmental awareness and education, we believe that children can achieve a better understanding and appreciation for the world in which they live.

Winning projects must: promote understanding of environmental issues; focus on hands-on involvement; promote interaction and cooperation within the group; help develop planning and problem solving skills and include adult supervision. Projects are generally school-based. Typical projects include planting community gardens, trees and native habitat restoration.

Eligibility: Non-profit sponsored projects involving youth age 6-18.

Award: $250 - $2,500

For more information:

Captain Planet Foundation   (404) 827-4130

One CNN Center, Suite 1090

Atlanta, GA 30303   www.captainplanetfdn.org

CARING AWARDS

Seeks to identify, honor, and reinforce the activities of particularly caring Americans who ennoble humanity by transcending self in service to others. Those who are selected for recognition reflect the best of the best. These select few, honored at a series of events in Washington, DC have dedicated the better parts of their lives to helping others. They have created solutions where others have despaired of finding answers.

For more information:

Caring Institute   (202) 547-4273

513 C Street, NE   www.caring-institute.org

Washington, DC 20002-5809

ChevronTexaco Conservation Awards

The ChevronTexaco Conservation Awards have recognized more than 1,000 volunteers, professionals and organizations since 1954. Recipients have contributed to the creation of wildlife refuges and preserves, the protection of species, the establishment of park and recreation areas, and heightening of environmental awareness.

Award: $10,000   # Given: 6

Apply by: mid-May   By nomination

For more information:

Chevron Texaco Conservation Awards   (415) 894-7040

575 Market Street, Room 3418   CONSERVN@chevrontexaco.com

San Francisco, CA 94105   www.chevron.com/community/conservation/consawards/

The Christophers

Video Contest for College Students

The Christophers, a nonprofit organization based on the Judeo-Christian concept of service to God and humanity, sponsors an annual video contest. College students are invited to interpret the Christopher belief that individuals can shape our world for the better, and that whether working alone or within the framework of a group, one person can make a difference.

Eligibility: Currently enrolled college student in good standing.

Award: $3,000   # Given: 1 $2,000   # Given: 1

$1,000   # Given: 1

Apply by: mid June

Poster Contest for High School Students

The Christophers sponsors an annual Poster Contest for HS students, with the theme "You Can Make a Difference."

Eligibility: Grade 9 through 12

Award: $1,000   # Given: 1 $500   # Given: 1

$250   # Given: 1

Apply by: mid January

For more information:

The Christophers   (212) 759-4050

Poster Contest or Video Contest   www.christophers.org

12 East 48th Street   tci@idt.net

New York, NY 10017

Civitan Shropshire Scholarship

Civitan is a worldwide community service organization, best known for hands-on work in the community. From projects to help people who are mentally and physically disabled to building youth recreation centers, Civitans are actively involved in bettering their communities and enjoy the feeling of knowing they are helping others. Scholarships are awarded to students pursuing careers which help further the ideals and purpose of Civitan International.

Eligibility: enrolled in a degree or certificate program at a community college, vocational school, four-year college. Civitan (or immediate family member) or Junior Civitan and has been a Civitan for at least two years. Financial need is a consideration.

Award: $1,000   Apply by: January 31

For more information send a self-addressed business size envelope with 2 stamps to:

Scholarship Coordinator   (205) 591-8910

Civitan International Foundation

PO Box 130744

Birmingham, AL 35213   www.civitan.org/schapp.pdf

COCA-COLA SCHOLARSHIPS

Coca-Cola Scholars

A merit-based scholarship awarded to high-school seniors, this is one of the largest corporate sponsored scholarship programs of its kind. Applicants are judged on leadership in school, civic and other extracurricular activities, academic achievement and motivation to serve and succeed.

Eligibility: HS seniors attending school in a participating bottler territory; a U.S. citizen, national, permanent resident, temporary resident (legalization program), refugee, asylee, Cuban-Haitian entrant or humanitarian parolee; and planning to pursue a degree at a U.S. post-secondary institution. To see if your HS is eligible check the Coca-Cola web site. If your counselor doesn't have an application, have them call with the school's "CEEB" code.

Award: $20,000   # Given: 50

$4,000   # Given: 100

Apply by: October 31   Apply to: your guidance counselor

For more information:

Coca-Cola Scholars   (800) 306-COKE

www.coca-colascholars.org/l   scholars@na.ko.com

First Generation Scholarship

Since 1994, this program has awarded millions to students who are the first in their immediate families to go to college. The program is available to students on 400 U.S. campuses in 31 states, as well as 32 American Indian Tribal colleges.

Eligibility:student must be the first in his or her immediate family to go to college, must demonstrate need, and possess a record of community service.

Award: $2,500/semester, renewable up to three years.

For more information: http://www.youthdevelopment.coca-cola.com/ach_fgs_how.html

www2.coca-cola.com/citizenship/education_firstgenerationscholars.html

Contact the student aid office at any one of the participating schools

Two-Year Colleges Scholarship Program

This program recognizes students attending two-year degree granting institutions for their unique contributions to community service and academic excellence.. Participating college campuses may nominate two students.

Eligibility: U.S. citizens or permanent residents, demonstrated academic success, first and/or second year students planning to continue their education at a two-year institution, 100 hours of community service within the previous 12 months. (Eligible students should contact the college's financial aid office to declare their interest in being nominated by their college.)

Award:400 awards given annually.   Apply By: May 31

For more information:

Coca-Cola Two-Year Colleges Scholarship Program 800-306-2653

P.O. Box 1615

Atlanta, GA 30301-1615

COLGATE YOUTH FOR AMERICA

Rewards clubs and troops which do something terrific for their community. If you are a member of one of the organizations listed below, your club can enter. Winning projects have included adult literacy campaigns, environmental preservation projects, community restorations, senior citizen assistance, and anti-substance abuse programs. Use your creativity to come up with a project that will help your town in some meaningful way. Winning groups are those which the judges consider the most innovative and successful. A bonus prize of an additional $1000 is awarded to the project voted 'Best in the Nation'.

Eligibility: ages 4 -19, and a member of Boy Scouts, Girl Scouts, Boys and Girls Clubs, Girls Incorporated, Camp Fire Inc., or National 4H Council.

Award: to $1,000   # Given: 300+

Apply by: March

For more information:

Colgate Youth For America   fcw001@aol.com

P.O. Box 1058   www.colgate.com/cp/corp.class/colgate_cares/youthForAmer.jsp

FDR Station

New York, NY 10150

CONGRESSIONAL HUNGER CENTER FELLOWSHIPS

Mickey Leland International Hunger Fellowship

This two year Fellowship begins with a one year field placement in countries throughout South Asia, Sub-Saharan Africa, and Latin America. Field placements include national and international non-governmental organizations, private commercial organizations, and bi-lateral and multi-lateral organizations. Fellows then spend a second year assisting with policy formulation in the headquarters of the organizations where they served during their field placements. Field and policy placements are coordinated so that timely, innovative information from the field translates into appropriate policies that address root causes of hunger.

Eligibility: US citizen with a graduate degree or equivalent experience; at least three months continuous work in a developing country; and written and spoken proficiency in language appropriate to field placement

Stipend:Year 1 $15,000; Year 2 $23,000; plus benefits and $5,000 end-of-service award.

Apply by: February 15   # Given: 11

Application Instructions: www.hungercenter.org/international/app_form.html

Bill Emerson National Hunger Fellowship

The Congressional Hunger Center sponsors this twelve month leadership development opportunity for individuals dedicated to eliminating hunger and poverty. Fellows are placed for six months with urban and rural community-based organizations all over the country involved in fighting hunger at the local level, such as food banks, community kitchens, and local advocacy agencies. They then move to Washington, DC to complete the year with six months of work at national organizations involved in the anti-hunger and poverty movement, including national advocacy organizations, think tanks, and federal agencies. The Fellows Program develops hunger-fighting leaders with a deep understanding of hunger and poverty at both the local and national level that enables them to find innovative solutions and create the political will to end hunger.

Eligibility: US citizen with a Bachelor's degree.

Stipend: $12,000 , benefits, travel, and an end- of-service cash award of $3,500.

Apply by: January 15   # Given: 26

Application Instructions: semd via email to fellows@hungercenter.org

For more information:

Congressional Hunger Center	(202) 547-7022
229 1/2 Pennsylvania Avenue, SE	fellows@hungercenter.org
Washington DC 20003	www.hungercenter.org

CONSERVATION FELLOWSHIPS

The New England Wild Flower Society sponsors six month Fellowships to work with the Plant Conservation Volunteer and New England Plant Conservation Programs, groups of professional and amateur volunteer botanists active in each state in New England.

The Fellows will assist in all aspects of administering the conservation programs of NEWFS, including data retrieval from the heritage programs, data entry, conducting training programs, obtaining landowner permission, and sending out volunteer assignments. Additionally, the Fellows will assist in the planning and implementation of restoration and management activities, invasive species initiatives, general floristic surveys and PCV field trips to botanically interesting locations throughout the region.

Stipend: $230 + housing   # Given: 2

Apply by: mid February

For more information:

New England Wild Flower Society	(508)-877-7630
180 Hemenway Road	
Framingham, MA 01701	www.newfs.org

CORO FELLOWSHIP IN PUBLIC AFFAIRS

If you are committed to public service and would like to build on your community service experiences in college, the Coro Fellowship may be a critical "next step" in your career. Coro is recognized nationally as one of the best training programs for leaders in all sectors of public life. The Fellows Program is a nine-month, full-time program offered in Los Angeles, New York, Pittsburgh, St. Louis and San Francisco. This remarkable fellowship may be of interest to college seniors and individuals with some work experience who are committed to improving this nation's system of democratic self-governance.

Fellows engage in field assignments, seminars, group and independent public service projects, and interact with leaders in the public, private and non-profit sectors. Fellows acquire an in-depth understanding of how leaders work to solve some of society's most complex problems. The bulk of the program is made up of rotations or internships through different sectors. Six rotations include a political campaign, government agency, labor or trade union, media organization, corporation, non-profit community agency. In January, fellows work together in various group projects for real-world clients producing projects.

The Coro Fellowship is an incredible experience for committed individuals interested in a different kind of graduate experience. The program is primarily experiential rather than academic and provides in nine months the kind of exposure and experience that few individuals receive in a lifetime.

Tuition for the Fellows Program is $3,500, but more than half of the Fellows receive a full tuition scholarships and many other fellows receive partial scholarships and stipends. Eligibility for scholarships is determined by each Center; there is no application process.

Eligibility: bachelor's degree or equivalent work experience. Post-graduate academic and work experience desired, but college seniors can compete.

Award: over half of the Fellows receive full scholarships

Apply by: January

For more information contact the nearest Coro center:

Coro Northern California Center (San Francisco)
recruitSF@coro.org   415-986-0521, x213
Coro Southern California Center (Los Angeles
recruitLA@coro.org   213-623-1234, x23
Coro New York Leadership Center (New York)
recruitNY@coro.org   212-248-2935, x230
Coro Midwestern Center (St. Louis)
recruitSTL@coro.org   314-621-3040, x11
Coro Center for Civic Leadership (Pittsburgh)
recruitPGH@coro.org   412-258-2675
                                   www.coro.org

Exploring Leadership

A summer program for eighteen rising 11th and 12th graders from San Francisco who are interested in expanding their leadership skills by examining community issues and existing public leadership. The 2002 Exploring Leadership program met for eight weeks and students received a $1,200 stipend upon completing the eight-week program.

Exploring Leadership begins during the selection process when candidates identify an issue that affects young people in San Francisco; much of the training is then focused on this issue. This year, students selected "Youth and Educational Opportunity". Additionally, Exploring Leadership has five major components: 1) a wilderness camping trip; 2) an orientation based on their selected issue; 3) internships; 4) training and interviews; and 5) a group project centering on the focus issue.

For more information:

    (415) 986-0521 ext. 106   lwhitcanack@coro.org

CORPORATION FOR NATIONAL SERVICE

Civil Society Nonprofit Scholars

The Corporation for National and Community Service and the Woodrow Wilson International Center for Scholars created the Civil Society Nonprofit Scholars program to increase understanding of the complex relationship between civil society, the nonprofit sector, volunteerism, and public policy in the U.S. Research is focused on three primary themes: (1) the relationship between democratic institutions and nonprofit organizations; (2) the role of service and citizenship in modern society and civil society; and (3) civic engagement and public policy.

Civil Society Nonprofit Scholars would serve nine months in residence at the Corporation for National and Community Service in Washington, DC, from September through May. Scholars will receive a stipend based on their current salary, be located at the Corporation in Washington and develop relationships with other Washington area organizations. Each scholar will also have access to the extensive research resources afforded by the Corporation, the Center, and the Washington area. In addition, scholars will be encouraged to participate in Corporation-sponsored activities as well as seminars and other events offered by the Center for the larger community of fellows and scholars.

After the program period, scholars will be expected to disseminate their research findings through various public media, including presentations, open forum discussions, publications, and Web postings.

Eligibility: Scholars from any country with a wide variety of backgrounds, proposing to explore preferred themes within an American context. For academic applicants, eligibility is limited to the postdoctoral level and these candidates should demonstrate scholarly development beyond their doctoral dissertation. For other applicants, an equivalent level of professional achievement is expected. Applicants working on degrees at the time of the application (even if the degree is to be awarded prior to the proposed scholarship year) are not eligible unless there is an equivalent level of professional achievement evidenced in work experience.

    Fellowship: Up to $85,000   Apply by: February

    # Given: 3

For more information:

    Corporation for National and Community Service   202/606-5000 x571

    1201 New York Avenue, NW, Rm. 8100-H   scholars@cns.gov

    Washington, DC 20525   www.nationalservice.org/scholars or www.wilsoncenter.org/scholars

Presidential Freedom Scholarships

An opportunity for schools and communities to recognize young people for outstanding service to their community by providing them with a college scholarship of at least $1,000.

The Corporation for National Service provides $500 toward the $1,000 President's Student Service Scholarship to students who have performed outstanding service or service-learning for at least a year. In order to award a scholarship, a school must first obtain matching funds of at least $500 from the school district, community or civic organizations, foundations, private sector institutions, or other groups or individuals.

High school principals can work with other school officials and teachers, community organizations, civic leaders, and students to determine how applications will be solicited and how scholarship recipients will be selected. Every principal may nominate one student per school, per year. Juniors will receive their scholarships in their senior year.

Eligibility: high school juniors or seniors who contribute at least 100 hours of service to their community within a 12-month period and are U.S. citizens or permanent residents. Students must be nominated by a public, private, charter, or parochial school located within one of the 50 states, the District of Columbia, an Indian tribe, a U.S. territory, or a Department of Defense school; and plan to attend an eligible institution of higher education in the U.S. No minimum GPA.

Award: $1,000	# Given: 10,000
Apply by: June	By nomination

For more information:

Presidential Freedom Scholarships   866-291-7700 (toll-free)
1150 Connecticut Avenue, NW, Suite 1100   202-742-5390 (local)
Washington, DC 20036   info@studentservicescholarship.org
www.nationalservice.org/scholarships/index.html

DAVIS-PUTTER SCHOLARSHIP FUND

Since 1961, the Davis-Putter Scholarship Fund has provided need-based grants to student activists who are able to do academic work at the college level and who are actively involved in the movement for social and economic justice. Early recipients fought for civil rights, against McCarthyism and to stop the war in Vietnam. More recently, grantees have included people active in the struggle against racism, sexism, homophobia and other forms of oppression; building the movement for economic justice; and creating peace through international, anti-imperialist solidarity.

Eligibility: Graduate or undergraduate students enrolled in an accredited school for the time period covered by their grant. Must live in the United States and plan to enroll in an accredited program in the U.S. U.S. citizenship not necessary.

Award: up to $6,000	#Given: 25 and 30
Apply by: May 1	

For more information (for application send a self-addressed stamped envelope):

Jan Phillips, Secretary
Davis-Putter Scholarship Fund

Post Office Box 7307
New York, NY 10116-7307   davisputter@hotmail.com.

DISCOVER® CARD TRIBUTE AWARD

Sponsored by Discover® Card, the Tribute Award recognizes student achievement in areas beyond academics by awarding scholarships for continuing education or training after high school. In addition to their academic achievements, winners must show evidence of outstanding accomplishments in four of the following five areas: Special Talents, Leadership, Obstacles Overcome, Community Service and Unique Endeavors.

Scholarships can be used for any type of education and/or training including certification or license, trade or technical school, two or four year colleges and universities. If winners postpone their education or enter military service, the scholarships will be reserved for them for four years.

Eligibility: high school juniors, 2.75 GPA

Award: $25,000   # Given: 9
         $2,500   # Given: 9
Apply by: January
For more information:
Discover® Card Tribute Award®   (703) 875-0708
c/o American Association. of School Administrators
PO Box 9338   www.aasa.org/Discover.htm
Arlington, VA 22219   tributeaward@aasa.org

EVELYN DUBROW/UNITE! FELLOWSHIP

This unique opportunity to work closely with community and labor leaders on important immigrant, labor, and civil rights issues is open to students, community activists, and workers with demonstrated leadership in supporting Asian Pacific American and/or labor issues. The program runs for 10 weeks.

Award: $3,000   Apply by: end April
For more information:
APALA   202-974-8051
815 16th Street, NW   apala@apalanet.org
Washington, DC 20006   www.apalanet.org

ECHOING GREEN FELLOWSHIP

The Echoing Green Fellowship program was created to provide social entrepreneurs who have original and compelling ideas for driving social change with the tools and resources to start new autonomous public service projects or organizations. The fellowships include a two-year stipend, technical assistance and the support structure of our Fellows' Community. Echoing Green has been providing seed funding to individuals and partners for over 10 years and has a community of over 350 active fellows and alumni.

They support programs domestically and internationally in all public service areas including but not limited to the environment, arts, education, health, youth service and development, civil and human rights and community and economic development. Projects must be thoughtful and original, sustainable and possibly replicable, address clearly defined needs and will have a measurable impact on the communities they serve.

Eligibility: Applicants who are 18 years of age or older starting projects that are the original idea of the individual applying. Applicants must make a full-time commitment to the project's development for at least two years.

Award: two-year $60,000 stipend+benefits #Given: 19

Apply by: January

For fellowship co-ordinator names only:

Echoing Green   general@echoinggreen.org
www.echoinggreen.org

EHRLICH FACULTY AWARD FOR SERVICE-LEARNING

Nominate faculty from your institution for one of the most prestigious awards in service and service-learning. Each year Campus Compact, with funding from TIAA-CREF, honors one faculty member for contributing to the integration of community or public service into the curriculum and for efforts to institutionalize service-learning, bringing recognition to the faculty's home campus.

The recipient will be featured in both the Campus Compact Current and the Campus Compact Reader, in addition to being offered the opportunity to present a keynote address at the National Gathering of the Educators for Community Engagement.

Award: $2,000   # Given: 1

Nominate by: mid-February

For more information:

Campus Compact   (401) 867-3929
Brown University   jstearns@compact.org
Box 1975   www.compact.org/ccawards/ehrlichaward/ehrlichawardtitle.html
Providence, RI 02912

ENVIRONMENTAL JOURNALISM FELLOWSHIP PROGRAM

The annual fellowship offers an intensive, five-day field course for 12 working environmental journalists providing deep back grounding to enhance reporting on tropical ecological issues and general understanding of environmental science. The fellowship will feature case studies on tropical biodiversity and conservation, restoration ecology, endangered species, ethnobotany and economic impact of plants on culture, and forest-sea links.

Apply by: mid-January

For more information:

Director of Education   (808) 332-7324 ext. 225 or 251
National Tropical Botanical Garden
3530 Papalina Road   tavana@ntbg.org
Kalaheo, HI 96741   www.ntbg.org/ejannounce.htm

Environmental Leadership Program

The ELP Fellowship is a highly experiential and innovative national program that aims to build the leadership capacity of the environmental movement's most promising emerging professionals. Fellows receive intensive training, institutional support, and mentoring for a three-year period. Fellows receive national recognition through the program and gain access to funding to pursue further skill training and develop new projects. ELP provides participants with the tools, support, and experience to lead public debates about environmental issues and to energize their home institutions and communities.

Retreats lie at the heart of the Fellowship. Through hands-on leadership training, retreats will teach practical skills of public intellectual leadership, help fellows hone leadership styles, and explore ways to achieve lifelong goals in public service. Topics include the challenges of stimulating public dialogue, negotiating institutional politics, building complex coalitions, and effectively managing time and resources. While the fellowship requires regular participation throughout the year, fellows are expected to continue their full-time jobs or studies.

Eligibility: newly established environmental practitioners (three to ten years of professional or post-undergraduate experience) eager to connect their specialized work to broader environmental and social concerns. Demonstrated talent for intellectual or public leadership. US residents working in US.

Award: $2,000-$10000 to support leadership-building activities + travel.

Given: 25   Apply by: October 1,

For more information:

Environmental Leadership Program   info@elpnet.org
P.O. Box 446   413.268.0035
Haydenville, MA 01039   www.ELPnet.org

Eureka Community Fellowship

Eureka Communities is a professional learning association which brings together community-based nonprofit leaders seeking to achieve new standards of excellence in their efforts to build self-sufficiency among, and improve the quality of life for, the people they serve. Through its programs Eureka provides the executive directors of community-based, organizations (CBOs) with: opportunities for improving leadership skills; developing supportive and cooperative relationships with peers; broadening understanding of their communities; and learning from the best examples of community self-help across the country.

Selected Fellows desire to improve their organizations' capacities to serve clients more effectively, and are committed to pursuing strategies for generating income and volunteer involvement. Fellows are organized into classes of seven, who experience the program together. The Eureka Fellowship is a two-year, 200 hour commitment.

Eligibility: CEOs of 501(c)(3) community service organizations (Directors of regional affiliates of national nonprofits will also be considered) providing a substantial portion of its services to clients in one of the Eureka Communities: Boston,

Detroit, Los Angeles, San Diego, or the San Francisco Bay Area.
For more information:

Eureka Communities Central Office	202-332-2070
1601 Conn. Ave. NW, Ste 802	info@eureka-communities.com
Washington, DC 20009	www.eureka-communities.org

Apply to the city where you intend to apply for a Fellowship.

Eureka Los Angeles	Eureka Detroit
523 West 6th Street Suite 240	1212 Griswold
Los Angeles, CA 90014	Detroit, MI 48226-1899
(213) 630-2128	(313) 226-9389
www.eureka-losangeles.org	
Eureka San Diego	Eureka Bay Area
555 West Beech Street, Suite 413.	425 Market Street 16th floor
San Diego, CA 92101	San Francisco, CA 94105
(619) 595-1850	(415) 546-3996
www.eureka-sandiego.org	www.eureka-sanfrancisco.org
Eureka Boston	(617) 859-8218
32 Rutland Street	
Boston, MA 02118	www.eureka-boston.org

EVERETT PUBLIC SERVICE INTERNSHIP PROGRAM

The Everett Internships consist of about 200 summer internships in over 50 public service organizations in New York City; Washington, DC; Boston; Boulder, CO; and Chicago. The Everett Program encourages students' future involvement in public life by allowing them to participate in the challenges and rewards of public interest work. It also provides the public interest community, which too often functions on limited resources, with much needed help from the dedication, energy and idealism interns bring to their work.

Everett interns engage in a variety of endeavors, from preparing Congressional testimony and legislative and legal research, to writing policy papers and implementing communication strategies. Interns come from public and private colleges and universities across the nation, major in subjects ranging from engineering to philosophy, from political science to social work. They span the ethnic, racial and political spectrum.

Look through the internship listings on the web site to see available internships and contact information. Apply to the organization(s) of your choice by their deadline, and mention that you're applying for the Everett intern position.

Eligibility: Current undergraduate (with at least two semesters of college completed) or graduate students attending a United States university, or have just graduated in the spring immediately preceding the summer of the Internship. (Recipients of post-graduate fellowships are not eligible.) Available to work full-time for 10-weeks at a participating organization (see web site for list) that have not worked at previously.

Stipend: $225 weekly for ten weeks   #Given: 200

For more information:
Everett Public Service Internship Program

c/o Co-op America
1612 K Street NW, Suite 600
Washington, DC 20006

www.everettinternships.org/default.html

Explorers Club Youth Activity Fund

Established to help foster a new generation of explorers and to build a reservoir of young men and women dedicated to the advancement of knowledge of the world by probing the unknown through field research. Enables students to participate in field research in the natural sciences under the supervision of a qualified scientist anywhere in the world.

Eligibility: high school and undergraduate students.

Award: to $1,500

Apply by: January 31

For more information:

The Explorers Club
46 E. 70th St.
New York, NY 10021

www.explorers.org
(212) 628-8383
membership@explorers.org

Federal Employee Education & Assistance Fund

FEEA awards are strictly merit based. Criteria include academics, extracurricular and community service activities, and an essay.

Eligibility: Current civilian federal and postal employees, dependent family members with at least three years of federal service, 3.0 GPA. Full-time students, enrolled or planning to enroll in a two- or four-year post-secondary, accredited undergraduate or graduate degree program.

Award: $300 to $1,500

Given: varies

Apply by: end of March

For more information send a self-addressed, stamped #10 business envelope to:

FEEA
8441 W. Bowles Ave., Suite 200
Littleton, CO 80123-3245

www.feea.org/scholarships.shtml

Florida College Student of the Year

Recognizes students who support themselves through school, earn excellent grades, and participate in community service, philanthropies and political activism.

Eligibility: undergraduate or graduate student attending a Florida college or university.

Award: $3,000

Given: 20

Apply by: February 1

For more information:

College Student of the Year
POB 14081
Gainesville, FL 32604-2081

(352) 373-6907
http://www.floridaleader.com/soty/

4-H

Community service project grants are awarded to youth that take leadership roles in identifying critical issues in their communities. Using the grant and other community resources, teams develop activities to address these issues and to educate other young people on ways to engage in community service. Awards and deadlines vary. See web site for most up-to-date information.

Eligibility: 4-H members

For more information:

Youth Grants

www.fourhcouncil.edu/programs

National 4-H Council

7100 Connecticut Avenue

Chevy Chase, MD 20815-4999

FUND FOR SOCIAL ENTREPRENEURS

The Fund invests in visionary young leaders who have bold, effective, and innovative ideas for national and community service ventures. It combines the risk-taking spirit which American entrepreneurs used to build our country with the commitment, idealism and spirit of today's emerging young leaders. Recipients become members of a class of Youth Service America social entrepreneurs for a three year period. The awards are given primarily to people starting innovative or model youth service non-profit organizations.

Entrepreneurs receive start-up funds, professional management and leadership development, technical assistance and mentoring to ensure the success of their youth service start-up non-profit venture. Years One and Two feature professional development retreats, program seed grants and living stipends.

YSA has a tradition of assisting up-and-coming organizations in the national and community service field. We have learned that successful ventures depend upon a combination of idealism and business savvy, as well as a support network in the development phase and beyond.

Ideally, selected entrepreneurs will be on the brink of establishing their new non-profit, or just incorporated and have done some community outreach, forward planning and program development.

Eligibility: under age 35 starting a youth service organization.

Stipend: $28,000 total for 2 years, up to $8,000 seed money.

Given: 5 - 7

For more information:

Youth Service America

(202) 296-2992

1101 Fifteenth St. NW, Suite 200

fse@ysa.org

Washington, DC 20005

www.ysa.org

WILLIAM C. FRIDAY FELLOWSHIP IN HUMAN RELATIONS

The core program of the Wildacres Leadership Initiative, the Fellowship is a two-year leadership development program that assists committed North Carolina residents in the public, private for-profit, or private not-for-profit sectors in both strengthening their own leadership skills and working in collaboration with others who bring different perspectives, resources, and skills.

Eligibility: nominated emerging leaders from North Carolina who have at least 3 but not more than 15 years of work experience.

For more more information:

    The Wildacres Leadership Initiative   www.wildacresleadership.org

GENERATIONS FOR PEACE ESSAY CONTEST

To request annual essay theme enclose a self-addressed stamped envelope, and $1.00 processing fee, with request for essay guide lines.

Eligibility: high school junior or senior, US citizen.

    Award: $750 - $1,500   # Given: 2

    Apply by: April 15

For more information:

    Saint James Lutheran Church   (503) 227-2439

    Attn: Generations For Peace Essay Contest

    1315 SW Park Avenue

    Portland, OR 97201   www.stjameslutheranportland.org

HERB SOCIETY

The Herb Society grant furthers the knowledge and use of herbs and contributes the results of the study and research to the records of horticulture, science, literature, history, art, and/or economics.

Previous research subjects have included: genetics of sex allocation in coriander; imagistic associations of garlic in Greek and Latin literature; landscape uses and hardiness of herbs in Tennessee and traditional dye plants of the Huichol Indians of Mexico.

Eligibility: Persons with a proposed program of scientific, academic, or artistic investigation of herbal plants. The grant is not given for financial aid to individuals, rather for specific research on herbal projects.

    Award: $5,000   Apply by: January 31

For more information:

    Research Grant   (440) 256-0514

    The Herb Society of America, Inc.

    9019 Kirtland Chardon Rd.

    Kirtland, OH 44094   membership@herbsociety.org

                         www.herbsociety.org/research.htm

HUMAN RIGHTS CENTER FELLOWSHIP PROGRAM

Designed to promote human rights by providing practical training in the varied aspects of human rights work worldwide. The fellowship placement should provide both training for the individual and assistance to the organization and foster links between communities in the Upper Midwest and communities and human rights organizations around the world. Therefore, participants will act as human rights ambassadors of their work after the fellowship appointment, by bringing human rights concerns back to their communities in the Upper Midwest.

Eligibility: residents of the Upper Midwest (USA)-including students, teachers, lawyers, other professionals, community leaders, activists and others.

Awards: $1,000-$4,500　　　　　　　# Given: 20

Apply by: early March

For more information:

University of MN Law School　　　　humanrts@umn.edu

Human Rights Center　　　　　　　(612) 626-0041

www.hrusa.org/field/fellowships/uppermidwest.shtm

Samuel Huntington Public Service Award

For a graduating senior to pursue public service anywhere in the world. The award allows recipients to engage in a meaningful public service activity for up to one year before proceeding on to graduate school or a career.

Eligibility: students graduating from accredited colleges.

Award: $10,000　　　　　　　　# Given: 1 - 2

Apply by: mid-February

For more information:

Samuel Huntington Fund　　　　　(508) 389-2877

Attn: Thomas G. Robinson

25 Research Drive

Westborough, MA 01582　　　www.narragansett.com/inside/edsvcs/samuel/index.htm

IFESH International Fellows Program

Sponsored by the International Foundation for Education and Self-Help (IFESH), the International Fellows Program (IFP) provides nine-month overseas internships for outstanding Americans who are graduate students or recent college and university graduates. IFESH has the following specific objectives: reduce hunger and poverty; empower people through literacy; train and place the unskilled and unemployed in jobs; provide preventive and basic health care to individuals in need; deal with population and environment problems; develop employment through economic development activities; foster cultural, social, and economic relations between Africans and Americans, particularly African Americans.

Fellows are placed with development-focused organizations working overseas and have a chance to gain practical, hands-on experience with a community organization or a grassroots program in a developing region of the world, with an emphasis on the continent of Africa. The opportunity to contribute to endeavors taking place in areas such as health care, literacy, skills training, agriculture and community development. Fellows depart in August following a one-week orientation program to be held in Phoenix, Arizona.

Eligibility: U.S. citizen, graduate student or college senior.

Stipend: $800/mo. plus travel, insurance and pre/post settling-in allowances.

Apply by: February 28

For more information:

IFESH)　　　　　　　　　　　(480) 443-1800

5040 E. Shea Boulevard, Suite 260
Scottsdale, Arizona USA 85254-4687
www.IFESH.org

(800) 835-3530
ifesh@ifesh.org

IMAGINE AMERICA

The award-winning Imagine America scholarship program helps thousands of high school seniors each year to pursue a post-secondary career education at hundreds of career schools across the nation. The Career Training Foundation (CTF), the not-for-profit affiliate of the Career College Association, in partnership with Peterson's, allows every high school in the United States and Puerto Rico to select up to three graduating seniors to receive an Imagine America scholarship.

Eligibility: Students must meet the standard admissions requirements of the 400 participating career colleges to which they apply; have a high school GPA of 2.5 or greater; financial need; and demonstrated voluntary community service during senior year.

Award: $1,000   # Given: 3/ high school

How to apply: At www.petersons.com/cca/apply.html, where you can view a list of participating schools. If your high school is not yet enrolled in the program, your guidance counselor can do so by calling 202-336-6711 or emailing scholarships@career.org.

For more information:

Career Training Foundation
10 G Street NE, Suite 750
Washington, DC 20002-4215

(202) 336-6800
www.career.org
scholarships@career.org

For a list of participating colleges: www.petersons.com/cca/members.html

INSTITUTE FOR POLITICAL SERVICE

United Leaders is a national nonpartisan non-profit created in 1999 to encourage the Millennial generation to see politics as a means for positive social change and pursue honorable careers in political service.

The Institute for Political Service (IPS) is an eight-week summer fellowship program designed to equip young people with the tools, resources, support, and network necessary to overcome the financial and social barriers to service. In 2003 the Institute will be in Boston, June 13-Aug. 9, and Washington D.C. June 6-Aug. 2 and consists of: 2 diverse 4-week political service internships; Skills training seminars; Meetings with elected officials, journalists, and authors; Service Learning Curriculum

Eligibility: individuals ages 18-24 who have not graduated from college.

Award: $2,000 stipend + room and board.

For more information:

www.UnitedLeaders.org   Admissions@UnitedLeaders.org.

JUNIOR MISS

Junior Miss seeks to recognize, reward and encourage outstanding college-bound high school girls who are striving to be the best they can be. A strong record of community service is an essential for consideration.

If you are chosen to be your state representative after competing for scholarships at the local and state level, you spend two weeks with all expenses paid in Alabama, where you compete in the national finals for a share in scholarships totaling more than $115,000 to be used at the college or university of your choice.

Over 200 colleges and universities support the program with scholarships offered to local, state and national participants. This nationwide scholarship and honors program recognizes, rewards and encourages excellence while promoting self-esteem.

The "Be Your Best Self" program is a nationwide outreach aimed primarily at influencing young people. Junior Misses incorporate a positive, personal approach into their work with young people to encourage self-esteem, thereby helping them successfully deal with challenges they face.

The program is a personalized message stressing the importance of incorporating six elements into one's life— morality, integrity, honesty, love, respect, and hope. Junior Misses reach out to young people and encourage them to make a commitment to being their best selves in areas including academics, physical fitness, morality, character, and social and civic concern and participation.

Eligibility: female, never married, U. S. citizen, high school senior.

Application forms available from your local Junior Miss Program. Contact your State Chairman during the summer between your sophomore and junior years, or as soon into your junior year as possible. Local program deadlines vary.

Award: $40,000	# Given: 1	$5,000	# Given: 3
$15,000	# Given: 1	$4,000	# Given: 1
$10,000	# Given: 1	$2,500	# Given: 5
		$1,000	# Given: 21

For more information: www.ajm.org/

Robert F. Kennedy Fellows

Robert Kennedy believed in youth as our country's greatest natural resource and inspired young people from Watts to Capetown to make a difference in their communities. Since 1968, more than 400 Robert F. Kennedy Fellows have played key roles in creating and leading more than 200 community organizations, fighting injustice and inequality throughout the country.

RFK Fellows are located in Los Angeles, San Francisco and Washington, DC and work to empower young people in under-served communities through programs tackling the spiraling cycles of gang violence, drug abuse, illiteracy and racism. Teams of young women and men are selected each year on the basis of their commitment to public service. Priority is given to individuals from the ethnic groups and neighborhoods served by the Fellows and their partner agencies. Fellows act as mentors and role models to at-risk youth while creating and implementing much-needed community service projects. Fellows also are members of AmeriCorps, and receive a federally funded modest living allowance (augmented by RFK Memorial funds) and education awards that can be used to help pay off student loans, and also finance college, graduate school or vocational training.

For more information:

Robert F. Kennedy Memorial   (202) 463-7575
1367 Connecticut Ave.. NW, Suite 200   info@rfkmemorial.org
Washington, D.C. 20036   www.rfkmemorial.org

LEADERSHIP FOR A CHANGING WORLD AWARD

Seeking to recognize, strengthen and support leaders and to highlight the importance of community leadership in improving lives, the program seeks to confirm that resourceful leaders are bringing about positive change in virtually every community. Each year, Leadership for a Changing World recognizes leaders and leadership groups not broadly known beyond their immediate community or field. Nominated community leaders may work in fields that include: economic development; community development; environment and environmental justice; human rights; citizen participation and government accountability; human development; sexual and reproductive health; education reform; religion and social change; arts and social action; and access to media, including new technologies.

Leadership for a Changing World seeks to recognize and support leaders by providing shared learning and networking opportunities: Over the course of the two year program, awardees will participate in four program-wide meetings designed to provide opportunities for shared learning and collaboration among awardees and with other leaders. Leaders may use these sessions to consider their leadership and program challenges and explore new opportunities to develop their programs, and deepen our understanding of community leadership.

Eligibility: candidates must be nominated

Award: $100,000 over two years to support their programs. Awardees will also receive $30,000 to explore new learning opportunities to support their work.

Given:20

For more information:

Leadership for a Changing World   (202) 777-7560
Advocacy Institute   info@leadershipforchange.org
1629 K St., NW Suite 200   www.leadershipforchange.org
Washington, DC 20006-1629

MAKE A DIFFERENCE DAY

Make A Difference Day is the most encompassing national day of helping others -- a celebration of neighbors helping neighbors. Created by USA WEEKEND magazine, Make A Difference Day takes place annually on the fourth Saturday of October. Projects can be as large or as small as you wish! See what needs to be done in your community and then send an entry form. Young and old, individuals and groups, anyone can carry out a volunteer project that helps others. It might be collecting truckloads of clothing for the homeless, or spending an afternoon helping an elderly neighbor.

If you want to participate make sure you take part in the next Make A Difference Day in October. You can also join someone else's project listed on the Web site. If you need more than one day for your project, do a good part of your volunteering on Make A Difference Day. If you are rebuilding a community soup kitchen, you may have to do some wiring the week before or some painting the week after, but a significant part of the construction needs to take place on that Saturday. If your volunteers are together on weekdays, do some of your project on Make A Difference Day. If students collect food for the homeless during the school week, get a group together on Make A Difference Day to deliver the food.

Each April, hundreds of good deeds done on Make A Difference Day are selected for honors, headlines and charitable donations. Paul Newman donates $10,000 each to 10 selected projects. Honorees are spotlighted in USA WEEKEND with articles and photographs, and on the Make a Difference Day web site.

Eligibility: employees of Gannett, The Points of Light Foundation or USA WEEKEND carrier newspapers are ineligible for awards.

Award: $10,000   # Given: 10
For more information:
    Make A Difference Day   (800) 416-3824
    USA Weekend   diffday@usaweekend.com
                                                     www.usaweekend.com/diffday/

Editors note: This information is edited from the Make A Difference Day web site. There is no connection between Make A Difference Day and Making A Difference Scholarships.

Charles H. Revson Fellows Program

Revson Fellows are mid-career urban activists and community leaders from diverse fields selected each year to pursue self-designed study programs for one academic year at Columbia and to meet together for weekly seminars on urban issues in order to enhance their ability to contribute to the improvement of New York City. This unique opportunity for self-development for those who have already made a substantial contribution in an urban area and who recognize that they can benefit from a year's study and reflection before embarking on the next stage of their careers.

The program seeks to bring together individuals from diverse backgrounds and fields of achievement. Fellows are chosen on the basis of their contribution to improving New York City or another urban center, and their potential for further contribution. There are no educational prerequisites for the fellowship. Rather, Fellows are required to have demonstrated intellectual interest and capacity to benefit from the University's teaching and research resources.

Award: $18,000 + free tuition and student health insurance
Given: 10   Apply by: February 1
For more information:
    The Charles H. Revson Fellows Program
    Columbia University   (212)280-4023
    Mail Code 6940   revson@columbia.edu
    New York, NY 10027   www.columbia.edu/cu/revson/

Ronald McDonald House Charities

Local Chapters of Ronald McDonald House Charities with support from RMHC Global, McDonald's Corporation and McDonald's Owner/Operators, offer scholarships to students from disadvantaged communities who face limited access to educational and career opportunities. The scholarship programs are designed to assist youth that face a widening education gap by providing financial support to students committed to pursuing post-secondary education in their chosen field at any accredited institution. It recognizes student accomplishments, potential and commitment to serve the community.

Eligibility: must have at least one parent of African American, Asian-Pacific or Hispanic origin, be eligible to enroll in and attend a two-year or four-year college with a full course of study in the United States, and reside in a participating area. For specific information about RMHC/Future Achievers scholarships in your area, please contact your Local RMHC Chapter. For information on which chapters sponsor which scholarship program, see web sites of programs below:

African American Future Achievers Scholarship Program
> www.rmhc.com/mis/scholarships_african/index.html

ASIA Scholarship Program
> For Asian-Pacific students.
> www.rmhc.com/mis/scholarships_asia/index.html

HACER Scholarship Program
> For Hispanic students.
> www.rmhc.com/mis/scholarships_hacer/index.html

> Award: $1,000   Apply by: February 1

For more information:
> RMHC/Future Achievers Scholarship Program
> Scholarship Program Administrators
> P.O. Box 22376
> Nashville,TN 37202   www.rmhc.com/mis/chapters/search/index.html

MARGARET McNAMARA MEMORIAL FUND

Supports education of women from developing countries who are committed to improving the lives of women and children. Previous winners studied fields such as agriculture, architecture and urban planning, civil engineering, education, forestry, journalism, nursing, nutrition, pediatrics, public administration, public health, social sciences and social work.

Eligibility: women at least 25 years old with a record of service to women and/or children in their country; financial need; enrolled in US educational institution during the entire period covered by the grant; national of a developing country that is currently eligible to borrow from the World Bank; residing in the U.S. at the time of application; cannot be a U.S. Green Card holder and must be planning to return to her country in about two years; not related to any World Bank Group staff member or his/her spouse.

Applications must be requested in writing.
> Award: $1,100   # Given: 6
> Apply by: February 1

For more information:

World Bank   (202) 473-8751
Margaret McNamara Memorial Fund   MMMF@worldbank.org
1818 H Street NW, Room H2-204
Washington, DC 20433

Seymour Melman Fellowship

The program supports fellowship grants each year to new scholar/activists to pursue original work on a range of issues from demilitarization to workplace democracy. Recipients will be encouraged to spend some time at IPS, either as summer interns or at some other time during the year, and will write an essay and/or articles on their research. When deemed useful and necessary, a Melman Fellow will be mentored by a Fellow or project director of IPS.

Award: up to $5,000   Apply by: March 1

For further information:
Miriam Pemberton
Peace and Security Program
Institute for Policy Studies   202-234-9382 ext. 214
733 15th Street NW, Ste. 1020   miriam@ips-dc.org
Washington, DC 20005   www.ips-dc.org

George J. Mitchell Scholarships

The US-Ireland Alliance is a proactive, non-partisan, non-profit organization dedicated to consolidating existing relations between the United States and Ireland--North and South--and building that relationship for the future. Scholarships are to educate future American leaders about the island of Ireland--North and South -- and to provide them with an understanding of, an interest in, and an affinity with the island. These Scholarships will allow American post-graduates to pursue one year of study at institutions of higher learning in Ireland and Northern Ireland.

Senator Mitchell's life and career have embodied a deep commitment to public service. Under his leadership a historic accord, ending decades of conflict, was signed by the governments of Ireland, the United Kingdom and the political parties of N. Ireland and was endorsed by the voters of Ireland in a referendum.

Prospective scholars must have a demonstrated record of intellectual distinction, leadership, and extra-curricular activity, as well as personal characteristics of honesty, integrity, fairness, and unselfish service to others -- indicating a potential for future leadership and contribution to society.

Eligibility: US citizens, 18 - 30 by October 1. Academic standing sufficient to assure completion of Bachelor's degree before beginning Mitchell Scholarship.

Award: $11,000 stipend, tuition, room and traveling expenses.

Apply by: October 15

For more information:
US - Ireland Alliance   www.MitchellScholar.org
2800 Clarendon Blvd. #502
Arlington, VA 22201

NATIONAL ASSOCIATION OF SECONDARY SCHOOL PRINCIPALS

National Honor Society Scholarships

Each National Honor Society chapter may nominate two seniors for this national scholarship. Nominees must be able to demonstrate that they possess outstanding character, scholarship, service, and leadership.

Eligibility: high school senior who is a member of National Honor Society.

Scholarship packet mailed to NHS Adviser in November.

Award: $1,000   # Given: 250

Apply by: January 24

Principal's Leadership Award

Principals use this program to recognize one outstanding student leader from the senior class. At the national level, school winners compete--on the basis of their application--for the scholarships. Any high school senior may be nominated by his or her school.

Award: $1,000   # Given: 150

Apply by: December 6

For more information

Trust to Reach Education Excellence   (703) 860-0200

National Association of Secondary School Principals

1904 Association Drive   www.nhs.us/schlr_awards

Reston, VA 20191-1537

NEW VOICES - NON-PROFIT DEVELOPMENT FELLOWSHIP

A capacity-building and leadership development grant program that assists nonprofit organizations and professionals entering the fields of human rights and international cooperation. Sponsored program areas include international human rights, women's rights, racial justice, migrant and refugee rights, peace and security, foreign policy and international economic policy.

New Voices addresses the scarcity of substantive jobs for talented professionals at the beginning stages of their careers in the sponsored program areas; the need for creating additional venues through which new perspectives and approaches can be incorporated into an organization's work; and the lack of resources and systems within small non-profit organizations.

New Voices helps community-based and nonprofit organizations to bring fresh innovative talent to their staffs and to cultivate and strengthen the leadership potential of these "new voices." Selected fellows are offered financial assistance, training, and opportunities for personal and professional development.

Eligibility: Graduating students (from undergraduate or graduate programs) who have a proposed host nonprofit organization to prepare a joint application with. Organizations should have annual budgets between $75,000 and $2 million.

Award: Full salary and benefits for fellow in Year One; 75% in Year Two, $1,500 per year in professional development activities. Financial assistance program to help meet outstanding student loan obligations (up to $6,000/year). A new computer for the Fellow's use.

Apply by: January 14

For more information:

AED/New Voices   (202) 884-8051
1825 Connecticut Ave., N.W.   newvoice@aed.org
Washington, D.C. 20009   newvoices.aed.org

NESTLÉ VERY BEST IN YOUTH

Cosponsored by Nestlé and RIF, honors 30 young people who have made reading a priority and in the process have made tangible contributions to the quality of life in their communities. The young people, selected from nominations from RIF coordinators, hundreds of volunteers, parents, and teachers. Nestlé will donate $1,000 in the name of each winner to the charity of his/her choice.

Eligibility: legal resident of the U.S., between 9 and 18 years of age.

For more information:

Nestlé Very Best In Youth
P.O. Box 29059202-673-1506.
Glendale, CA 91209   www.rif.org/news/events/vbiy2003.html

NUCLEAR AGE PEACE FOUNDATION

Swackhamer Peace Essay

Seeks suggestions for constructive approaches to the problems of war and peace. The topic for 2003 is "How would a Peace Education course in your school benefit students, the school, the community and the world? What lessons and issues do you think should be included in such a course?"

Eligibility: high school students from any country.

Award: $1,500   # Given: 1
      $1,000   # Given: 1
      $500   # Given: 1
Apply by: June 1

Barbara Mandigo Kelly Peace Poetry Awards

Encourages poets to explore aspects of peace and the human spirit.

Award: $1000 adults
      $200 teen (13-18)
      $250 youth (12 & under)
Apply by: June 30

For more information:

Nuclear Age Peace Foundation   805-965-3443
1187 Coast Village Road, Suite 1   wagingpeace@napf.org
Santa Barbara, CA 93108   www.wagingpeace.org

OPEN SOCIETY INSTITUTE COMMUNITY FELLOWSHIPS

Supports work with nonprofits in either New York City or Baltimore for 18 months. The goals of these fellowships is to encourage public and community service careers, expand the number of mentors and role models available to youth in inner-city neighborhoods, and promote entrepreneurial initiatives that empower communities to increase opportunities and improve the quality of life for residents.

Eligibility: Applicants may come from any field, including, but not limited to, business management, law, medicine, education, architecture and engineering; legally able to work in the U.S.

Award: $48,750 for a term of 18 months   # Given: up to 10

Apply by: early April

For more information:

New York City   (212) 548-0603

www.soros.org/fellow/community

Baltimore   (410) 234-1091

www.soros.org/baltimore/fellowships.htm

THE PAUL AND PHYLLIS FIREMAN PUBLIC SERVICE FELLOWSHIP

Awarded annually to a talented individual who will join City Year's national headquarters for a minimum of one year. The Fireman Fellow will work on high priority projects that are essential to helping City Year achieve its organizational goals. City Year unites a diverse group of 17 to 24 year-old young people for a year of full-time, rigorous community service, leadership development, and civic engagement

An "action tank" for national service, City Year seeks to demonstrate, improve, and promote the concept of national service as a means of building a stronger democracy. City Year envisions a day when service will be a common expectation - and a real opportunity - for citizens all around the world.

The Fellowship is designed for graduates of MBA, MPP, MPA and other advanced studies programs with demonstrated commitment to social enterprise, national service, and nonprofit management and/or social entrepreneurship, or those who are seeking a career change in order at apply their management experience to a dynamic organization in the nonprofit sector. Fellowship begins in July.

Award: up to $70,000/year + benefits   Apply by: January 17

For More information:

Danielle McNeil   617-927-2401

City Year, Inc.   617-927-2500

285 Columbus Avenue   dmcneil@cityyear.org

Boston, MA 02116   http://www.cityyear.org/about/fireman.cfm

PRUDENTIAL SPIRIT OF COMMUNITY AWARDS

Spirit of Community seeks to help rekindle America's community spirit by encouraging young people to become actively involved in making their communities better places to live. The initiative aims to create visible role models for young people by recognizing exemplary, self-initiated community service students across the US; help young Americans learn how they can make worthwhile contributions to their communities; and to promote greater public attention to the issue of community service by young people.

In partnership with the National Association of Secondary School Principals, Prudential sponsors the national awards program to recognize young people for outstanding self-initiated community service. Two top individuals are chosen in each state, in Washington D.C. and in Puerto Rico. These State Honorees are celebrated with several days of recognition events in Washington, D.C. Ten National Honorees receive an additional award of $5,000.

Eligibility: grades 5-12 as of the last weekday in October during the applying year (except for children of employees of participating firms).

Award: $6,000   # Given: 10

   $1,000   # Given: 94

Apply by: October 30   By nomination

For more information:

   Prudential Spirit of Community Awards

   CSFA

   1505 Riverview Road

   PO Box 297

   St. Peter, MN 56082   http://www.prudential.com/community/spirit/awards/

Public Education Fund

Louis Feinstein Memorial Scholarship

Honors students who best exemplify the qualities of brotherhood, compassion, integrity, leadership, a dedication to public service and a determination to make a positive difference in the lives of others.

Criteria include public and community service activities for which no compensation was received, an essay, recommendations and special awards.

Eligibility: high school juniors planning to attend college in RI.

Award: $10,000   Apply by: June 30

Charles A. Morvillo Scholarship

This scholarship is for students who demonstrate financial need, integrity, leadership, a determination to gain a higher education despite socio-economic adversity and the desire to make a positive impact on the community. Students who are selected will become Morvillo Scholars. Scholars who attend an institute of higher education will receive a $2,500 scholarship per year for a maximum of four years and $2,500 upon graduation.

Eligibility: high school seniors in North Providence and Providence public Schools., RI.

Award: $2,500/year up to four years, $2,500 upon graduation

Apply by: June 1

For more information:

   Public Education Fund   (401) 454-1050

   15 Westminster Street, Suite 824   www.ri.net/PEF/scholarships.htm

   Providence, RI 02903   info@publiceducationfund.org

Quest Scholars Program

A five-year long educational/leadership program for exceptionally gifted low-income, at-risk, predominantly minority, high school juniors and seniors who are concerned with the environment."

Apply by: mid-March

For more information:

Quest Scholars Program

(650) 328-8591

PO Box 20054

questions@syesp.stanford.edu

Stanford, CA 94309

www.questscholars.org/

JACKIE ROBINSON FOUNDATION SCHOLARSHIP PROGRAM

Serving as an advocate for talented young people with the greatest financial need, the Jackie Robinson Foundation helps promising students realize their full potential as well-educated, active participants in the process of social change. The Scholarship Program provides comprehensive support services to minority students enrolled at institutions of higher education.

Eligibility: minority high school seniors accepted by a four-year college or university, U.S. citizen, high academic achievement, minimum 900 SAT or 23 ACT scores, leadership potential, financial need.

Award: To $6,000 annually for 4 years.

Apply by: April 1

For more information:

JRF Scholarship Application

(212) 290-8600

3 West 35th Street

www.jackierobinson.org/Scholars/

New York, NY 10001-2204

dwalters@jackierobinson.org

ROTARY SCHOLARSHIPS

Ambassadorial Scholarships Program

The Rotary Ambassadorial Scholarships Program seeks to further international understanding and friendly relations among people of different countries.

While abroad, scholars serve as ambassadors of goodwill to the people of the host country and give presentations about their homelands to Rotary clubs and other groups. Each scholar is assigned a sponsor and a host Rotarian counselor who provide orientation, advice and assistance.

Recent winners are studying to help Amazon Indians live and work with encroaching modern cultures; studying public health in Namibia; and studying non-violent conflict resolution techniques in India.

Eligibility: at least two years of university coursework or equivalent professional experience. Rotarians, spouses or descendants of Rotarians not eligible.

Academic-Year Ambassadorial Scholarships are for one academic year abroad and provide funding for transportation, tuition, room and board, educational supplies and language training.

Award: $25,000 Academic-Year Ambassador

$12,500 Multi-Year Ambassador per year for 2 or 3 years

$12,000 Cultural Ambassador (3 months)

$19,000 6 months of language study in another country

Given: 1,250+   Apply by: varies (Spring)

The Rotary World Peace Scholarships

The Rotary Foundation has partnered with eight leading universities around the world to establish the Rotary Centers for International Studies in peace and conflict resolution. Each year, Rotary will select 70 scholars to study at one of the seven Rotary Centers worldwide. The selected Rotary World Peace Scholars will enroll in two-year master's-level degree programs in conflict resolution, peace studies, and international relations.

Eligibility:Must have an undergraduate degree from an accredited college or university or its international equivalent (based on a four-year curriculum); proficiency in a second language ; hold citizenship in a country where there is a Rotary club. Rotarians, spouses or descendants of Rotarians not eligible.

Award: tuition, fees, room, board, transportation, and contingency expenses

Apply by: varies, Rotary clubs submit applications by October 1

Apply to: Your local Rotary club, each Rotary district may nominate one candidate.

For more information:

Contact a local Rotary club or   (847) 866-3236

The Rotary Foundation   www.rotary.org

http://www.rotary.org/foundation/educational/index.html

SeaWorld/Busch Gardens Environmental Excellence

These awards recognize outstanding efforts of students across the country who are working at the grass-roots level to protect and preserve the environment. The award categories correspond to each of our nonprofit conservation and education partners.

Projects should offer creative solutions to environmental problems, demonstrate significant environmental and educational impact, and be primarily student-driven. Awards are made on behalf of and for the benefit of winning projects, and are not given to individual students.

My Own Backyard Award / National Wildlife Federation

Whether you live in the city or the country, in the mountains or on the beach, you have the opportunity to connect with nature. Tell how you bettered your own backyard, public park, a vacant city lot or your own school grounds.

Environmental Outreach Award / National Geographic Society

Education is key to ensuring the planet stays in good global hands for generations to come. Show how you created an original education outreach program about the environment that you've already shared with your school, other school districts, other states even other countries.

Citizen Scientist Award / The Ocean Conservancy

Whether testing, sampling, measuring, hypothesizing, or using the latest technologies, science is necessary to pass laws, create awareness and solve some of our most challenging environmental issues. Tell how your group made a difference by using science and technology to help the environment.

Planet Ocean Award / American Oceans Campaign

Marine habitats such as coral reefs, kelp forests and coastal great lands are being threatened by pollution and other human activities. Tell how your group has explored humanity's impact on our oceans, raised public awareness or restored a marine habitat.

Community Conservation Award / Conservation International

Local communities hold the key to conservation success. Conservation strategies must make ecological and economic sense in order to have long-term impact on the environment. Indicate how your school creatively solved a challenge by meeting the needs of both people and nature.

Wildlife Partners Award / National Fish and Wildlife Foundation

Working together for solutions can practically guarantee success. Creative partnerships between schools, businesses, government and private citizens are great ways to get things done. How has your school group worked with your community to protect wildlife and habitats in your area?

Last Great Places Award / The Nature Conservancy

This planet is filled with many great places supporting a diversity of wildlife. But some of them are fragmented by human impact, making them unfriendly for plants and animals. Award recognizes students working to preserve some of Earth's last natural areas or land crucial to long-term species survival.

Energy Wise Award / The Izaak Walton League of America

Increased use of fossil fuel poses one of the largest threats to the environment. Alternative energy solutions such as solar, wind, water and even waste products are being found all the time. How has your group rescued resources by coming up with alternative solutions in your school or community?

Award: $10,000 + trip for 3 students & chaperone /teacher to a SeaWorld.

Given: 8 (1 per category)

$5,000 + trip for educator plus guest to Busch Gardens Adventure Camp and all-expenses-paid trip to the National Science Teachers Association (NSTA) conference.

Given: 1

Eligibility: All schools (grades K-12) in the United States and Canada. Projects must be sponsored by a formally recognized grade level, classroom or club. Public, private, charter and home schools are all eligible to apply.

Apply by: December

For more information:

SeaWorld/Busch Gardens Environmental Excellence Awards

Education Department   (877)792-4332

7007 SeaWorld Drive

Orlando, FL 328821   www.seaworld.org/EEAwards/main.htm

SIERRA CLUB

Joseph Barbosa Award

This award recognizes club members under the age of 30 who have a demonstrated record of service to the environment.

Eligibility: Sierra Club member.

Award: $2,000   # Given: varies

Apply by: June 1   By nomination

For more information:

Ellen Mayou   mayou@flash.net
4161 Heartstone Dr.
Grapevine TX 76051   www.sierraclub.org/awards/

START SOMETHING

Sponsored by Target Stores and the Tiger Woods Foundation, Start Something is a program designed to help young people ages 8 to 17 identify and achieve their dreams and goals. It is a 20 hour curriculum that shows youth how to take positive actions that will bring them closer to their goals, and helps build qualities like initiative, leadership and community stewardship.

Youth who finish the program can apply for a Start Something scholarship which can be used to pursue a goal or dream. Examples include music lessons, sports camps, special educational programs, travel and equipment.

Eligibility: Ages 8 to 17. Scholarships are not available outside the U.S., or to employees of Target Corporation or their immediate families.

Award: $100 to $5,000 for a total of $300,000

Apply by: Awarded three times/ year, applications due May 1, September 1 and January 1.

For more information:

Start Something
3701 Wayzata Blvd., MS 2BF
Minneapolis, MN 55416
startsomething.target.com

PATRICK STEWART HUMAN RIGHTS SCHOLARSHIP

Awarded to youth displaying a strong past and future commitment to human rights work. This is an excellent opportunity for students to design their own projects for practical, applied field-work over the summer. Most applicants arrange internships with local or global human rights organizations to deepen skills as a human rights activist and enhance career opportunities in the human rights workforce.

By working directly in the field with practitioners, you strengthen the work and open the channels of communication between activists. The more connections that are made among the global movement, the greater the effect we will have upon perpetrators of rights violations.

Eligibility: high school, college and graduate students.

For more information:

Attn: Patrick Stewart Human Rights Fellowship
Urgent Action Network   aisuanfpo@aiusa.org
Amnesty International USA   (303) 258 1170
P.O. Box 1270
Nederland, CO 80466

H. SWEARER STUDENT HUMANITARIAN AWARD

Recognizes students for their outstanding public service, and supports their efforts to address social needs. Swearer believed "universities should be communities of compassionate people involved in serious intellectual pursuits, but never divorced from the reality of their communities."

Candidates should show outstanding public service during the preceding twelve-month period and develop an innovative approach to a social, educational, environmental, health, economic, or legal issue within a community. The committee is especially interested in efforts that linked service to academic study, designed structures for the long-term support for the project, or linked service with the larger social context of the need.

Eligibility: must attend a Campus Compact member school.

Award: $1,500	# Given: 5
Apply by: February 21,	By nomination

For more information:

Howard R. Swearer Student Humanitarian Award

Amy Umstadter	(401) 867-3939
Campus Compact, Box 1975	swearer@compact.org
Brown University	www.compact.org
Providence, RI 02912	

TARGET ALL-AROUND SCHOLARSHIP

Every year Target gives millions of dollars to deserving students, teachers and schools across the country to help support and enhance their education efforts. Each Target store awards scholarships annually to well-rounded high school seniors who are committed to their communities through volunteer service, education and family involvement.

Eligibility: High school seniors, high school graduates and current undergraduate college students (age 24 and under) who are legal U.S. residents are eligible to apply. Must be enrolled in a full–time undergraduate course of study no later than the fall term following application at an accredited two–or four–year college, university or vocational–technical school in the U.S. Employees of Target Corporation are not eligible to apply. Program is not offered in Alaska, Hawaii, Puerto Rico, or outside the United States.

Store Award: $1,000	# Given: 2 per store - over 2,100
National award: $10,000	# Given: 4
Apply by: November 1	

Applications available each summer at a Target store near you.

For more information:

Contact your local Target store	or	Scholarship Program Manager
(800) 316-6142		Target All-Around Scholarship
		c/o CSFA (800) 537-4180
		1505 Riverview Rd.
		St. Peter, MN 56082-0480

target.com/common/page.jhtml?content=target_cg_scholarship

TEMPLE AWARDS FOR CREATIVE ALTRUISM

Presented annually to one or more outstanding altruists whose lives and work embody the inspirational light of unselfish service motivated by love. People from every age, race and walk of life are candidates. An award fund of $25,000 is divided among recipients each year.

Nominees tend to inspire altruism - the gift of generosity and caring in others; make significant contributions to humanity that serve as a model of creative altruism and to manifest sustained commitment to altruistic ideals. Nominees also have personal qualities that support this commitment; engage in regular and consistent actions which benefit others; and are loving, compassionate, kind and non-violent in relationships.

Recent winners include a woman who founded a nonprofit organization dedicated to showcasing the work of local Navajo artists and to providing literacy and health awareness programs to indigenous people in the area. Another winner decided the best way to help end world hunger was to replenish the earth's trees. Through his efforts, trees have been planted in his native India, Guatemala and Brazil. Tens of millions of trees have been planted through Trees for Life. A third recent winner founded the Tibet Child Nutrition and Collaborative Health Project to cure Tibetan children whose growth was being severely stunted.

Award: $25,000   Apply by: December 1

By nomination: contact Rose Welch (707) 779-8238   rose@noetic.org

For more information:

Temple Awards for Creative Altruism	707.775.3500
Institute of Noetic Sciences	www.noetic.org/ions/new.html
101 San Antonio Road	membership@noetic.org
Petaluma, CA 94952	

DONALD TERNER RESIDENCY PROGRAM

An opportunity in social entrepreneurship for a special individual who will work at BRIDGE Housing Corporation for a two-year tenure. BRIDGE is a nonprofit housing developer whose basic mission has always been to build and maintain large volumes of extremely high-quality housing at exceptionally affordable prices. BRIDGE participates in community development and is committed to enhancing the value of every neighborhood it serves.

For more information send a resume and a letter of interest to:

hr@bridgehousing.com   www.bridgehousing.com/residency/index.html

THIRD WAVE

For female students involved as activists, artists, or cultural workers working on issues such as racism, homophobia, sexism, or other forms of inequality.

Eligibility: full-time or part-time students age 30 and under enrolled in, or have been accepted to, an accredited university, college or community college.

Award: $1,000 - $5,000   # Given: varies

Apply by: April 1, October 1

For more information:
Third Wave   (212) 675-0700
116 East 16th St. 7th floor   thirdwavef@aol.com
New York, NY 10003   www.feminist.com

TOYOTA COMMUNITY SCHOLARS PROGRAM

The Toyota Community Scholars program awards scholarships to outstanding high school seniors for excellence in academics and for making meaningful contributions of service to their schools and their communities.

Participating high schools select a student who best exemplifies the outstanding academic leadership potential and dedication to community service that the scholarship program seeks to recognize. In addition, the nominee must be actively involved in, or have initiated, a service program that addresses a school or community need. Recognized and documented community service work will be an important selection criterion. Students who meet these criteria should contact the school guidance counselor to learn about the nomination process.

Eligibility: high school senior, 3.0 GPA or better, rank in the top 10 % of graduating class. US citizen, national or permanent resident. Not available to children or grandchildren of Toyota Motor Sales, employees or other U.S. Toyota subsidiaries, and Toyota and Lexus dealers.

Award: $10,000 - $20,000   # Given: 100
Apply by: December 1   Renewable for 4 years

For more information:
Contact School guidance counselor for details on nomination process.
Or
Scholarship and Recognition Programs
Educational Testing Service
Rosedale Road, MS 86D
Princeton, NJ 08541   www.toyota.com/about/community/education/scholars.html

HARRY S. TRUMAN SCHOLARSHIP

Merit-based scholarships to college students who plan to pursue careers in government or elsewhere in public service. Awarded on the basis of merit to outstanding students with extensive records of public and community service, outstanding leadership potential and communication skills. Truman Scholars participate in leadership development programs and have special opportunities for internships and employment with the federal government.

Priority given to candidates proposing to enroll in graduate and professional programs specifically oriented to careers in public service such as law; public administration; public policy analysis; public health; international relations; government; social services delivery; education; conservation; and environmental protection.

Eligibility: attend an accredited U.S. college or university and be nominated by the institution's Truman Faculty Representative [candidates MAY NOT apply directly], be U.S. citizens or U.S. nationals, be in the upper quarter of their junior class, except for residents of Puerto Rico, the Virgin Islands, Guam, American

Samoa or the Northern Marianas who must be in their senior class. Materials must be submitted by the institution's president or the Truman Faculty Representative. A listing of Faculty Representatives are available on the Foundation's home page.

Award: $3,000 for the senior year of undergraduate education and $27,000 for graduate studies.

Given: 75-80   Apply by: late January (By nomination)

For more information:

The Harry S. Truman Scholarship Foundation
712 Jackson Place NW
Washington DC 20006   www.truman.gov

MORRIS K. UDALL SCHOLARS

The Udall Foundation is committed to educating a new generation of Americans to preserve and protect their national heritage by the recruitment and preparation of individuals skilled in effective environmental public policy conflict resolution. Based on Congressman Udall's legacy of 30 years of public service, the Program encourages outstanding students to pursue careers related to environmental public policy, especially Native Americans and Alaska Natives who are studying tribal public policy and health care. Typical majors include environmental engineering, natural sciences, natural resource management, and social sciences.

Eligibility: Be a matriculated sophomore or junior pursuing a degree at an accredited institution of higher education at the time of nomination with a college grade-point average of at least a "B" or the equivalent. Be a United States citizen, a permanent resident alien, or, in the case of nominees from American Samoa or the Commonwealth of the Mariana Islands, a United States national. For scholarships in the areas of tribal policy and health care, nominees must be Native American or Alaska Native.

Award: up to $5,000   # Given: 80
By nomination

Excellence in National Environmental Policy Fellowship

The Udall Foundation awards dissertation fellowships to doctoral candidates entering the final year of writing dissertations concerning environmental public policy and/or environmental conflict resolution.

Eligibility: U.S. citizens, permanent residents, or, in the case of applicants from American Samoa or the Commonwealth of the Mariana Islands, U.S. Nationals. The fellowship must be used for the final year of writing a dissertation for a doctoral degree to be received at the end of the fellowship year. Applicants must have completed all coursework, passed all preliminary exams, and had the dissertation research proposal or plan approved by February 3. Students already holding a fellowship for the purpose of writing the dissertation the year before the fellowship year are not eligible to apply.

Award: $24,000   # Given: 2
Apply by: February 3

For more information:

Morris K. Udall Foundation   (520) 670-5529 or (520) 670-5542

130 South Scott Avenue
Tucson, AZ 85701

millage@udall.gov
www.udall.gov/prog.htm

U.S. Institute of Peace

National Peace Essay Contest

Contest is intended to promote serious discussion among high school students, teachers, and national leaders about international peace and conflict resolution. The U.S. depends on knowledgeable and thoughtful students - the next generation of leaders - to build peace, freedom and justice among nations and peoples.

State winners meet with national and international figures, explore questions of peacemaking, participate in briefings by officials at foreign embassies, visit sites of historical and cultural interest and more. 2002–2003 Essay Topic "The Justification of War: Is there such a thing as a just war?"

Eligibility: grade 9 - 12 attending HS or in a high school correspondence program in the US, US territories, or US citizens attending school overseas.

Award: $10,000   # Given: 1
$5,000   # Given: 1
$2,500   # Given: 1
$1,000   # Given: 53

Apply by: late January

Jennings Randolph Program for International Peace Senior Fellowships

The Institute funds projects in preventive diplomacy, ethnic and regional conflicts, peacekeeping and peace operations, peace settlements, post-conflict reconstruction and reconciliation, democratization and the rule of law, cross-cultural negotiations, U.S. foreign policy in the 21st century, and related topics.

Eligibility: Open to citizens of all nations.

Award: up to $80,000 for ten-months   Apply by: mid September

Peace Scholar Dissertation Fellowships

The Jennings Randolph Program for International Peace, Peace Scholar Fellowship program supports doctoral dissertations that explore the sources and nature of international conflict, and strategies to prevent or end conflict and to sustain peace.

Eligibility: Citizens of all countries are eligible, but must be enrolled in an accredited college or university in the United States. Must have completed all requirements for the degree except the dissertation by the commencement of the award (September).

Award: $17,000   Apply by: November 1

For more information:

United States Institute of Peace   (202) 457-1700
National Peace Essay Contest   www.usip.org/
1200 17th Street NW   essay_contest@usip.org
Washington DC 20036   jrprogram@usip.org

Volvo for Life Awards

This a public service program designed by Volvo Cars of North America to honor "ordinary people who act with conscience, care, and character to help others in need." Volvo is conducting the program in an effort to inspire people nationwide to make outstanding contributions in their own communities. Nominations will be accepted in the areas of safety, environment, and quality of life.

Eligibility is limited to lawful residents of the United States. To be considered for this year's aAwards, a nominee's achievements must have occurred at least in part during the calendar year of application. Group entries will be considered, but only if a single individual is designated by name to accept any or all awards on behalf of the group.

Award-Finalist: $10,000   # Given: 10

Award-Winner: $50,000 donation made in the name of winner to the charities of their choice. Top winner will receive a Volvo car for the rest of his or her life.

#Given: 3   Apply by: February 28

For more information:
http://www.volvoforlifeawards.com

The Washington Center

The Washington Center for Internships and Academic Seminars provides students with a comprehensive participatory learning experience in Washington, D.C. The unique format of the program promotes future leadership for the public, private and nonprofit sectors of society. The Washington Center's academic one- or two-week seminars focus on a specific topic or current issue. Each seminar offers lectures, panel discussions, briefings, site visits, small group discussions, readings and journals. Certain programs within The Washington Center automatically guarantee financial assistance once you have been accepted.

Environmental Internship Program
Award: Many of the students enrolled in the EIP receive financial assistance for housing from the organizations they are assigned.

Women in Public Policy, and Nonprofit Leaders Programs
Award: $1,000

Mass Communications
Award: $250

Diversity in Congress Program, NAFTA Program (U.S. students)
Award: $2,000

NAFTA Program (Mexico, Canada) Minority Leaders Fellowship
Award: Eligible for financial assistance..
Apply by: see www.twc.edu/DatesDeadlines/DatesDeadlines.htm for details

For more information:

Enrollment Services	(800) 486-8921
Washington Center	www.twc.edu
2301 M Street NW 5th Floor	info@twc.edu
Washington DC 20037	

White House Fellows Program

White House Fellows work hand-in-hand with leaders in government. They enjoy private, informal meetings with leading representatives from the worlds of business, the arts, science and technology, media, and politics in the US and abroad. White House Fellowships offer outstanding people the opportunity to learn and grow, to connect with each other and with the world around them. The WHFP is the nation's most prestigious fellowship for leadership development and public service.

Engagement in the work of the federal government lies at the center of the Fellowships. Work assignments can bring broad access and ever changing issues and challenges, but also long hours and unglamorous chores requiring as much perseverance as ability. White House Fellows spend a year as full-time, paid assistants to senior White House staff, the Vice-President, Cabinet officers and other top-ranking government officials. Fellows write speeches, help draft and review proposed legislation, answer Congressional inquiries, and conduct briefings.

The Fellowship's education program augments and amplifies the work experience. Fellows travel to major U.S. cities, domestic military bases, and foreign countries to talk with locals about conditions and concerns which shape policy-making and problem-solving. Fellows have walked with community leaders through diverse neighborhoods in L.A. and New York City. Fellows rose before dawn with cutters in the sugarcane fields in Miami, flew over the Panama Canal in helicopters, witnessed the end of apartheid in South Africa and the crumbling of the Berlin Wall, and explored ethnic tensions in Greece, Turkey and Cyprus.

The application is designed to reveal remarkable achievement early in an applicant's career, demonstrated leadership qualities, a commitment to serve others, and the skills required for a successful year as a special assistant to a high level government official. Evidence of growth potential is also a key criterion in the selection process.

National finalists are interviewed by The President's Commission which recommends to the President those individuals it finds most qualified.

Eligibility: US citizens, out of school and working in their chosen profession. Federal gov't. employees are not eligible unless they are career military personnel.

Award: $83,000 (approx.) + benefits   # Given: 11 - 19

Apply by: February 1

For more information:

The President's Commission on White House Fellowships

712 Jackson Place NW   (202) 395-4522

Washington, DC 20503   www.whitehouse.gov/fellows/

Wiedner and Vandercook Peace & Justice Scholarship

Grandmothers for Peace International awards scholarships to students across the United States and the world. Students must write a brief biography of their activities relating to nuclear disarmament, conflict resolution, or community service; describe their plan for contributing to a healthy planet and provide information on his or her school and community activities.

Eligibility: high school senior or college freshman from any country.

Award: $250   # Given: 50

        $500   # Given: 1

Apply by: March 1

For more information send a self-addressed and stamped legal-size envelope to:

Wiedner & Vandercook M.S.F.   www.grandmothersforpeace.org

c/o Leal Portis, Chairperson

16335 Patricia Way

Grass Valley, CA 95949

ELIE WIESEL PRIZE IN ETHICS

The Elie Wiesel Foundation for Humanity's mission is to advance the cause of human rights and peace throughout the world by creating a new forum for the discussion of urgent ethical issues confronting humankind. Its essay contest challenges students to examine and analyze urgent ethical issues confronting them in today's complex world. Essays may be developed from any point of view and can be a case study or an analysis that is literary, philosophical, historical, biographical, sociological, theological, or psychological.

Themes may include such topics as: Why has humanity failed to learn from history the lessons of tolerance and respect for others? Why must individuals speak out when confronted with human suffering and injustice? What are our ethical obligations to preserve and protect our physical environment and natural resources? How does the behavior of our leaders or heroes influence our own sense of ethics? How does an individual reconcile desire for autonomy with the need for cooperation within a community?

Eligibility: Full-time undergraduate juniors and seniors at accredited colleges and universities in the US and Canada. International or non-citizen students are eligible, as are enrolled juniors studying abroad.

Award: $5,000   # Given: 1

        $2,500   # Given: 1

        $1,500   # Given: 1

        $500   # Given: 2

Apply by: early January

For more information send a self-addressed stamped envelope by December 15 to:

Elie Wiesel Foundation For Humanity   (212) 221-1100

1177 Avenue of the Americas, 36th Floor

New York, NY 10036

WILDLIFE CONSERVATION SOCIETY RESEARCH FELLOWSHIP

The Research Fellowship Program (RFP) is designed to support individual field research which is based on sound and innovative conservation science, and aims to build capacity for the next generation of conservationist.

Eligibility: The RFP does not limit any individual from applying, however, most grantees are Professional conservationists from the country of research, and/or Post-graduates pursuing a higher degree. Applications will be accepted for field research in Africa, Asia, and Latin America (including Mexico). Additionally, the RFP will entertain proposals for research in North America only from Native Americans and First Nation People.

Award: $1,000 -$25,000   Apply by: January 2 and July 1

For more information

Program Coordinator, Research Fellowship Program

International Conservation

Wildlife Conservation Society   718-220-6828

2300 Southern Blvd.   fellowship@wcs.org

Bronx, NY 10460   wcs.org/home/wild/researchfellowship/1267/

World of Children Awards

Nominations are invited from around the world for the program's three awards to recognize those individuals who dedicate their lives to serving the world's youngest citizens.

Cardinal Health Children's Care Award

Recognizes an individual who has made a significant lifetime contribution to the health and well-being of children, including work in medical care, sanitation, nutrition, and research.

Award: $100,000

Kellogg's Child Development Award

Honors an individual who has made a lifetime contribution to children's futures by greatly improving their opportunities to learn and grow. Contributions in this area include providing shelter, improving living conditions, fostering safety, and working against discrimination, poverty, violence, and child labor.

Award: $100,000

Founder's Scholarship

For a young person who is making an extraordinary contribution to children. The nominee must be 21 or younger, and must have contributed at least three consecutive years of service to helping children.

Award: $15,000   Apply by: end April

For more information:

World of Children, Inc.   (614) 491-3633

301 Obetz Rd.

Columbus, Ohio 43207   www.worldofchildren.org/

World Population Film/Video Festival

The Festival is an international competition for college and secondary students to encourage critical thought and self-expression regarding population growth, resource consumption, the environment, and our common global future.

Entries must address the festival's inter-related themes: world population, resource consumption, the environment, and a sustainable future. Entries may be any length, and originate in any format - film, video, or multimedia -- and be any style: documentary, narrative, music video, animation, etc. Prize winning and honorable mention programs will be chosen for each category.

Eligibility: produced by a current high school or college student, or by a group of such students.

Award: $10,000 total prize money   Apply by: June 15

For more information:

WPFVF   (800) 638-9464
46 Fox Hill Road   info@wpfvf.com
Bernardston, MA 01337   www.wpfvf.com
(800) 638-9464

YOSHIYAMA AWARD FOR EXEMPLARY SERVICE

Yoshiyama Award recipients are positive forces within their communities and will be the future leaders of their states, regions, and their country. They exemplify the kind of citizen initiative and community responsibility needed in the globally interdependent society of the twenty-first century. Awardees have courageously and tenaciously addressed issues of deep concern in American communities - problems such as substance abuse, homelessness, gang violence, teen pregnancy, prejudice and discrimination, crime, the needs of special populations, and environmental degradation.

"Making the world a more peaceful, better place to live is the desire of people everywhere. Although poverty, sickness, suffering, and fighting are widespread, they can be overcome - but only with sustained, thoughtful effort. It is important for us to join hands toward making whatever improvement we can. Any step forward, no matter how small, is far better than none at all.

The young men and women selected to receive the Yoshiyama Award have shown they care deeply about much more than just themselves. They have demonstrated their continuing concern for and commitment to society. It is gratifying and reassuring to know there are such extraordinary young people in the world.."

Hirokichi Yoshiyama, Benefactor, The Yoshiyama Award

Eligibility: H.S. seniors in U.S. & U.S. territories., need not be college bound.

Award: $5,000 dispensed over two years

Apply by: April 1   By nomination

For more information:

The Yoshiyama Award   (202) 457-0588
PO. Box 19247   www.hitachi.org/yoshiyama/index.html
Washington, DC 20036-9247

YOUTH ENGAGED IN SERVICE AMBASSADORS

Points of Light Foundation

The YES Ambassador program places community-minded young people with statewide "Partner" organizations for one year to provide technical assistance, training, advocacy and program development around youth service, service-learning and youth leadership. Ambassadors and partner organizations determine needs and how they can improve the youth service infrastructure. Ambassadors develop action plans for the group they will work at the local, state and national level, to help build capacity of organizations to create service and leadership opportunities for youth and to mobilize more young people to become problem solvers.

A YES Ambassador might provide training to youth and adults on a variety of topics including youth leadership, adult-youth partnerships, service-learning, service project development, reflection, agency readiness, and diversity; consult with individuals, organizations, and institutions on the development of national and community service programs for youth; connect individuals, organizations and institutions to local, state and national networks and resources in the national and community service field, and build and support youth leadership opportunities in policy setting for national and community service initiatives.

Eligibility: ages 18 - 25

Stipend: Salary with benefits

For more information:

Points of Light Fdn, Youth Outreach	(202) 729-8000
1400 Eye Street NW, Suite 800	youth@PointsofLight.org
Washington, DC 20005	www.PointsofLight.org

YOUTH IN ACTION

Offers awards and recognition to youth who take action on their ideas, hopes and dreams for improving themselves, their communities and our nation.

Youth Action Guides helps find and create support for youth teams working together, combining ideas and solutions to create a project that improves their community. Winning projects fulfill community needs and create positive impact.

Eligibility: youth-initiated projects only that have demonstrable results, and are under 2 years old.

Award: $1,000   # Given: 50

Apply by: Mid-March   Apply through your school or youth club.

For more information:

Foundation of America
Youth In Action Campaign
43 Malaga Cove Plaza, Suite D
Palos Verdes Estates, CA 90274   www.youthlink.org/us/

YOUTH VENTURE

Youth Venture changes the role of young people in our society by allowing them to create their own organizations, thereby taking greater responsibility for their own lives and their communities. Young people receive grants and loans, technical support, and training to launch and run businesses and organizations. Organizations fall into three categories: community service organizations such as student-run tutoring, teen hotlines, or park cleanups; small business ventures, such as local landscaping; or after-school clubs, such as athletic, music or computer clubs. Young people themselves come up with the ideas and control the initiatives.

Many young people create such organizations today. Many more can and would, if they could overcome attitudinal barriers and resource constraints. We work with local community leaders, school principals, and heads of youth groups to change rules and provide seed money to start the ventures.

Youth must own the idea and actively control the venture, which must involve a team of young people -- partners and allies committed to its independence and success -- and must improve the Venturers' community.

Eligibility: high school and middle school students

Award: $200 - $1,000

Apply to: partner organizations (local & nat'l. youth organizations and schools.)

For more information:

Youth Ventures   (703) 527-4126
1700 North Moore Street, Suite 2000
Arlington, VA 22209   www.youthventure.org

MAKING A DIFFERENCE

SCHOLARSHIPS

FOR

UNDERGRADUATES

❖ ❖ ❖

If you wait, all that happens is that you get older.
Leonard Nimoy

Until the great mass of the people shall be filled with the sense of responsibility for each other's welfare, social justice can never be attained.
Helen Keller

American Geological Institute

Minority Geoscience Scholarships

Supports students majoring in geoscience, including the geoscience subdisciplines of geology, geophysics, geochemistry, hydrology, meteorology, physical oceanography, planetary geology, or earth-science education.

Eligibility: US citizens with verifiable ethnic minority status as Black, Hispanic, or American Indian, Eskimo, Hawaiian, or Samoan; financial need.

Award: $250-$1,000   # Given: over 20

Apply by: March 1

For more information:

American Geological Institute   (703) 379-2480

4220 King Street   www.agiweb.org/education/mpp/

Alexandria, VA 22302-1507

American Humanics Association

Pendleton, Qubein and Academic Scholarships

American Humanics' mission is to prepare and certify future nonprofit professionals to work with America's youth and families. This national alliance of colleges, universities and nonprofit organizations provides various scholarships for preparing undergraduates for careers with youth and human service agencies. AHA also provides leadership opportunities and internships.

Eligibility: entering or enrolled in a AHA program at a participating college (see AHA website).

Award: $1,000   # Given: over 30

For more information:

American Humanics Association   (816) 561-6415

4601 Madison Avenue   (800) 343-6466

Kansas City, MO 64112   www.humanics.org

American Meteorological Society

Majors in atmospheric or related oceanic and hydrologic sciences who show clear intent to make the atmospheric or related sciences their career.

AMS Undergraduate Scholarships

These are memorial scholarships designed to encourage outstanding undergraduate students to pursue careers in the atmospheric and related oceanic and hydrologic sciences.

Eligibility (all): entering final undergraduate year in fall of application year, majoring in atmospheric or related oceanic and hydrologic science full time in an accredited U.S. institution, 3.25 gpa, (financial need for some scholarships). Must be U.S. citizens or hold permanent resident status, pursuing a degree at a U.S. institution.

Award: $700-$5000   #Given: 11

Apply by: mid-February

AMS/Industry Undergraduate Scholarships

Sponsored by leading environmental science and service corporations and one government agency and are designed to encourage outstanding undergraduate students to pursue careers in the atmospheric and related oceanic and hydrologic sciences.

Eligibility: full-time students entering their junior year in the fall of application year with a minimum gpa of 3.25 on a 4.0-point scale . Must be U.S. citizens or hold permanent resident status, pursuing a degree at a U.S. institution.

Award: $2000/ year for 2 years   Apply by: mid-February

AMS/Industry Minority Scholarships

Funding minority students who have been traditionally underrepresented in the sciences, especially Hispanic, Native American, and Black/African American students.

Eligibility: Minority students entering freshman year of college in the fall of application year, who plan to pursue careers in the atmospheric or related oceanic and hydrologic sciences. Must be U.S. citizens or hold permanent resident status, pursuing a degree at a U.S. institution.

Award: $3000/ year for 2 years   Apply by: mid-February

For more information:

Education Program   202-737-1043
American Meteorological Society
1120 G Street, NW, Suite 800
Washington, DC 20005   amsedu@dc.ametsoc.org
     www.ametsoc.org/AMS/amsedu/scholfeldocs/

AMERICAN OCCUPATIONAL THERAPY FOUNDATION

For students in undergraduate Occupational Therapy programs, or in the final year of an Occupational Therapy Associate program.

Eligibility: juniors, seniors, member of the AOTA, enrolled full-time in accredited OT program, financial need. Preference given to US citizens & permanent residents.

Award: to $250-2,000   # Given: 53
Apply by: January 15

For more information:

Scholarship Administrator
American Occupational Therapy Foundation
4720 Montgomery Lane   800-729-2682
PO Box 31220   (301) 652-6611
Bethesda, MD 20824-1220   www.aotf.org

AMERICAN PLANNING ASSOCIATION SCHOLARSHIPS

See graduate listings.   www.planning.org/institutions/scholarship.htm

ARIZONA HYDROLOGICAL SOCIETY

AHS Scholarship

Scholarships to encourage students in hydrology, hydrogeology, and other water resources related fields at any Arizona university or college.

Eligibility: college junior, senior fitting the above category.

Award: $1,500   # Given: 3

Apply by: June 30

CAP Scholarship Announcement

The Central Arizona Project Award is for papers on water research that focus specifically on water issues that affect central and Southern Arizona and the Colorado River. Papers can focus on legal, economic, political, environmental, or water management issues, as well as any other issue that might be of interest to CAP or Arizona water users.

Eligibility: students at any college or university in the State of Arizona. Papers should represent the student's original, unpublished research.

Award: $500   # Given: 1

Winners will also be invited to present their research at the Arizona Hydrological Society's annual symposium, expenses paid.

Apply to: submit a one page abstract electronically to vcampo@cap-az.com.

Deadline: May 23

For more information:

U.S. Geological Survey   (928) 556-7142

2255 N. Gemini Drive, Bldg. 3

Flagstaff, AZ 86001   www.azhydrosoc.org

ARKANSAS ENVIRONMENTAL FEDERATION

An education association for businesses and industries that deal with environmental, safety, and health regulations on a day-to-day basis, the AEF focuses on waste minimization and pollution prevention. Awards students majoring in environmental, health and safety, or natural resource programs.

Eligibility: Resident of Arkansas, fulltime undergraduate or graduate student at time of application and for year scholarship is awarded, at an Arkansas University. Minimum 2.8 gpa.

Award: $1,500   # Given: 1

Apply by: March 31

For more information:

Arkansas Environmental Federation   (501) 374-0263

1400 W. Markham St. Suite 250

Little Rock, AR 72201   www.environmentark.org

ASSOCIATION OF CALIFORNIA WATER AGENCIES

Clair A. Hill Scholarship

The program is administered by the ACWA member agency that received the Clair A. Hill Water Agency Award the previous year. In 2002, Mid-Peninsula Water District (MPWD) was honored with the Clair A. Hill Water Agency Award for its "Our Water" educational curriculum.

Eligibility: college juniors and seniors. CA residents preferred.

Award: $3,000   # Given: 1

For more information:

MPWD   650.591.8941

ACWA Scholarships:

Eligibility: California resident full time junior or senior college students in water resources-related fields at selected California schools.

Award: $1,500   # Given: 6

Apply by: April 1

For more information:

ACWA   (916) 441-4545

910 K Street, Suite 250

Sacramento, CA 95814   www.acwanet.com

ASSOCIATION OF STATE DAM SAFETY OFFICIALS

Dam Safety Scholarship

One of the keys goals of the ASDSO is the development of well-trained technical persons with an interest in one of the many scientific fields related to dam safety. The basis for selection will generally follow these guidelines: academic scholarship, financial need and work experience/activities.

Eligibility: 3.0 GPA for first two years of college, recommended by academic advisor. U.S. citizens enrolled at the junior/senior level in a civil engineering program or related field; interest in pursuing career in hydraulics, hydrology or geotechnical disciplines; or discipline related to dams.

Award: to $5,000   # Given: 2

Apply by: February 14   Renewable

For more information:

Ass'n. of State Dam Safety Officials   (606) 257-5140

450 Old Vine Street, 2nd Floor

Lexington, Kentucky 40507   www.damsafety.org

BAT CONSERVATION INTERNATIONAL

Scholarships for research that best helps document the roosting and feeding habitat requirements of bats, their ecological or economic roles, or their conservation needs.

Eligibility: Students enrolled in any college or university worldwide.

Award: $500 to $2,500   # Given: 15

Apply by: mid-December

For more information:

Bat Conservation International

Student Scholarship Program

P.O. Box 162603   apuntch@batcon.org

Austin, X 78716-2603   www.batcon.org/schol/schol.html

BLINKS RESEARCH FELLOWSHIP PROGRAM

See Graduate listing: depts.washington.edu/fhl/stuops.html

CABELL BRAND FELLOWSHIPS

Center for International Poverty and Resource Studies

A research study and action center to examine, understand, and network on the interrelation of two of society's most import issues: The short and long term implications of international poverty; World resource usage and potential limitations with environmental interrelationships.

Provides high school and college students with an opportunity to study, research and suggest possible solutions to social and environmental issues which affect their community. Fields of study include but are not limited to: poverty, day care, health, crime, homelessness, hunger, recycling, land use, biodiversity, wildlife preservation, waste disposal, and the quality of life in all aspects.

Fellowship students develop projects with the assistance of a professor or teacher who oversees their work, and hopefully provide academic credit. A student can also apply to work with a local organization which receives a mini-grant to compensate student.

Eligibility: students currently enrolled in a learning institution such as a local high school or college in the Virginia New Century Region.

Award: $500-Fellowship

      up to $1,000-Mini-grant   # Given: varies

For more information:

Cabell Brand Center   (540) 387-3402

P. O. Box 429   www.cbcenter.org/application.html

Salem, VA 24153   cbc@cbcenter.org

CALIFORNIA ADOLESCENT NUTRITION AND FITNESS

The mission of the California Adolescent Nutrition and Fitness (CANFit) Program is to engage communities, and build their capacity to improve the nutritional status and physical fitness of California's low-income multi-ethnic youth 10-14 years of age. Undergraduate scholarships are available for African American, American Indian/Alaska Native, Asian/Pacific Islander or Latino/Hispanic students expressing financial need to study nutrition, physical education, or culinary arts in the state of California.

The application essay for 2003 is entitled "The junk food industry often targets urban youth, negatively impacting their nutrition and health. What steps can the average adult take on a personal, community, and national level to combat these negative influences?"

Eligibility: Enrollment in an approved bachelors (50 semester units of college credits with a 2.5 or better cumulative GPA) program in Nutrition, Public Health Nutrition, or Physical Education; or American Dietetic Association Approved Pre-professional Practice Program at an accredited university in California. Financial need, minority students affiliation (see above).

Award: $1,000   # Given: 5-10
Apply by: March 31
For more information:
CANFit   (800) 200-3131
2140 Shattuck Avenue, Suite 610   www.canfit.org
Berkeley CA 94704   info@canfit.org

CA ASSOCIATION OF BLACK SOCIAL WORKERS

The Los Angeles Chapter of the NABSW gives an annual book scholarship to social work students.

Eligibility: member or potential member of ABSW.

For more information:
CA Ass'n. of Black Social Workers   CABSW.org
7100 S. Western Ave.   FAX (909) 788-0894
Los Angeles, CA 90047   www.cabsw.org

CA CONGRESS OF PARENTS & TEACHERS

Acknowledges the achievements of HS seniors for volunteer service in the school and community. The scholarship program also provides continuing education opportunities for teachers, school nurses and PTA volunteers to continue their education.

Eligibility: Applicant must be a California resident graduating from a high school in California with a PTA/PTSA unit in good standing, and must be a member of that PTA/PTSA. Planning to attend an accredited CA college, university or trade and technical school.

Award: $500   # Given: 100+
Apply by: February 1
For more information:
CA Congress of Parents & Teachers   (213) 620-1100
930 Georgia Street   info@capta.org
Los Angeles,CA 90015-1322   capta.org/State_PTA/scholar_grant/

CALIFORNIA SEA GRANT

John D. Isaacs Memorial Scholarship

Recognizes excellence in research by high school seniors to encourage interest in marine science at the high school level, and to encourage pursuit of scholastic excellence in higher education. Each year a student who presents an outstanding marine science project at the California State Science Fair receives a scholarship to study at a college or university in California.

Eligibility: California high school senior.

Award: $12,000 over 4 years   # Given: 1
Apply by: April 4
For more information:
Isaacs Scholarship Committee   Isaacs@seamail.ucsd.edu

California Sea Grant College System
University of California, San Diego
9500 Gilman Drive
La Jolla, CA 92093-0232   www-csgc.ucsd.edu/EDUCATION/Isaacs.html

CALIFORNIA TEACHERS ASSOCIATION

Martin Luther King Jr Memorial Scholarship

For ethnic minority persons obtaining degree credentials for teaching-related careers in public education.

Eligibility: member of a defined ethnic minority group. Applicants must also be an active member of CTA, or a dependent child of an active, retired-life or deceased CTA member, or a member of Student CTA (SCTA).

Award: $250 - $2,000   # Given: varies
Apply by: March 15

L. Gordon Bittle Memorial Scholarship for Student CTA (SCTA)

For active member of Student California Teachers Association (SCTA) pursuing a career in public education.

Eligibility: Undergraduate, credential or graduate student in approved credential or degree program in an accredited institution of higher learning. High school grade point average should reflect a 3.5 average. This scholarship is not available for those currently working in public schools as members of CTA.

Award: $2,000   # Given: 3
Apply by: Feb. 15

For more information:

Scholarship Coordinator   650/552-5370
CTA - Human Rights Dept   scholarships@cta.org
PO Box 921   www.cta.org/InsideCTA/TrainingHR/Scholarship
Burlingame, CA 94011

CALIFORNIA WATER ENVIRONMENT ASSOCIATION

Kirt Brooks Scholarship

Provides annual scholarships for individuals attending a college or technical trade school with major related to Water Environment Industry (wastewater). Involvement in CWEA activities taken into consideration.

Eligibility: Full or part-time student members of CWEA and their immediate family. CWEA membership in the past year is mandatory.

Award: $500 - $2,000   4 year college or university
$250 - $500   2 Year college or technical trade school
Apply by: February 1

For more information:

California Water Environment Ass'n. (510) 382-7800
7677 Oakport Street, Suite 525
Oakland, CA 94621-1935   www.cwea.org/

Center for Environmental Citizenship

Summer Training Academy

The Center for Environmental Citizenship is committed to training and organizing young voters to protect the environment. The Summer Training Academy, held in Washington DC, trains students how to impact critical environmental issues through electoral organizing. The Academy seeks young people of diverse backgrounds from the U.S and Puerto Rico.

Award: free tuition, travel scholarships to DC are available

Apply by: May 1   # Given: 100

For more information:

Center for Environmental Citizenship www.cgv.org/cgv

200 G Street, NE #300   sta@envirocitizen.org

Washington, DC 20002   202.547.8435

Congressional Hispanic Caucus Institute

See Graduate listing: www.chci.org/chciyouth/scholarship/scholarshipawards.htm

Connecticut Ass'n. of Latin Americans in Higher Ed.

For Latino students involved with and committed to activities that promote Latinos' pursuit of education. For both high school seniors (or GED equivalent) and undergraduate college students.

Eligibility: Accepted for admission to, or enrolled in, an accredited institution of higher education, "B" average (3.0 College GPA), U.S. citizen or permanent resident. Must have been a Connecticut resident during the preceding 12 months. Limited to Latino students from Connecticut with financial need.

Award: $500   Apply by: April 15

For more information:

CALAHE   Dr. Wilson Luna

P.O. Box 382   Gateway Community Tech. College

Milford, CT 06460-0382   60 Sargent Drive

www.CALAHE.org   New Haven, CT 06511

Connecticut Forest and Park Association

James L. Goodwin Memorial Scholarships for students in silviculture or forest resource management programs.

Eligibility: Connecticut residents with financial need.

Award: $1,000 - $3,000

For more information:

Goodwin Memorial Scholarship   (860) 346-2372

Connecticut Forest and Park Association

16 Meriden Road   info@ctwoodlands.org

Rockfall, CT 06481-2961   www.ctwoodlands.org

CONSERVATION FEDERATION OF MISSOURI

Charles P. Bell Scholarships

For studies related to conservation. Group grants will also be awarded to Missouri HS classes or youth groups for projects related to natural resource conservation. Projects involving education or physical involvement in the protection of the environment receive special consideration.

Eligibility: Undergraduates with at least 60 credit hours in a field of study related to management of natural resources, specifically fish, wildlife, forest, soil, and water. Applicants must be Missouri residents, and those applicants enrolled in Missouri schools will be given preference.

Award: $500   # Given: 2
$250 elementary - H.S. groups   # Given: 6
Apply by: January 15

For more information:

Bell Scholarships   (314) 634-2322
728 W. Main St.   confedmo@socket.net
Jefferson City, MO 65101   www.confedmo.com/scholarships.asp

COUNCIL ON INT'L EDUCATIONAL EXCHANGE

Robert B. Bailey Scholarship

Intended to promote increased participation in the Council's International Study Programs, by members of groups which have traditionally been under-represented in study abroad -- especially ethnic minority students.

Eligibility: CIEE Study Center (CSC) applicants that are U.S. citizens, and self-identified as belonging to an underrepresented group. Financial need considered.

Award: $500   # Given: 10
Apply by: late October for spring programs
April 1 for summer, fall and academic year programs.

Bowman Travel Grants

Provides assistance to students participating in educational programs in non-traditional destinations. Preference for educational programs, projects and work/internship/volunteer activities in which applicants interact in a significant way with the host population. No restrictions are placed on the specific focus of the program, project, or activity, although reviewers are particularly interested in activities that enhance an applicant's language skills and/or understanding of cultural and social issues.

Eligibility: US citizens and permanent residents participating in a CIEE study or volunteer abroad program. Must attend a CIEE Member or CIEE Academic Consortium member institution and plan to study or volunteer in a non-traditional destination (see website for more details).

Award: Awards vary in amount to help defray the cost of travel
Apply by: April 1 (summer, fall & academic year programs)
late October (January - May programs)

Jennifer Ritzmann Scholarship for Studies in Tropical Biology

In honor of Jennifer Ritzmann who had a dream to do forestry work in Costa Rica and was committed to preserving the rain forest. A scholarship is awarded each year to a participant in the Monteverde program.

Eligibility: Students accepted to Council's Study Center program in Monteverde, Costa Rica will automatically be considered for this award.

Award: $1,000   # Given: 1

International Study Programs Scholarships

For students planning international study with CIIE.

Eligibility: Council Study Center applicants only. Applicants must be from Academic Consortium member institutions (see website). Students should demonstrate preparation for the program through course work, volunteer work, or internships. Students should indicate how they plan to integrate this international experience into academic, community, professional, and extracurricular activities. Financial need and merit are taken into consideration.

Award: $1,000   Apply by: as above

Council on International Educational Exchange (CIEE) Scholarships

To make study abroad opportunities available to the widest possible audience, these scholarships are for students who demonstrate both academic excellence and financial need.

Eligibility: CIEE Study Center (CSC) applicants from Academic Consortium member institution website). Financial need is strongly considered.

Award:$500-$1,000

Department of Education Scholarship for Programs in China

The U.S. Department of Education has awarded CIEE funding under the Fulbright-Hays Group Projects Abroad Program to provide financial assistance to students who are participating in the Chinese language programs offered by the CIEE Centers at Peking University, East China Normal University (Shanghai), Nanjing University, and National Chengchi University (Taipei).

Eligibility: U.S. citizen or U.S. permanent resident junior or senior enrolled in an institution of higher learning who plans a teaching career in modern foreign languages or area studies' completed 2 years of college-level Mandarin Chinese language training at the beginning of the program or the equivalent. Equivalency may be based on a language professor's evaluation or a language proficiency exam score.

Award: $500 - $4000.

Apply by: Academic Year Programs is April 15
Spring programs is November 15

For more information:

Council on International Educational Exchange   1-800-40-STUDY
205 E. 42nd St.   www.ciee.org/council_isp_scholarships.cfm
New York, NY 10001   scholarships@ciee.org

Darling Marine Center

University of Maine

The Summer Undergraduate Research Experience is an eleven week internship program funded in part by the Gulf of Maine Foundation (GMF). GMF is a nonprofit organization concerned with education and research in marine related topics, and in the understanding and preservation of the Gulf of Maine. . Students work along side faculty, staff and graduate students on a variety of research projects.

Eligibility: preference for juniors and seniors currently enrolled in a marine science program. Foreign students, minorities and women encouraged to apply.

Stipend: $2,600 + housing   # Given: 4

Apply by: February 15

For more information:

Darling Marine Center   darling@maine.edu

193 Clark's Cove Road   server.dmc.maine.edu

Walpole, ME 04573   (207) 563-3146 ext. 200

Demonstration of Energy-Efficient Developments

DEED Scholarships

Scholarships support research projects and education in energy-related fields and increase awareness about career opportunities in public power. DEED encourages activities that promote energy innovation, improving efficiencies and lowering the cost of providing energy services to the customers of publicly owned electric utilities.

Eligibility: energy related major. Students must obtain a DEED member sponsor for their scholarship project. Find a DEED member utility from your state, and contact DEED to request the specific contact information for the utility from which you wish to request sponsorship.

Award: $4,000   # Given: up to 10

Apply by: January 31

Senior Technical Design Project

Promote the involvement of students studying in energy-related disciplines in the public power industry.

Eligibility: students studying in energy-related disciplines from accredited colleges or universities are eligible for scholarships.

Award: $5000   # Given: 1

Apply by: October 15

For more information:

American Public Power Ass'n.   (202)467-2993

2301 M St. NW   www.appanet.org

Washington DC 20037

ENTOMOLOGICAL SOCIETY OF AMERICA

Scholarships designed to encourage student interest in entomology.

Eligibility: Students in entomology, zoology, biology, or a related science in the US, Mexico, or Canada; 30 college credits by August. Preference to students with demonstrated financial need.

Apply by: May 31

Stanley Beck Fellowship

Assists needy students in entomology and related disciplines at a college or university in the United States, Mexico or Canada. The is based on physical limitations or economic, minority, or environmental conditions. This fellowship was established as a tribute to Stanley D. Beck, a notable scientist who pursued his profession despite the effects of a debilitating disease. Made annually, amount of the fellowship varies each year.

Award: varies each year   Apply by: September 1

For more information:

Entomological Society of America   (301) 731-4535
Attn.: Undergraduate Scholarship Coordinator
9301 Annapolis Road
Lanham, MD 20706-3115   www.entsoc.org

THE FINANCIAL WOMEN'S ASSOCIATION OF SAN FRANCISCO

To encourage leadership and provide opportunities for Bay Area women in the field of finance.

Eligibility: Female students in finance or related field who will be juniors or seniors in the fall semester at an accredited Bay Area college or university, minimum GPA of 3.4. Financial need and community involvement and leadership considered.

Award: $5,000   # Given: 7
Apply by: February 28

For more information:

FWA Scholarship Committee   (415) 333-9045
PO Box 26143 Gateway Station   www.fwasf.org
San Francisco, CA 94126   info@fwasf.org

FIRST SCHOLARSHIPS

Eligibility: Students with a major or minor in Horticulture or a related field, with a minimum 3.0 gpa for most scholarships. Applicants with lower grade point averages may be considered if they have otherwise outstanding qualifications or extenuating circumstances. Must either be a citizen or resident of, or be enrolled in an accredited educational institution in, the U.S. or Canada.

Award: $500-$2,000   # Given: 23
Apply by: May 1

For more information:

Scholarship Applications   scholarship@firstinfloriculture.org

Floriculture Industry Research and Scholarship Trust
P.O. Box 280
East Lansing, MI 48826

(517)333-4617
www.firstinfloriculture.org

FLORIDA EXCELLENCE IN SERVICE AWARDS

For students involved in outstanding campus-based community service.
Eligibility: full-time student at accredited Florida higher ed. institution.

Award: $1000   # Given: 3
Apply by: March 1

For more information:
Florida Campus Compact
325 John Knox Road
Building F, Suite 210
Tallahasse, FL 32303

www.floridacompact.org
(850) 488-7782
info@floridacompact.org

FOREST LANDOWNERS FOUNDATION

Presented to outstanding students currently enrolled in a certified forestry program. Also support for a summer internship in Washington, D.C., for an advanced forestry student interested in forest policy issues.

Award: $1000

For more information:
Forest Landowners Association   (800) 325-2954
Research and Education Foundation
PO Box 450209
Atlanta, GA 31145   www.forestlandowners.com/foundation.html

FREEHOLD SOIL CONSERVATION DISTRICT

Munch, Clark and Freehold Soil Conservation District Scholarships

For students majoring in a field such as forestry, conservation, soil science, resource management, environmental studies, agriculture, environmental science or environmental education.

Eligibility: NJ resident from Middlesex or Monmouth County, entering junior or senior year.

Award: $1,000   # Given: 3
Apply by: mid April

For more information:
Freehold Soil Conservation District   (732) 446-2300
211 Freehold Road   www.webspan.net/~fscd/educate.htm
Manalapan, NJ 07726-3452   FSCD@webspan.net

GARDEN CLUB OF AMERICA

Clara Carter Higgins / GCA Summer Environmental Award

Provides financial aid toward summer courses in environmental studies. Offers students who have demonstrated a keen interest in the betterment of the environment an opportunity for further study in the field of ecology.

Some summer programs students completed recently include: oil spill cleanup and control; hazardous wastes, effects on coastal shellfish and wetlands; barrier island ecology, plant resources of the tropics; and mapping dimensions of sustainable development in Costa Rica.

Eligibility: college sophomores through seniors

Award: $1,500   # Given: 2+

Apply by: Early February

For more information:

The Garden Club of America   (212) 753-8287

14 East 60th Street   www.gcamerica.org/scholarships.htm

New York, NY 10022   csutton@gcamerica.org

Katharine M. Grosscup Scholarships

To encourage the study of horticulture and related fields.

Eligibility: college juniors, seniors or graduate students at the masters degree level, preferably from IN, KY, MI, OH, PA and WV. Personal interview in Cleveland is required of all finalists.

Award: To $3,000   # Given: 2+

Apply by: February 1

For more information:

Grosscup Scholarship Committee   Fax: (216) 721-2056 No phone calls.

Cleveland Botanical Garden   www.gcamerica.org/scholarships.htm

11030 East Boulevard

Cleveland, OH 44106

Francis M. Peacock Scholarship for Native Bird Habitat

For study of U.S. winter or summer habitat for threatened or endangered native birds. Opportunity to pursue real habitat-related issues that eventually benefit bird species and lend useful information for management decisions.

Eligibility: college seniors and graduate students

Award: $4,000   # Given: 1

Apply by: January 15

For more information:

Scott Sutcliffe   Fax: (607) 254-2415 No phone calls.

Cornell Lab of Ornithology   lh17@cornell.edu

159 Sapsucker Woods Road   www.gcamerica.org/scholarships.htm

Ithaca, NY 14850   lbirdsource.cornell.edu

GATES MILLENNIUM SCHOLARS

The Bill & Melinda Gates Foundation funds this program, administered by the United Negro College Fund, to provide outstanding African American, American Indian/Alaska Natives, Asian Pacific Islander Americans, and Hispanic American students with an opportunity to complete an undergraduate college education, in all discipline areas and a graduate education for those students pursuing studies in mathematics, science, engineering, education, or library science.

The program rewards leadership abilities proven through participation in community service, extracurricular, or other activities and GMS also provides opportunities for Scholars to prepare for leadership roles in their profession and in their communities.

Eligibility: is African American, American Indian/Alaska Native, Asian Pacific Islander American or Hispanic American; is a citizen or legal permanent resident or national of the United States; GPA of 3.30; entering an accredited college or university as full-time, degree-seeking freshmen in the fall of year; eligible for a federal Pell Grant; Nominated by a principal, teacher, guidance counselor, tribal higher education representative, or other professional educator.

Award: based on the cost of tuition, fees, books, and living expenses and financial need. Renewable for ongoing undergraduate and eligible graduate education.

Apply by: February 1

For more information:

Gates Millennium Scholars	(877)690-4677
P.O. Box 1434	
Alexandria, Virginia 22313	www.gmsp.org

GLAMOUR'S TOP TEN COLLEGE WOMEN

Recognizes exceptional achievements and academic excellence. Applicant must demonstrate leadership experience, involvement on campus and in her community, excellence in her field of study, and unique goals.

Eligibility: any woman, full-time junior at accredited college or university.

Award: $1,000   # Given: 10

Apply by: January 31

For more information:

Glamour's Top Ten College Women Competition	us.glamour.com
4 Times Square	(800) 244-GLAM
New York, NY 10036	ttcw@glamour.com

GOLDEN APPLE SCHOLARS OF ILLINOIS

Teachers, counselors, principals and non-family adults are invited to nominate high school juniors who demonstrate an interest in or commitment to teaching as a profession. The Golden Apple Scholars program prepares bright high school graduates who represent a rich ethnic diversity, for successful teaching careers in high need schools throughout Illinois. There is a particular shortage of minority and bilingual teachers. Students need teachers with similar backgrounds and experiences to serve as role models and give them the hope of a promising future.

Scholars participate in three times the amount of classroom experience as their peers in traditional education programs. Scholars experience the realities of teaching in a high need setting, observe different subjects and grades so they can decide on their specialty, and receive support from veteran teachers.

Eligibility: Nominated juniors at any Illinois HS. Must earn a bachelor's degree at a participating IL university, obtain IL teacher certification, and teach for five years in an IL school of high need. A limited number of positions in the program are also open to college sophomores nominated by the liaison of a participating university.

Award: $5,000 per year for 4 years   # Given: 60
    $2,000 stipend for summer institute

For more information:

Pat Kilduff, Director of Recruitment/Placement   (312)407-0433, ext. 105

Rocio Manriquez, Director of Selection   (312)407-0433, ext. 118

Golden Apple Foundation Scholarship Program

8 South Michigan Ave.

Chicago, IL 60613   www.goldenapple.org/programs-text-scholars.html

HAWAII COMMUNITY FOUNDATION

Offers a number of different scholarships for students in Hawaii of good moral character who show potential for filling a community need, and who demonstrate intent to return to, or stay in, Hawaii to work.

For more information:

Hawaii Community Foundation

900 Fort St. Mall, Suite 1300

Honolulu, HI 96813   www.hawaiicommunityfoundation.org

HAWKINSON FOUNDATION FOR PEACE AND JUSTICE

For students who have demonstrated a commitment to peace and justice through study, internships or projects that illustrate their commitment.

Eligibility: resident or student in MN, IA, WI, ND or SD. Must be available for personal interview in Minneapolis and attend an award ceremony in the fall.

Award: $1,500   Apply by: late April

For more information:

Vincent L. Hawkinson Foundation   (612) 331-8125

c/o Grace University Lutheran Church

324 Harvard Street SE

Minneapolis MN 55414   www.graceattheu.org

HEARST MINORITY/PHILANTHROPIC/NON-PROFIT

See Graduate listing.

EMILY HEWITT MEMORIAL SCHOLARSHIP

For students with an active commitment to nature and conservation.
Eligibility: Junior or senior standing.

Award: $500   Apply by: early May

For more information:

CBTA

Hewitt Scholarship Fund

POB 2053

Arnold, CA 95223

Hudson River Foundation

See Graduate listing.

Indiana Wildlife Federation

Students taking course work to major or minor in a field related to resource conservation or environmental education.

Eligibility: Indiana residents, college sophomores or above.

Award: $1,000.   # Given: 1

Apply by: April 30,

For more information:

Indiana Wildlife Federation   (317) 571-1220
Scholarship Committee
950 North Rangeline Road Suite A
Carmel, IN 46032-1315   www.indianawildlife.org

Institute for International Public Policy

To increase awareness of and interest in careers in international service among undergraduate students, especially members of underrepresented minority groups, by preparing them through a sequential program of policy institutes, study abroad, language training, internships and graduate education.

Sophomore Year Summer Policy Institute

Course work, seminars and field trips covering international politics, quantitative methods, international economics, peace/conflict resolution, U.S. foreign policy. Fellows pay for their travel to and from the SSPI. IIPP covers the costs of tuition, books, site visits, room and board, and a modest stipend.

Junior Year Study Abroad

Fellows may study abroad for up to one academic year at an accredited institution. IIPP will cover one-half of one semester of study abroad.

Junior Year Summer Institute

Eight weeks of intensive academic preparation for graduate school. IIPP covers the costs of travel to and from the JSPI, tuition, room and board, and a modest stipend.

Senior Language Institute

Intensive study in a five- to six-week program. IIPP covers the costs of travel to and from the SLI, tuition, room and board, and a modest stipend.

Eligibility: Underrepresented minority full-time sophomore student at a four year institution. 3.2 GPA or higher. U.S. citizens or permanent residents.

Apply by: March 1

For more information:

Institute for International Public Policy
http://161.58.87.106/content/index.cfm

2750 Prosperity Ave. Suite 600   (800) 530-6232
Fairfax, VA 22031   (703) 205-7624

Kentucky Environmental Protection

Seeks to promote environmental education at the undergraduate and graduate level in the state universities, and to assist the State's environmental protection agencies in their effort to hire qualified professional staff. Scholarship recipients are provided employment by state agencies during the summer while in school. Following graduation, each recipient is obligated to work for the Cabinet for one year for each year of scholarship support.

Eligibility: Kentucky undergraduate juniors and seniors, and graduate students in environmental academic areas critical to the staffing needs of the state.

Award: Tuition, room, board, books and fees at a Kentucky university.

\# Given: 4 (on average)

For more information:

Jim Kipp

Environmental Protection Scholarship

Kentucky Water Resources Research Institute

233 Mining and Minerals Resources Bldg.

University of Kentucky   kipp@pop.uky.edu

Lexington, KY 40506-0107   www.uky.edu/WaterResources/UK-EPS.HTML

Kettle Range Conservation Group (WA)

Applicants must submit a brief essay describing how to help society solve environmental problems.

Eligibility: Washington state HS seniors in Colville, Curlew, Inchelium, Kettle Falls, Republic and Tonasket.

Award: $1,000   # Given: 4

Apply by: May 1   Apply to: On-line

For more information:

KRCG - Project Scholarship

P.O. Box 150

Republic, WA 99166   www.kettlerange.org/scholarship.htm

Key Club International

Key Club is a student-led organization that teaches leadership through serving others. There are a number of scholarships available to active members.

Key Club International Scholarships

Eligibility: college-bound graduating high school senior involved in Key Club for at least two years, has completed 100 service hours in Key Club career, has paid dues and has held an elected officer position on the club, district, or international level. 3.5 GPA.

Awards: $1,000, renewable   Apply by: mid February

Key Club District Matching Scholarships

The Kiwanis International Foundation and Key Club International have designed a scholarship program to recognize graduating seniors who have excelled in leadership and have provided service to others. Interested students need to contact their district administrator (listed on web site) to determine the district's participation in the program. Most districts have their own scholarship application forms and deadlines.

Eligibility: active Key Club member for two years in good standing, has paid dues and appears on the roster on file at Key Club International,is a college, university, technical, or vocational school-bound graduating high school senior with a gpa of at least 3.0. Financial need is not a factor in this award. Key Club International Board members and Key Club district governors are not eligible for the District Matching Scholarship program.

Award: $1,000   Apply by: Each district determines deadlines.

For more information:

Youth Funds Manager   (800) KIWANIS,ext. 244
Kiwanis International   (317) 875-8755, ext. 244
3636 Woodview Trace   youthfunds@kiwanis.org
Indianapolis, IN 46268   www.keyclub.org/resources_opportunities.html

LEADERS OF TOMORROW SCHOLARSHIP PROGRAM

This program recognizes students for their outstanding demonstration of community service, leadership skills, positive attitude and academic achievement.

Award: $1,000 to be used toward higher education.

For more information:

www.comcast.com/InTheCommunity/scholarships/scholarship_intro.html

LOUISIANA WATER ENVIRONMENT ASSOCIATION

Deiler, Keffer and Norman Memorial Scholarships

Scholarships assist students pursuing either a baccalaureate or masters degree at a college or university within Louisiana in environmental related curriculum in engineering, physical or natural science, or public health.

Eligibility: LA resident; 3.0 GPA, at least a Junior (undergraduate) and no higher than a Master's level candidate during the year of award.

Award: $1,500   # Given: 3
Apply by: April 1

For more information:

LWEA Scholarship Selection Committee Chairman
c/o LCA
One American Place, Suite 2040
Baton Rouge, LA 70825   (225) 344-2609
                                        www.lweaonline.org

MAINE COMMUNITY FOUNDATION

R.V. Gadabout Gaddis

Awarded to Maine high school graduates who are college juniors or seniors majoring in outdoor writing or a related environmental field, and/or to accredited Maine colleges or universities with programs in this area.

Apply by: April 1

For more information:

Gadabout Gaddis Scholarship Fund (207) 667-9735
c/o Maine Community Foundation
P.O. Box 148
Ellsworth, ME 04605 www.mainecf.org/scholarships

MAINE MITCHELL SCHOLARS

Each year the Senator George J. Mitchell Scholarship Research Institute awards one scholarship to a student from every public high school in the state of Maine. Academic performance/academic potential, community service and financial need all weighed equally in selection process.

Eligibility: senior at a public high school in Maine entering a two- or four-year degree program, in or out of state.

Award: $1000 for up to 4 years   Apply by: April 1

For more information:

The Mitchell Institute (207) 773-7700
22 Monument Square, Suite 200 (888)-220-7209
Portland, ME 04101 info@mitchellinstitute.org
www.mitchellinstitute.org

MARINE SCIENCE SUMMER

Rosenstiel School of Marine & Atmospheric Science

Introduces bright and energetic undergraduates to research in the marine sciences. The intensive summer program allows undergraduate students the opportunity to experience graduate level research and school. A faculty member is assigned to each student, according to their educational background and interests. Students will spend ten weeks engaged in laboratory research.

Eligibility: United States citizens or permanent residents, juniors or seniors enrolled full-time at a four-year college or university, 3.0 GPA.

Award: $2,000 stipend, campus housing, possibility of travel expenses.

Apply by: February 10

For more information:

Rosenstiel School of Marine and Atmospheric Science
Dr. Frank Millero, Associate Dean
4600 Rickenbacker Causeway
Key Biscayne, FL 33149   www.rsmas.miami.edu/grad-studies/sumfel.html

McDONALD'S® "SERVE YOUR COMMUNITY" SCHOLARSHIP

McDonald's New York Tri-State restaurant owners sponsor this program to reward students who have made a difference in their communities by taking an active role in community service activities.

The scholarship program will award scholarships to high school seniors in the

New York Tri-State Area who have consistently demonstrated exemplary community service. Students are asked to write a 300-word essay on "How they bring the McDonald's mantra of giving back to the community to life."

Eligibility: Students must be a high school senior attending college in the fall of application year.

Award: $5,000   # Given: 5
Apply by: February 1

For more information:
McDonald's "Serve Your Community" Scholarship
        Scholarship Program Administrator
        P.O. Box 22492   www.mcdonaldsnymetro.com
        Nashville TN 37202

MANA Raquel Marquez Frankel Scholarship

Based on leadership potential, academic promise and commitment to improving the quality of life of the Hispanic community.

Eligibility: Hispanic/Latina women with financial need, must attend or be admitted to a postsecondary or vocational institution.

Award: $500 - $1,000   Apply by: April 1

For more information:
        MANA Scholarship Committee   (202) 822-7888
        1201 16th Street, N.W. Suite 300
        Washington, D.C. 20036   www.hermana.org

Mellon Minority Fellowship for Ecology

Focuses on the effects of biological diversity on the stability, productivity, and nutrient dynamics of ecosystems. The program is located on a 5500 acre research site that has a great range of native, old-growth habitats including prairie, savanna, hardwood forest, pine forest, and wetlands. Interns and visiting researchers live in on-site housing. Interns work in a series of well-replicated field experiments in which biological diversity is controlled and the impacts of diversity are measured. The program culminates in an individual research project.

Stipend: $3,500 -$4,000 + housing and transportation

For more information:
        Cedar Creek Natural History Area
        1997 Upper Buford Circle
        University of Minnesota
        St. Paul, MN 55108   www.mmuf.org

Migrant Scholarships

Mattera National Scholarship Fund for Migrant Children

Assists those migrant youth who have the potential and the desire to further their education so as to achieve their personal and career goals.

Eligibility: entering college or other types of post-secondary programs and high school dropouts and potential dropouts.

Award: $150 - $500

Frank Kazmierczak Memorial Migrant Scholarship

Eligibility: Child of a migrant worker or a migrant worker whose goal is to teach, academic achievement, financial need.

Award: $1,000   # Given: 1

For more information :

Scholarship Fund for Migrant Children   info@migrant.net

BOCES Geneseo Migrant Center   www.migrant.net/scholarships.htm

27 Lackawanna Avenue   (800) 245-5681

Mt. Morris, New York 14510   (585) 658-7960

Migrant Farmworker Baccalaureate Scholarship

Provides financial support to a deserving student with a history of migrating for employment in agriculture. Designed to assist the youth in obtaining a baccalaureate degree without substantial debt.

Eligibility: Completed freshman year

Award: to $2,000   Renewable for 3 years

For more information :

Migrant Farmworker Baccalaureate Scholarship Committee

Geneseo Migrant Center, Inc.   info@migrant.net

P.O. Box 549   (800) 245-5681

Geneseo, New York 14454-0549   www.migrant.net/scholarships.htm

MOTE MARINE LABORATORY

Gilbert Scholarship

MML offers scholarships to fund financially disadvantaged undergraduates for twelve week internships during the spring or summer. Internships available in research areas, education, communications, and the aquarium.

Eligibility: 3.2 GPA, completed the Free Application for Federal Student Aid (FAFSA) and demonstrated financial need.

Award: stipend for living expenses and research supplies for 8 to 16 weeks

Given: 2

Apply by: February 1 (it is recommended that students apply in the fall).

For more information:

Intern Coordinator   (941) 388-4441

Mote Marine Laboratory   adavis@mote.org

1600 Ken Thompson Parkway   www.mote.org

Sarasota, FL 34236

NATIONAL NETWORK FOR ENVIRONMENTAL MANAGEMENT

See Graduate listing.

NATIONAL PATHFINDERS SCHOLARSHIP

Awarded to women seeking careers in chemical, biological, or medical research on substance abuse and/or its causes; effect of substance abuse on the family, society, and/or abuser; counseling of substance abusers and/or others affected, etc.

Eligibility: College sophomores, juniors, seniors, and Masters students in fields related to substance abuse such as: chemistry, sociology, and psychology.

Award: $2,0500   # Given: 2

Apply by: February 1 (to local state Federation for nomination)

For more information send a self-addressed stamped envelope to:

NFRW headquarters

Attn: Scholarships and Internships   (703) 548-9688

124 North Alfred Street

Alexandria, VA 22314-3011   www.nfrw.org/programs/scholarships.htm

NATIONAL SECURITY EDUCATION PROGRAM

David L. Boren Undergraduate Scholarships

Provides American undergraduates with the resources and encouragement to acquire skills and experience in countries and areas of the world critical to the future security of our nation. You begin to acquire the international competence you need to communicate effectively across borders, understand other perspectives and analyze fluid economic and political realities. NSEP educates citizens to understand foreign cultures, strengthen economic competitiveness, and enhance international cooperation and security.

NSEP focuses on geographical areas, languages and fields of study deemed critical to national security. The program recognizes that the scope of national security includes not only the traditional concerns of protecting and promoting American well-being, but also the challenges of a global society, including: sustainable development, environmental degradation, global disease and hunger, population growth and migration, and economic competitiveness.

Recipients are required to seek employment with a federal agency or office involved in national security affairs. Duration of the service requirement is equal to the length of the scholarship support under NSEP auspices. Undergraduate recipients are eligible to apply for NSEP graduate fellowships.

Eligibility: US citizen freshman, sophomore, junior, or senior in an accredited U.S. post-secondary institution.

Award: to $20,000 for an academic year, renewable

Apply by: early February-IIE, December-January-your campus representative.

For more information:

Institute of International Education   nsep@iie.org.

809 United Nations Plaza   www.iie.org

New York, NY 10017-3580   1-800-618-NSEP or (202) 326-7697

info@worldstudy.gov   www.worldstudy.gov

Nation Institute

See Graduate listing.

National Council of State Garden Clubs

Promotes study in horticulture, floriculture, landscape design, botany, biology, plant pathology, forestry, agronomy, environmental concerns, city planning, land management and/or allied subjects.

Eligibility: full-time juniors, seniors and graduate students. Applications may be made by sophomores for grants to be awarded for the junior year. 3.0 GPA. Applicants must be majoring in one of these fields of study. Approval must be granted by the NCSGC Scholarship Committee for application to be made in any major other than the ones listed.

Applications must be sent to the State Garden Club Scholarship Chairman for the state in which student is a legal resident, not the NCSGC Scholarship Chairman. See website for individual state chairmen.

Award: $3,500   # Given: 32
Apply by: March 1 (received by date)
For more information:
NCSGC Scholarship Chairman   (512) 360-2738
Renee D. Blaschke   enee_blaschke@juno.com
Fourth Vice-President, NGC, Inc.
307 Garwood Street
Smithville, Texas 78957-1504   www.gardenclub.org/scholar.htm

New Education Foundation College Grants

Education is Freedom, a new national education organization founded by 7-Eleven, Inc. president and CEO James W. Keyes, provides funding to U.S. high school seniors or graduates who show academic promise and wish to attend college but who do not qualify for financial assistance programs. Scholarships awarded on the basis of merit, financial need, community service, and leadership.

Eligibility: a U.S. resident for at least a year; a U.S. high School senior or graduate with 3.0 GPA; be enrolled for the first time in a full-time undergraduate course of study at an accredited two- or four-year college or university; and be 24 years of age or younger.

Award: $500-$5,000   # Given: approx. 250
Apply by: March 15
For more information:
Education Is Freedom   (866)EIF-EDUCATE
c/o 7-Eleven, Inc.
2711 North Haskell Avenue
Dallas, TX 75204   www.educationisfreedom.org/

New York City Government Scholars Program

Offers a select group of college students, who are interested in pursuing a career in government and public service, a unique opportunity to learn about New York City Government through a ten-week program combining full time employment in City government with a comprehensive seminar series.

Eligibility: sophomores, juniors, or graduating seniors; all majors.

Stipend: $3,500   Apply by: early January

For more information:

NYC Government Scholars Program

NYC Department of Citywide Administrative Services

1 Centre Street, Rm 2425   (212) 669-3695

New York, NY 10007   www.nyc.gov/html/dcas/html/intern.html

New York Water Environment Association

Students enrolled in an environmental program which will allow them to pursue a professional career in the environmental field.

Eligibility: children of NYWEA members, students enrolled at a college or university where there is a NYWEA student chapter, high school students who will be enrolled in an environmentally related program in a four year college or university.

Award: $1,500   # Given: 6 (2 in each category)

Apply by: March 15

For more information:

NYWEA, Executive Office   (315) 422-7811

126 N. Salina Street, Suite 200   www.nywea.org/scho-ann.htm

Syracuse, NY 13202

NSF Research Experience for Undergraduates (REU)

National Science Foundation's Research Experience for Undergraduates (REU) Program is an autumn program for basic research skills, analytical techniques, and interpretation and presentation proficiency. Research areas include ecology of marine and estuarine fish; plant-animal interactions in seagrass beds; microbial ecology; hydrodynamic effects on marine organisms; biomechanics of marine invertebrates; and phytoplankton and zooplankton ecology.

Eligibility: College juniors and seniors with interests in biology, chemistry, geology and environmental sciences. US citizens or permanent residents of the U.S. and its possessions.

Stipend: $3,000 for 12 weeks, travel assistance, on-campus housing, food allowance.

Apply by: March 1

For more information:

University Programs Registrar, Sally Brennan

REU Research Fellowships   (251) 861-7502

Dauphin Island Sea Lab   www.disl.org

101 Bienville Blvd.   sbrennan@disl.org

Dauphin Island, AL 36528   univ-prog.disl.org/graduate.html

OTS Minority Scholars Program

OTS has a mission to provide leadership in education, research, and the responsible use of natural resources in the tropics. The program offers opportunities for African American, Native American, and Hispanic American students to participate in its field-based science courses in Costa Rica.

Undergraduate Semester Abroad

Mellon Fellowships available for African Americans, Hispanic Americans, Native Americans, and Costa Rican nationals; fellowships cover all program-related expenses and are available for the fall semester only.

Apply by: early March

Summer Tropical Ecology and Ethnobiology

Partial and full scholarships available for African Americans, Hispanic Americans, and Native Americans.

Apply by: mid-February

Research Experiences for Undergraduates (REU)

Funding available to U.S. citizens of all ethnic backgrounds; NSF funding for selected students covers all program-related expenses.

Apply by: mid- January

Fore more information:

OTS North American Office   (919) 684-5774
www.ots.duke.edu   nao@duke.edu

Park People

Dedicated to preserving and enhancing parks and green space in the Houston area by providing financial support to undergraduate or graduate students pursuing a degree in Urban Forestry, Parks and Recreation, Horticultural Sciences, Landscape Architecture, Architecture with an emphasis on urban greenery, Urban Planning or a closely related field.

Eligibility: Full-time students in eligible programs at the following Universities: Rice University, Stephen F. Austin State University, Texas A&M University, Texas Southern University, Texas Tech University, University of Houston. Applicants must be intending to stay in Texas upon graduation, those planning to live in the Houston/Harris County area after completion of their studies are preferred. Financial need is considered.

Award: $2,000   Apply by: March 1

For more information:

The Park People, Inc.   (713) 942-7275
Attn: Scholarship Chair   info@parkpeople.org
3015 Richmond, Ste. 210   www.parkpeople.org/
Houston, Texas 77098

The Posse Foundation-For High School Seniors

The Posse Foundation identifies, recruits and selects student leaders from public high schools to form multicultural teams called "Posses". These teams are then prepared, through an intensive eight-month Posse Training Program, for enrollment at top universities nationwide to pursue their academics and to help promote cross-cultural communication on campus. The Posse Program has exhibited great success over the past twelve years placing 359 students into top colleges and universities. These students have won over $27 million in scholarships from Posse partner universities and are persisting and graduating at close to 90% -- a rate higher than the national averages at institutions of higher education.

The focus of the program is two-fold: 1) To recruit students who have extraordinary leadership ability and academic potential that might be overlooked by the traditional university selection process, and 2) To devote the resources and support necessary to allow those students to achieve personal and academic excellence, reach graduation and effect positive changes on their college campus and in their community. Responsibility for the final selection of students is shared by both the participating universities and Posse.

For more information:

Posse Foundation	212/405.1691
14 WALL STREET, 11TH FLOOR	info@possefoundation.org
NEW YORK, NY 10005	www.possefoundation.org

Public Service Scholarship

For students planning a career in government service in local, state, or federal government. Preference given to applicants with previous public service work or volunteer experience, including community service experience.

Eligibility: Full-time students having completed at least one year of college. 3.5 GPA. Graduate students may be either part-time or full-time.

Award: $1,000 for full-time students
$500 for part-time graduate students

For more information send a self-addressed stamped envelope to:

Public Employees Roundtable	202.927.4926
Scholarship Committee	www.theroundtable.org
PO Box 75248	
Washington, DC 20013-5248	nfo@theroundtable.org

Resource Conservation - San Diego County

Conservation Scholarships to encourage students to obtain expertise and pursue careers in resource conservation and agriculture.

Eligibility: residents of the Resource Conservation District, nearing completion of senior year of HS, 2.5 GPA, and planning to enroll in undergrad college courses related to conservation or agriculture.

Apply by: Mid-May

For more information:

Resource Conservation District of Greater San Diego County
Attn: Scholarship Committee   (760) 745-2061
332 S. Juniper Street, Suite 110   scott@rcdsandiego.org.
Escondido, CA 92025   www.rcdsandiego.org/educational/scholarship.html

RHODE ISLAND FOUNDATION

Michael P. Metcalf Memorial Grant

To subsidize experiences intended to broaden students' perspectives and enhance their personal growth beyond the classroom and curriculum. May include travel in this country and abroad, and a variety of internships and public service programs. Experience must include either an established program or be well-constructed by the student, and have a clear purpose.

Eligibility: RI residents, college sophomores and juniors.

Award: To $2,000 - $5,000   # Given: 2 - 4
Apply by: mid-January

Association of Former Legislators Scholarship

To promising students with a distinguished record of public service, planning to pursue an education beyond high school.

Eligibility: RI resident, graduating high school senior, history of substantial voluntary community service, financial need.

Award: $1,000   # Given: 5
Apply by: Mid-June

For more information:

Rhode Island Foundation   www.rifoundation.org
Scholarship Coordinator   (401) 274-4564
One Union Station
Providence, Rhode Island 02903

ROCKEFELLER STATE WILDLIFE SCHOLARSHIP (LA)

Awarded to high school graduates, college undergraduates and graduate students majoring in forestry, wildlife or marine science.

Eligibility: Must attain a degree in one of the three eligible fields at a LA public college/university; US citizen or eligible noncitizen; LA resident; annually submit a Free Application for Student Financial Aid (FAFSA) prior to the annual deadline; have no criminal convictions other than misdemeanor traffic violations; have graduated from an accredited high school with at least a 2.50 gpa and have an ACT score or have earned 24 or more graded college credit hours and have at least a 2.50 cumulative grade point average

Award:$1,000 with a cumulative maximum award of $7,000 for up to five years of undergraduate and two years of graduate study.

Given: 30 new, 30 continuing   Apply by: July 31

For more information:

Rockefeller Scholarship
LOSFA   (800)259-5626 ext 1012
POB 91202   (225)922-3258
Baton Rouge, LA 70821   www.osfa.state.la.us

ROCKY MOUNTAIN ELK FOUNDATION

The mission of the Rocky Mountain Elk Foundation is to ensure the future of elk, other wildlife and their habitat.

High Schools for Habitat Conservation Scholarship

One of the Elk Foundation's education programs is High Schools for Habitat (HSH). The rationale of HSH is to raise up a new generation of citizen conservationists who understand the principles of wildlife management and wise stewardship ethics, and who practice philanthropic and charitable giving through fundraising. The scholarship promotes leadership by high school students who are actively involved in the High Schools for Habitat Program.

Eligibility: Be or have been an active participant in a local HSH program of a recognized member school showing a minimum of two years of active involvement, planning to enroll as a freshman undergraduate in a recognized wildlife program in the United States or Canada, with at least one semester or two quarters remaining in degree program for the following fall semester/quarter. Applicants who completed their military service immediately after graduating from high school or deferred their college education for up to and including four years after graduation from high school are eligible to apply.

Award: $1,000   # Given: 10
Apply by: March 1

For more information:

High Schools for Habitat   814-833-7996

Carole Biletnikoff   carole@highschoolsforhabitat.org

www.highschoolsforhabitat.org

Wildlife Leadership Awards

Established to recognize, encourage and promote leadership among future wildlife management professionals.

Eligibility: undergraduate in a recognized wildlife program in the United States or Canada; junior or senior standing, with at least one semester or two quarters remaining in degree program; enrolled as a full-time student for the following semester/quarter.

Award: $2,000   # Given: 10
Apply by: March 1

For more information:

Wildlife Leadership Awards
Jodi Bishop   jodi@rmef.org
Rocky Mountain Elk Foundation   (800) 225-5355 ext. 572
P. O. Box 8249   www.elkfoundation.org
Missoula, MT 59807-8249

Saw Mill River (NY) Audubon Society

Environmental Summer Program Scholarship

For youth who desire to attend a summer camp, workshop or class that focuses on environmental study. Past scholarships have been used for a variety of programs including sessions at the summer youth camps for the National Wildlife Federation, National Audubon Society, and NYS Department of Environmental Conservation.

Eligibility: Age 13 to 17. Priority to applicants within the Saw Mill River Audubon Society membership area -- the western third of Westchester County from Peekskill to Irvington. Background in conservation or environmental activities helpful.

Award: Varies   Apply by: February 15
For more information:

Saw Mill River Audubon Society   (914) 666-6503
275 Millwood Road   office@sawmillriveraudubon.org
Chappaqua, NY 15014   www.sawmillriveraudubon.org

J.W. Saxe Memorial Prize

Awarded to students working in public service to enable them to gain practical experience by taking a non-paying or low-paying job or internship during the summer or other term.

Eligibility: students working toward a career in public service. Preference for applicants who have already found a position but require additional funds.

Award: $1,500   # Given: varies
Apply by: March 15
For more information:

J.W. Saxe Memorial Fund   www.jwsaxefund.org
1524 31st Street NW
Washington, DC 20007

Albert Schweitzer Fellowship

See listing in Health section.

Smithsonian

See listings in graduate section as well.

Native American Community Scholar and Visiting Scholar Awards

Appointments in residence at the Smithsonian are awarded to Native Americans, undergraduate and graduate students who are related to a Native American community, to undertake projects on a Native American subject.

Award: $100 per day up to 21 days plus travel and research allowance.

Native American Internship Awards

Internships in residence at the Smithsonian are awarded to undergraduate and graduate Native American students to participate in research or museum activities related to Native American studies for 10 weeks.

Award: $500 per week plus travel allowance.

Apply by: March 1, July 1, November 1

For more information:

Smithsonian Office of Fellowships	202-275-0655
PO Box 37012	siofg@si.edu
Victor Bldg, 9300, MRC 902	
Washington, DC 20013-7012	www.si.edu/ofg

Smithsonian Environmental Research Center: Work/Learn Program

An opportunity to conduct individual projects in environmental studies under the supervision of professional staff members. Areas of study include terrestrial or estuarine environmental research, resource planning and decision making, environmental education research and development.

Eligibility: graduate or undergraduate students. U.S. citizenship is not a requirement to participate in this program.

Award: $350.00 per week for 10-16 weeks.

Apply by: Spring - December 1   Summer - March 1

For more information:

Smithsonian Environmental Research Center	
P.O. Box 28	(301) 798-4424
Edgewater, MD 21037	www.serc.si.edu

SOIL AND WATER CONSERVATION SOCIETY

Melville Cohee Student Leader Conservation Scholarship

For SWCS members pursuing studies in natural resource conservation such as agricultural economics, soils, planned land use management, forestry, wildlife biology, agricultural engineering, hydrology, rural sociology, field agronomy, water management.

Eligibility: member of SWCS for more than one year; 3.0 gpa; junior or senior at an accredited college or university.

Award: $1,000   # Given: 2

Apply by: mid-February

Donald Williams Soil Conservation Scholarship

The Donald A. Williams Soil Conservation Scholarship provides financial assistance to members of SWCS who are currently employed but who wish to improve their technical or administrative competence in a conservation-related field through course work.

Eligibility: a member of SWCS pursuing undergraduate level coursework at an accredited college or through a program of special study; completed at least one year of full-time employment in a natural resource conservation endeavor; financial need.

Award: $1,500   # Given: up to 3

Apply by: Mid-February

See web sites of local SWCS chapters for more scholarships specific to your state:

www.SWCS.org/f_aboutSWCS_chrel.htm

For more information:

SWCS

945 SW Ankeny Road

Ankeny, Iowa 50021-9764

www.SWCS.org/f_aboutSWCS_chrel.htm

(515)289-2331

STUDENT ENVIRONMENTAL ASSOCIATE PROGRAM AND DIVERSITY INITIATIVE

A cooperative venture between EPA and the Environmental Careers Organization. Last year, EPA sponsored 114 students from a wide variety of communities and tribes across the country. Each student completed a paid, full-time, on-site training opportunity of three to six months. Interns were chosen based on academic achievement, extracurricular activities and stated interest in pursuing an environmental career.

For more information:

The Environmental Careers Organization

179 South Street

Boston, MA 02111

(617) 426-4783

www.eco.org

SUMMER ECOSYSTEM EXPERIENCES FOR UNDERGRADUATES

A five week field ecology program held at Black Rock Forest, NY -- a 1500-hectare preserve of eastern deciduous forest 1.5 hours outside of New York City. Students will have a rich field experience combined with instruction in some of the most advanced digital tools in environmental research. SEE-U allows students to be physically present in one field site or biome while using previously collected data to study two other biomes (Brazil and Arizona). Participants receive 6.0 Columbia University credits in environmental biology.

There is a limited amount of scholarship monies available to aid students who have both academic merit and financial need. Students who do not feel that they qualify for financial aid can apply to be a student organizer. A student organizer is a student who volunteers to help organize other students and distribute information, posters etc. These students who assist in organizing and motivating 3 additional students to participate will be given a stipend to cover their transportation expenses to and from the field site of their choice.

Eligibility: Undergraduate student, who has completed Introductory biology (or high school equivalent)

Apply by: April 1

For more information:

Center for Environmental Research and Conservation

Columbia University

New York, NY

www.see-u.org

212.854.8179

see-u@cerc.columbia.edu

Telacu Educational Foundation (So. CA)

The TELACU Scholarship Program, in partnership with corporations, individuals, and a network of Southern California's finest, most prestigious colleges and universities, annually awards scholarships to qualified Latino students. TELACU Scholars receive not just monetary assistance, but also counseling, leadership training, classes in time management and other subjects that help the students succeed in college.

Eligibility: a low income, full-time, first generation college student attending one of 23 partnering colleges and universities; resident of the following target communities: Bell Gardens, City of Los Angeles (including SF Valley), Commerce, unincorporated East Los Angeles, Huntington Park, Montebello, Monterey Park, Pico Rivera, Santa Ana, and South Gate; must be a U.S. Citizen or Permanent Resident of the U.S.; minimum gpa of 2.5.

Apply by: First Saturday in April

For more information:

Telacu Education Foundation	(323) 721-1655
5400 E. Olympic Blvd, Suite 300	www.telacu.com
Los Angeles, CA 90022	info@telacu.com

Toad Suck daze Scholarships Program (AR)

Jim Stone and Woody Cummins Scholarships

Encourages community service and provides an opportunity for educational and community growth. Awards two categories of scholarships on the basis of scholarly achievements, attitude, and community service.

Eligibility: Faulkner County, Arkansas high school students with GPA of 2.5 planning to attend 1. either Central Baptist College, Hendrix College and the University of Central Arkansas or 2. a local vocational/technical school. There are specific community service requirements for for each category of applicant.

Award: $3,000 (College/University)   # Given: 6
$1,000 (vocational/technical)   # Given: 2

For more information:

Toad Suck Daze Scholarships	(501) 327-7788
The Conway Area Chamber of Commerce	
900 Oak St.	www.conwayarkcc.org
Conway, AR 72032	www.toadsuck.org

Transportation Fellowship

Provide scholarships and field experience to persons traditionally underrepresented in the field of transportation (economically disadvantaged persons, women, and ethnic minorities).

Award: tuition (at Texas resident rates), paid internship placements, and funding for books, conferences, and memberships in professional organizations.

For more information:

North Central Texas Council of Governments

616 Six Flags Drive

P.O. Box 5888

Arlington, TX 76005-5888

(817) 608-2325

vpruittj@dfwinfo.com

www.dfwinfo.com/trans/fellowship/index.html

TRIBAL LANDS ENVIRONMENTAL SCIENCE SCHOLARSHIP

See Graduate listing.

UNCOMMON LEGACY FOUNDATION

Scholarships for lesbian students actively working to improve conditions for gay, lesbian and transgender communities.

Eligibility: full time students at an accredited US college or university, 3.0 GPA, financial need.

Award: $2,500   Apply by: July 1

For more information:

Legacy Scholarship Committee

P.O. Box 33727

Washington DC 20033

202-265-1926

scholarship@uncommonlegacy.org

www.uncommonlegacy.org

Every man must decide whether he will walk in the light of creative altruism or the darkness of destructive selfishness. This is the judgement. Life's most persistent and urgent question is, what are you doing for others?

Martin Luther King Jr.

UNITED NEGRO COLLEGE FUND

The College Fund/UNCF awards scholarships primarily to students attending its member colleges/universities with financial need as verified by the Financial Aid Director.

Cisco/UNCF Scholars Program

This scholarship is designed to provide financial support and Cisco internship opportunities for African American Electrical Engineering or Computer Science majors, with a special focus on women and students who demonstrate community service.

Eligibility: Undergraduate sophomore with a minimum 3.2 GPA attend one of the participating Colleges/Universities (see web site for list).

Award : $4,000   Apply by: january 10

Malcolm Pirnie Scholars

Scholarships and summer internships for students majoring in civil, chemical or environmental engineering or one of the environmental sciences.

Eligibility: Undergraduate Junior; 3.0 GPA; majoring in Engineering, Physical Sciences at any UNCF associated school.

Award: $3,000

Grumman Scholarship for Peace and Justice

Competitive scholarships are awarded annually to students involved with organizations seeking peaceful social change.

Eligibility: Pre-Law, Political Science, Sociology, Religion major at any UNCF associated school, with a 2.5 GPA.

Malcolm X Scholarship

Awarded for demonstrated academic excellence, campus and community leadership, and exceptional courage.

Eligibility: Attend any UNCF associated school, with a 2.5 GPA.

Award: $4,000, Renewable   Apply by: mid November

For more information:

Contact your financial aid office at your UNCF school

www.uncf.org/scholarship/general.asp

WASTE MGM'T. EDUCATION RESEARCH CONSORTIUM

The WERC fellowship program is designed to encourage students to take environmentally focused courses while pursuing higher education. Fellowships and scholarships are available to undergraduate and graduate students who are pursuing degrees in an environmental field.

Fellowships are available to U.S citizen or permanent resident full-time students taking an environmentally related course of studies pursuing an Environmental Management Certificate or Minor.

Research Fellowship

Eligibility: GPA of 3.2; complete the WERC minor requirements (a minimum of 18 credits, at least nine credits must be upper-division) upon receipt of a baccalaureate degree; conduct a research project under the mentorship of a professor; mentor a WERC fellowship recipient; have already completed eight credits of environment courses.

Award: $1,000/semester

Certificate Fellowship

Eligibility: GPA of 3.0.; complete 9-12 credits upon the time receipt of a baccalaureate degree; continuously take one or more credits of WERC-approved environmental courses; have already completed three credits of environment courses; mentor a WERC fellowship recipient (12 hours total, four hours a month).

Award: $500/semester

Book Fellowship

Eligibility: GPA of 2.75; enroll in one or more credit hours of WERC-approved environmental courses; perform six hours involvement in an environmental activity (two hours a   month).

Award: $300/semester

Freshman Fellowship

Eligibility: Posses an environmental interest; participate in WERC activities and be mentored by a WERC Fellowship recipient (four hours a month);

maintain a GPA of 2.75 or higher.

Award: $150/semester

For more information:

New Mexico State University
Environmental Fellows Program   (505) 646-7821
Box 30001, Dept. 3805   www.werc.net/students/aid.htm
Las Cruces, NM 88003

WATER ENVIRONMENT FEDERATION

Stockholm Junior Water Prize

Engages and stimulates youth in water-environment issues regionally, nationally and internationally by sponsoring a US student to compete in the Stockholm Junior Water Prize in Sweden. Representatives will be selected at local International Science and Engineering Fair (ISEF) for the national competition. To find science fair date, location, and contact information visit the ISEF website www.sciserv.org/isef and click on "Affiliated Fairs."

Eligibility: high school students (grades 9-12).

Award: $2,500 and a five-day, all expense paid trip to Stockholm, Sweden. Up to four finalists will receive $500 each.

For more information

Lorraine Loken   (703) 684-2487
Manager of Public Education
Water Environment Federation
601 Wythe Street   lloken@wef.org
Alexandria, VA 22314-1994   www.wef.org

WOODROW WILSON FELLOWSHIPS

Thomas R. Pickering Foreign Affairs Fellowship Program

Provides undergraduate and graduate funding to ethnically-diverse students, as they are prepared academically and professionally to enter the US Department of State Foreign Service. The Fellow must commit to pursuing a graduate degree in international studies at one of the graduate schools identified by the WWNFF. Participating graduate schools provide financial support in the second year of graduate study based on need.

Fellows must meet Department of State Foreign Service entry requirements. Each successful candidate is obligated to a minimum of four and one half years service in an appointment as a Foreign Service Officer.

Eligibility: College sophomores, financial need, extracurricular/community/volunteer activities and leadership roles, U.S. citizenship, 3.2 GPA.

Award: Tuition, room, board, and fees during the junior and senior years and the first year of graduate study, reimbursement for books and round-trip travel.

Apply by: February 21

For more information:

Dr. Richard Hope, Director   pickeringfaf@woodrow.org

Foreign Affairs Fellowship Program
The Woodrow Wilson National Fellowship Foundation
P.O. Box 2437
Princeton, NJ 08543-2437

YOUNG FEMINIST SCHOLARSHIP

Encourages and recognizes young feminists interested in writing. Scholarship to be awarded each year to the female student who submits the best essay on feminism, and what it means to her. Essay not to be longer than three pages, double-spaced, typed. Winner will receive a scholarship plus publication of her essay in a national magazine for young women.

Eligibility: Female high school senior.

Award $1000   # Given: 1
Apply by: December 31

For more information:

Spinsters Ink Publishing House   (800) 301-6860
Young Feminist Scholarship
P.O. Box 22005
Denver CO, 80222   www.spinsters-ink.com/scholarship.html

MAKING A
DIFFERENCE
SCHOLARSHIPS

◇ ◇ ◇

COLLEGES
&
UNIVERSITIES

Why read about scholarships from colleges?

The scholarships listed by individual colleges are either awarded automatically as part of your application to the college (sometimes through applying for financial aid) or are for students already in attendance. Do not contact these colleges for information regarding these scholarships unless you are applying/attending there.

Lots of colleges today claim they will help you make a difference. How many colleges back up their words with money for students who are engaged in activities or studies for a better world? Not many. While this section is not exhaustive, you can assume these colleges are more serious than most about the importance of community service and/or social change. So, if you want to attend a college which puts its money where its mouth is, as well as be rewarded for your history of community service and activism, the colleges listed here are a good place to start.

Another source of information is our Making A Difference College and Graduate Guide, which profiles colleges with concerns for peace, social justice, the environment and service.

For more information:

www.making-a-difference.com

AMERICORPS MATCHING SCHOLARSHIPS AND AWARDS

Some colleges and universities provide matching funds and other incentives for AmeriCorps graduates. To ensure accurate information, contact schools early in your application process. This list was provided by AmeriCorps Alums.

Colleges and Universities that offer Matching Funds

Augsburg College: see listing	Contact: Sally Daniels	
Brown University: see listing		
Sterling College: see listing	Contact: Barbara Stuart	
Bryant College, RI	Contact: (401) 232-6009	
Community College of RI	Contact: Rebecca Yount	(401) 333-7159
Defiance College, OH		
The Evergreen State College, WA		
Johnson & Wales, RI	Contact: Rose Banister	(401) 598-2871
NE Institute Of Technology, RI	Contact: Larry Blair	(401) 467-7744
University of Rhode Island	Contact: Horace Amaral	(401) 874-5106
RI School of Design	Contact: Peter Reifler	(401) 454-6636
Roger Williams University, RI	Contact: Lynn Fanthrop	(401) 253-1040
Salve Regina, RI	Contact: Laura McPhie	(401) 847-6650
Union College, New York	Contact: Lisa Payne	(606) 546-4151
University of Charleston, WV	Contact: Fin. Aid Office	(800) 995-4682

Brandeis University, MA

Heller school will offer $5,000 to one incoming AmeriCorps alumni as well as wave the application fees for all applicants.

Clark University, MA   (508) 793-7201   idce@clarku.edu

Department of International Development, Community Planning, and Environment offers a tuition-free scholarship

Springfield College, MA   Contact: Peter Guimette

The S.A.G.E. AmeriCorps Program matches the Education Award for members in graduate programs at the college with a scholarship of up to $7,600.

Olivet College, MI: Contact: Terry Langston

Up to $6,000 to full-time; up to $3,000 to part-time.

Cleveland State University, OH   Contact: Contact: Marcie Rechner

No match, but student may receive up to 8 internship credit hours, graduate or undergraduate in urban affairs.

Providence College, RI   Contact: Rick Battistoni

Up to $5,000/ yr. for anyone majoring in Public and Community Service

Rhode Island College   Contact: James Hanbury

Full tuition and fee; match for 1st year-undergraduates only

For more information:

AmeriCorps Alums, Inc.   (202) 729-8180
1400 I Street, NW Suite 800   alumni@americorpsalums.net
Washington, DC 20005   www.americorpsalums.org

ALLEGHENY COLLEGE

Trustee Scholarships

In addition to academics, awards achievements in areas such as: art, communications, community service, creative writing, dance, debate, leadership, music, science or math, religious activities, scouting.

Eligibility: Allegheny college applicants in top 25% of their high school class with an SAT score of approximately 1200 or ACT score of 24.

Award: To $12,500 per year, guaranteed for four years

Given: Approximately 200

Apply by: February 15 through regular admissions application process

For more information:

Office of Admissions   (800) 521-5293

admiss@allegheny.edu

AmeriCorps Bonner Leaders Program

Students complete 900 hours of service and training over two years (including one or two summer components) in exchange for a summer stipend, work study funding during the academic year, training in leadership and service, and a post-service education award from AmeriCorps.

Eligibility: Low-income sophomores and juniors.

Award: cash award from AmeriCorps (students receive work study funds and summer stipends from Allegheny when applicable.)

For more information:

David Roncolato   (814) 332-5318

Director of Community Service   droncola@allegheny.edu

Box 22, Allegheny College   www.allegheny.edu

Meadville, PA 16335

ANTIOCH COLLEGE

Horace Mann Presidential Scholarship

Awarded to first-year students. with a demonstrated commitment to humanitarian values, civil rights, or environmental issues.

Award: $5,000

Arthur Morgan Public Service Scholarship

Awarded to students with demonstrated academic promise and an interest in a career in public/community service. Essay required.

Award: $5,000

Beatrice Kotas Social Service/Work Scholarship

To a student interested in a career in social work or social services.

Award: to $1,000

Foreign Exchange Scholarship

For students who have lived and/or worked abroad in an American Field Service, or other foreign exchange program.

Award: to $3,000

Bonner Scholar Program: Americorps matching
>Eligibility (all): Students applying to or attending Antioch.

For More Information:

Admissions Office   (800) 543-9436

Antioch College

Yellow Springs, OH 45387   www.antioch-college.edu

AUGSBURG COLLEGE

Hoversten Peace Scholarship

Recognizes students who have a demonstrated commitment to peace, service, community, and social justice issues. Involvement in Amnesty International, Habitat for Humanity, and church activities relating to peace and justice are examples of service performed by current scholarship recipients.

>Eligibility: incoming freshmen and transfer students.

>Award: $2,000 - renewable

Adeline M. Johnson, Community Service Scholarships

Awarded to students of any class or major, based on community or public service involvement.

>Award: $2,000   Renewable for 4 years

># Given: 5 - one for each class, and one other, 4 are renewable.

Americorps Matching Scholarships

>Award: $5,000 per year   Renewable for up to 4 years

For more information:

Augsburg College   (612) 330-1294

2211 Riverside Ave.   (612) 330-1208

Minneapolis, MN 55454   www.augsburg.edu

BATES COLLEGE

Vincent Mulford Service Internship and Research Fund

For summer service-learning project anywhere in the world.

>Award: $2,500   # Given: 4

Arthur Crafts Service Awards

Helps fund service-learning projects.

>Award: to $300   # Given: 12

Philip J. Otis Fellowships

Offers students grants to support off-campus projects that explore an environmental or eco-spiritual topic.

>Award: $2,000 - $5,000   # Given: 2-5

Bates Science Education Outreach Grants

Designed to enhance K-12 science education in under-resourced schools, and to build lasting collaborations among Bates students and faculty, public school teachers and administrators. Students involved in student teaching or service-learning in area classrooms may apply for funds to support science education or curriculum development.

Award: $200 - $10,000

Hoffman Mellon Grants

These grants provide modest summer stipends to undergraduates pursuing their own independent research, assisting a faculty member conducting research, or undertaking a service-learning project.

Eligibility: For all awards - enrolled Bates students.

Award: $1,000   # Given: 20

For more information:

Center for Service-Learning   (207) 786-8273
Bates College
Lewiston, ME 04240

BENTLEY COLLEGE

Bentley Service-Learning Scholarship

Awarded to freshman students with excellent academic records who have demonstrated a commitment to community service.

Award: $5,000, renewable   # Given: 24

National Black MBA Association Scholarship

For a black freshman with the strongest record of academic achievement and community service. NBMBAA is a business organization that leads in the creation of economic and intellectual wealth for the black community. The recipient will participate in the association's community outreach activities such as serving as a mentor to high school students.

Award: full tuition, renewable   # Given: 1

INROADS Scholarship

Awarded to a freshman ALANA student (African-American, Latino, Asian and Native American), the INROADS program develops and places talented youth of color in business and industry, and prepares them for corporate and community leadership.

Award: full tuition, renewable   # Given: 1

Sullivan Scholar Award

Awarded to a freshman urban ALANA student with an interest in business ethics and community service. Student will participate in Bentley's Center for Business, which fosters an ethical framework for the conduct of business and establishes cooperation on ethical issues among academic, corporate, government, labor and public interest groups (application required). All applicants to Bentley are automatically considered for all but the Service-Learning and Sullivan Scholar scholarships.

Award: $6,000, renewable   # Given: 1

For more information:

Office of New Student Financial Assistance Services
Bentley College   (617) 891-3441
Waltham, MA 02154-4705   www.bentley.edu

Bonner Foundation Scholar and Leadership Program

Like you, the Bonner Foundation believes that a merit scholarship, based on community engagement, should be available at all colleges and universities. They sponsor two programs to encourage and reward service.

Bonner Scholar Program

These four-year community service scholarships given to approximately 1500 students annually at twenty-five specific colleges and universities transform the lives of students as well as their campuses, local communities, and nation through providing access to education and opportunities to serve. The scholarship serves those who have high financial need and a commitment to service. It is designed to heighten the overall education a Scholar receives by asking students to engage in ongoing service work and helping them develop the tools and the knowledge necessary to make that work meaningful and lasting.

Bonner Scholars are expected to maintain good academic standing, participate in educational enrichment activities, and to engage in 10 hours a week of community service during the school year and 240 hours in the summer.

You may submit the on-line Bonner Scholars application to all 25 schools at once, or apply individually through the participating colleges. All of the following colleges operate under a set of broad guidelines, but each has developed a unique program to match the student body and culture of its campus.

Antioch College, OH	800-543-9436
Berea College, KY	800-326-5948
Berry College, GA	800-237-7942
Carson-Newman College, TN	800-678-9061
College of the Ozarks, MO	800-222-0525
Concord College, WV	800-344-6679
Davidson College, NC	800-768-0380
DePauw University, IN	800-447-2495
Earlham College, IN	800-428-6958
Emory & Henry College, VA	800-848-5493
Ferrum College, VA	800-868-9797
Guilford College, NC	800-992-7759
Hood College, MD	800-922-1599
Mars Hill College, NC	800-543-1514
Maryville College, TN	800-597-2687
Morehouse College, GA	800-851-1254
Oberlin College, OH	800-622-6243
Rhodes College, TN	800-844-5969
Spelman College, GA	800-982-2411
Union College, KY	800-489-8646
University of Richmond, VA	800-700-1662
Warren Wilson College, NC	800-934-3536
Waynesburg College, PA,	800-225-7393
West Virginia Wesleyan College, WV	800-722-9933
Wofford College, SC	

Expands the Bonner Scholars Program model of service-based scholarships by using funds from federal work-study, AmeriCorps education awards, and AmeriCorps stipends. Institutions create scholarship stipends for students who complete community service each week for one or two-year term of service.

Each of these campuses has a core group of 5-30 student members who commit to completing the required hours of community service during their term (approximately 300 hours of service/year and the summer between). The Bonner Leaders work on issues such as improving educational opportunities and fighting hunger through community programs that focus on literacy issues, mentoring and nutrition/anti-hunger initiatives. These students/members also participate in regular training and reflection activities sponsored by their campuses, their community partners, and the Bonner Foundation.

Different schools house the Bonner Leaders Program in different offices, which usually report to a Director of Community Service or Service-Learning at the following colleges in addition to the Bonner Scholar Campuses listed above:

Allegheny College, PA	814-332-5318
Bluefield College,VA	276-326-3682
Brigham Young University,ID	
California State University - Chico, CA	
California State University - LA, CA	323-343-3370
Centre College, KY	800-654-7798 ext. 4212
Coro Foundation, NY	212-248-2935x230
Juniata College, PA	814-641-3365
Lees-McRae College, NC	
Mercer County Community College, NJ	
Middlesex County College, NJ	732-548-6000
Millikin University, IL	217-362-6461
Montana Campus Compact,MT	406-243-5177
Pfeiffer University, NC	704-463-1360 ext. 2706
Philadelphia Higher Ed. Network for Neighborhood Dvlpmnt,	215-573-2379
Princeton University,NJ	609-258-7260
Rider University, NJ	609-896-5000
Rutgers University - Cook College,NJ	
St. Mary's College of California, CA	925-631-4755
Southwest Virginia Community College, VA	540-964-7286
The College of New Jersey, NJ	
Tusculum College, TN	423-636-7300 ext. 256
University of California at Berkeley, CA	
University of Louisville, KY	502-852-4333
Washburn University, KS	785-231-1010
Washington and Lee University, VA	540-463-8784
Wheeling Jesuit College, WV	

For more information:

The Bonner Foundation	609-924-6663
PO Box 712, 22 Chambers Street	info@bonner.org
Princeton, NJ 08542	www.bonner.org

BREVARD COMMUNITY COLLEGE

Outstanding Student Humanitarian Scholarship

Annually recognizes and honors a student who has performed an exceptional humanitarian service during the preceding twelve-month period.

Award: $1,000

On Campus Community Service Scholarship

Honors and recognizes a student for outstanding "on-campus sponsored" community service contribution during preceding twelve-months.

Award: $400

Leadership / Service Scholarship

Student must have demonstrated leadership and service at Brevard Community College. Depending on the student's schedule, the recipient of will have the opportunity to intern at the Foundation Office for a limited number of hours per semester and/or assist with Foundation events.

Award: $1,500

Terraphile Society Environmental Scholarship

For a student with a major related to environmental issues.

Eligibility: Brevard County resident and Cocoa campus student, attending BCC full time, completed a minimum of 12 credit hours. 3.0 GPA.

Award: $150   Apply by: May 1

James Oxford Memorial Scholarship

Horticulture or agriculture majors. First priority given to a freshman.

Eligibility: As above

Award: $600   Apply by: May 1

For more information:

Brevard Community College   (407) 632-1111 ext. 62410

Center for Service-Learning, Student Center - Room 214

1519 Clearlake Road

Cocoa, FL 32922   www.brevardcc.edu

BROWN UNIVERSITY

Brown University, because of the Ivy League Athletic Conference rules, offers no merit scholarships of any kind. Different departments at Brown do offer service-related fellowship funding to matriculated students. Among the departments that offer such funding is the Howard R. Swearer Center for Public Service.

Funding individuals with good ideas is one way that the Swearer Center supports entrepreneurism in the civic sector. Through a number of fellowships, we have been able to both recognize outstanding accomplishments and provide seed funds for the exploration and implementation of new ideas. Fellowships include support for service projects, community-based research, project integrating service and academic study, as well as full-time post graduate work in social change.

Royce Fellowship Program

Recognizes undergraduates who have gained distinction through their research, creativity, service and leadership, with awards to support a proposed research or public service project.

Award: to $4,000   Apply by: February

C.V. Starr National Service Fellowship/Americorps Matching

Recognizes and encourages student participation in voluntary public service. The Program will also match the $4,725 stipend any selected Starr Fellow receives for Americorps service.

Award: $2,500   Apply by: February

Aided Internship Program

Sponsored by Brown University Career Services

Apply by: March

Hazeltine/Rosenthal Intern Scholar Program

Sponsored by Career Services

Apply by: March

Howard R. Swearer International Service Fellowship

Apply by: March

Luce Undergraduate Environmental Fellows Program

Sponsored by Brown University Watson Institute for International Studies

Apply by: November

Richard Smoke Summer Internship Program

Sponsored by: Watson Institute, OIP, and Swearer Center

Eligibility: Brown students and faculty. Please do not contact the Swearer Center for information if you are not a Brown student or faculty member.

Apply by: March

For more information on these and other fellowships:

www.brown.edu/Departments/Swearer_Center/

Brigham Young University

Bonner Scholars Program

See Bonner Scholars listing.

Canisius College

Canisius College Community Service Scholarship

As a Jesuit Institution, Canisius places a high value on service and its role in forming students to be "men and women for others". Canisius encourages students to become involved in service in order to increase their awareness of and commitment to social responsibility.

Eligibility: Admission to Canisius as a full-time student. High School B average or higher. Previous volunteer experience.

Award: $1,500 - $2,500   # Given: 10-15

Apply by: February 1   Renewable

For more information:

Service Scholarship Coordinator   (716) 888-2200
Canisius College-Campus Ministry Office
2001 Main St.
Buffalo, NY 14208   www.canisius.edu/camp_minist/scholarships.asp

CENTER FOR GLOBAL EDUCATION

Undergraduate Semester Program Abroad Scholarships

Scholarships have been established to enable students of color, who otherwise may not have sufficient funding, to participate in the semester abroad programs such as: Women, Gender and Development or Gender & the Environment-- Latin American Perspectives (Mexico); Multicultural Societies in Transition -- or Women/ Gender and Development -- Southern African Perspectives; Sustainable Development & Social Change (Central America).

The Center is committed to facilitating the exchange of diverse perspectives not only between students and resource people within Southern Africa and Latin America, but also among the student participants themselves.

Eligibility: Financial need, secure funding for the program costs beyond the scholarship, and willingness to assist the Center upon return to U.S.

Award: $500 - $2,500   # Given: 12
Apply by: October 15 or May 15

For more information:
Academic Programs Abroad   (612) 330-1159
Center for Global Education
Augsburg College
2211 Riverside Avenue
Minneapolis, MN 55454   www.augsburg.edu/global/studyabd.html

CHATHAM COLLEGE

Leadership Scholarship

Girl Scout Gold Award recipients are eligible for the Leadership Scholarship, and the opportunity to be considered for additional scholarships.

Students requesting consideration must forward a copy of their Girl Scout Gold Award to the Office of Admissions and Financial Aid.

Award: $2,000   Renewable

For more information:
Director of Financial Aid   (800) 837-1290
Chatham College
Woodland Road
Pittsburgh, PA 15232   www.chatham.edu

CLEMSON UNIVERSITY

The Department of Forest Resources offers a number of Scholarships
For more information:
Financial Aid Office   virtual.clemson.edu/groups/finaid/

G-01 Sikes Hall
Clemson University
Clemson, SC 29634

COLORADO STATE UNIVERSITY

The College Of Natural Resources offers a number of Scholarships.

For more information:

Scholarship Committee   (970) 491-3916
101 Natural Resources, College of Natural Resources
Colorado State University
Fort Collins CO 80523-1401

www.cnr.colostate.edu/development/scholarships/index.html

CORNELL UNIVERSITY

The Center for Community Partnership seeks to foster student leadership and social responsibility by encouraging students to take action against social problems. Projects aim to promote Cornell and community partnerships, address social inequities through community and student empowerment, and facilitate student leadership. Recent projects include a grant to renovate a church and community day care center, a hydro-electric education project in the Dominican Republic, and to help housing renovation in Ithaca.

James A. Perkins Prize for Interracial Understanding and Harmony

Recognizes the Cornell student, faculty, staff member, or program making the most significant contribution to furthering the ideal of university community while respecting the values of racial diversity.

This prize is awarded at a special ceremony each spring. Other individuals devoted to advancing University community through interracial understanding and harmony will also be honored. The Perkins Prize will be awarded with the understanding that the money will be used to further projects which promote interracial understanding and harmony at Cornell University.

Award:$5,000   # Given: 1
Apply by: February 22 (Nomination Deadline is February 1)

For more information:

Office of the Dean of Students   (607) 255-6839 or 255-1115
401 Willard Straight Hall www.dos.cornell.edu/dos/PerkinsPrize.html

REACH Fellowships

REACH is a Cornell student movement that partners with the community in the national campaign for children's literacy. The REACH AmeriCorps Fellowship recognizes students who are willing to provide leadership, support, and resources to America Reads and America Counts student tutors to ensure a high-quality, structured and stable service environment. Fellows work closely with Cornell Public Service Center (PSC) School Programs staff, as well as teachers and community members, to support the academic achievement of children and youth in the Ithaca community.

Eligibility: A full-time continuing undergraduate student who is work study, Tradition or COSEP eligible, with basic understanding of literacy methods and strategies, tutoring experience in a classroom or informal setting; U.S. citizenship/permanent residence. Able to work an average of 10.5 hours/week during the Cornell academic year in order to complete 300 hours of service.

Award: $7-$7.50/hour + opportunity to earn an additional $1,000 educational award from AmeriCorps upon completion of 300 hours of service.

Given: 15-20   Apply by: February-March

For more information: america_reads@cornell.edu

Robinson-Appel Humanitarian Award

Honors students who have made outstanding contributions to community service, and supports projects addressing a community's social needs.

Eligibility: Cornell undergraduate or graduate student.

Award: $1,500   # Given: 3

Apply by: March 7

For more information:

Public Service Center   www.cornell.edu
200 Barnes Hall
Cornell University
Ithaca, NY 14853-1601

Kieckhefer Adirondack Fellowships

Aims to stimulate original research focused on the Adirondack region. All fields of study pertaining to life and biological sciences are appropriate.

Eligibility: Graduate students enrolled in the College of Agriculture and Life Sciences and the Division of Biological Sciences.

Award: to $5,000   Renewable

For more information:

Office for Research
College of Agriculture and Life Sciences
245 Roberts Hall
Cornell University
Ithaca, NY

CUMBERLAND COLLEGE

Community Service Scholarships

For students who have shown outstanding service in their community. Applicants must be currently involved in service to others.

Award: $1,000   # Given: 5
Renewable   Apply by: March

For more information:

Office of Financial Planning   (800) 532-0828
Cumberland College
6190 College Station Drive
Williamsburg, KY 40769-1372
cserve.cumberlandcollege.edu/admissions/financial_planning/aid_descriptions/scholarships/

DEFIANCE COLLEGE

Presidential Service Leadership Award

A strong sense of civic and social responsibility is necessary to be a member of this prestigious group. Recipients participate in a variety of local and national service projects such as the Red Cross Blood Drive, Make a Difference Day, March of Dimes Walk America, United Way Day of Caring, and many more. In addition to weekly volunteering, the recipients join forces in one major project each year.

Eligibility: Entering freshmen, 2.5 GPA, strong record of community and/or church-related service.

Award: $7,500   # Given: 15 - 20
Renewable up to 4 years

For more information:

Defiance College   (419) 783-2374
Office of Admissions   admissions @defiance.edu
701 N. Clinton St
Defiance, OH 43512   www.defiance.edu/pages/leadership_award.html

DEPAUW UNIVERSITY

Key Club International Bonner/Wright Scholarship

Selection is based on academic achievement, commitment to community service, and leadership. Women, ethnic minorities, and high-need students are encouraged to apply. Through the creation of the Bonner/Wright Scholarship Program with Key Club International, DePauw University is recognizing Key Club members' commitment to leadership and service.

Bonner scholars are expected to: maintain good academic standing at DePauw, participate in educational and enrichment activities; successfully complete the Bonner Program First-Year Student Seminar; participate in community-service programs for an average of ten hours per week during the school year; and complete a summer internship consisting of 200 hours.

The Bonner Scholar Program provides scholarship funds to qualified, high-need, first-year students who wish to continue community-service activities while pursuing their collegiate academic studies.

Eligibility: College-bound graduating high school senior, 3.0 GPA, active member of Key Club for two years.

Award: $56,000 total over 4 years   # Given: 2
Apply by: March 1 priority deadline.

For more information:

Rodney G. Haywood   (800) 447-2495
DePauw Univ. Office of Admission   rhaywood@depauw.edu
Bonner/Wright Scholarship Program   www.depauw.edu
Greencastle, Indiana 46135-1778 www.keyclub.org/Winner/BW-BeAWinner-depauw.htm

Duke University

The biology department at Duke sponsors a number of fellowships for undergraduates.

For more information:

www.biology.duke.edu/undergrad/fellowships_research.htm

Earlham College

Bonner Scholars Program

See Bonner Scholars Listing.

Earlham College Community Service Award

Recognizes students who have provided service to others through volunteer work on the local, regional, national or international level. Students must complete the CSA application found in the admission application folder.

Award: $1,000   # Given: 50

Apply by: February 15

For more information:

Admissions Office   (800) 327-5426

Earlham College

Richmond, IN 473744095   www.earlham.edu/%7Eadm/

Eckerd College

Special Talent Scholarship

For extensive community service and/or leadership experience.

Award: $1,000 - $5,000   Renewable

For more information:

Office of Admissions   (800) 456-9009

Eckerd College

4200 54th Avenue

South St. Petersburg, FL 33711   www.eckerd.edu/catlas/scholarship_programs

Emory & Henry College

Bonner Scholars Program

See Bonner Scholarship Listing

Appalachian Center Associates

For students with demonstrated commitment to service in high school, but don't qualify for the Bonner Scholarship. Appalachian Associates usually work in the local community as tutors in reading skill and language arts, targeting learners in grades K-3.

Award: $1,200   # Given: 12

Renewable for 4 years

For more information:

Gloria Surber   gwsurber@ehc.edu

The Appalachian Center for Community Service

Emory & Henry College
Emory, VA 24327   www.ehc.edu/serve/index.html

THE EVERGREEN STATE COLLEGE

First Peoples' Scholarship

Entering students of color who have distinguished themselves in academic achievement, community service, music, etc.

Award: Same value as undergraduate resident tuition.

Thayer Raymond Memorial Scholarship

For new and continuing juniors and seniors. Awards will go to students with financial need and involvement in the betterment of society.

Award: $1,800

The Evergreen State College Foundation Scholarship

For entering undergraduates who have distinguished themselves in a wide range of areas (academics, community service, music, art, etc.).

Award: same value as undergraduate resident tuition.

Merv Cadwallader Scholarship

New or current enrolled juniors or seniors who demonstrate a personal commitment to the betterment of society, through good citizenship and community involvement. Preference given to students with financial need.

Award: $500   Apply by: (all) February 1

For more information:

Dean of Enrollment Services Office   (360) 866-6000 ext. 6310
The Evergreen State College
Olympia, WA 98505   www.evergreen.edu/scholarships/scholars.htm

FLORIDA STATE UNIVERSITY

The Service Scholar Program

Recognizes students with an outstanding record of service and promotes service as an integral part of the liberal arts education at FSU. Awarded to students who have demonstrated excellence in service to the community, and who have an interest in continuing to enhance their learning through service while doing good in the community.

Each student has a service advisor, performs 5 hours of service weekly, attends reflection/educational seminars, and writes reflective journals.

Eligibility: Starting first year of college at FSU

Award: $2,000   # Given: 10 each year (40 total)

Apply by: January 1   Renewable: up to 4 years

Ben Rosenbloom Memorial Service Scholarship?

Designed to recognize students with an outstanding record of service and to foster their commitment to a lifetime of service.

Eligibility: Any rising sophomore, junior, or senior who will be returning to FSU for the 2002-2003 term with a minimum 2.0 GPA is eligible to apply.

Award: $1,000

For more information:

Service Scholarship Program Co-ord. (850) 644-3342
930 West Park Avenue www.fsu.edu/~service
Florida State University
Tallahassee, FL 32306-4180

CA STATE UNIVERSITY - FRESNO

Community Service Scholarship Program

Students are placed with volunteer agencies related to the student's academic major and, in order to provide enough time for a "real world" experience, each student performs assignments ranging from 100-200 hours. Students are placed in a variety of community assignments related to education, crime, youth programs, and public health. Students also earn 3 units of academic credit.

Award: $1,000

For more information:

Admissions Office (209) 278-2261
CSU Fresno
5241 North Maple St.
Fresno, CA 93740-0047 www.csufresno.edu/

GREEN MOUNTAIN COLLEGE

Leadership Scholarships

There are many service agencies and organizations in which students can exercise talents related to their chosen degree or particular special interests. Students can participate in community recycling, youth intramurals, centers for aging, animal shelters, environmental education, health care, and many other programs. Resourceful students can create their own service projects. If you are entering college with limited service experience, Green Mountain College provides the needed opportunity to help you get involved in worthy causes and earn scholarships.

Each year students will be evaluated on the level of service contribution and be awarded service scholarships based on performance. Service and Leadership Scholarships generally range from $500 to $1,500.

For more information:

Office of Admissions (802) 287-8000
Green Mountain College www.greenmtn.edu
Poultney, VT 05764

UNIVERSITY OF HAWAII AT MANOA

Hiroki Kaku Memorial Scholarship

For students with demonstrated commitment in some area or specific field leading to opportunities for self-sufficiency of people in Pacific Basin.

Eligibility: productive or innovative community service; exhibits community involvement. Junior, senior or Graduate student.

> Award: varies

For more information:

College of Trop. Agr. & Human Res.	(808) 956-8236
University of Hawaii at Manoa	
Dept. of Food Science & Human Nutrition	
Honolulu, HI 96822	www.uhm.hawaii.edu

HOOD COLLEGE

Trustee Scholarship

Awarded to incoming freshmen with demonstrated academic ability and leadership in school and community activities.

> Award: $8,000 - $10,000

Achievement Award

$2,000 - $8,000

Awarded to incoming freshmen with demonstrated financial need who have the potential to succeed academically and have demonstrated leadership, commitment to community service, and/or demonstrated talent.

> Award: $2,000 - $8,000

For more information:

Admissions Office	(301) 663-3131 ext. 235
Hood College	
401 Rosemont Avenue	
Frederick, MD 21701-8575	www.hood.edu/admissions/finaid/

HUNTER COLLEGE

Child Welfare Leadership

Encourages and assists students interested in entering the field of child welfare as agents of change and becoming leaders in the field. Recipients must participate in a two-semester weekly seminar for credit and a one year, eight hour per week field placement, and take two child welfare-related courses.

> Eligibility: Matriculated undergraduate Hunter College students.

> Award: $2,000   # Given: 15

> Apply by: Early Spring

For more information:

Judy Blunt, Program Director	(212) 772-4256
Center for the Study of Family Policy	
East 1036	
Hunter College	
New York, NY	
maxweber.hunter.cuny.edu/psych/leadsch.htm	

Indiana-Purdue U. Indianapolis

Community Service Scholarship

Recognizes students who have made exemplary service contributions to the community and/or the campus during the past two years. The scholarship fosters continued service contributions to the community, enhances the development of civic responsibility, and helps meet community needs.

Scholars will volunteer six hours per week throughout the academic year and complete a service learning course.

Eligibility: Students who have completed 15 hours at IUPUI.

Award: $2,500   # Given: 6
Renewable for 1 year

For more information:
Center for Public Service & Leadership   (317) 278-2370

Charles O. McGaughey Leadership Awards

For qualifying upper class students with demonstrated leadership abilities and a record of achievement in community service, and service to IUPUI.

Award: $2,000

Zora Neale Hurston - Mari Evans Scholarship

These scholarships encourage the study of subjects which transcend gender, race, age, culture and economic status.

Award: $2,000   # Given: 5 (3 undergrad)
Renewable for $500

Make a Difference Scholarship

Students who have participated in school or community service that are interested in careers the "make a difference" and who want to be involved with helping others.

Eligibility: Must be accepted to IUPUI, must agree to be enrolled full-time and maintain a 2.5 GPA, and must meet with the American Humanics Campus Director in the Center of Philanthropy to develop a service plan. Incoming Freshman must be in the top 50% of their High School class and have a 950 SAT/20 ACT score.

Award: $500   Apply by: March 1 st

Sam Masarachia Scholars

New beginning full-time students in Liberal Arts who are interested in studies related to labor, senior citizens and/or community activism are encouraged to apply for this scholarship. Recipients will participate in Masarachia seminars, internship, and related activities.

Eligibility: Top 40% of graduating class, SAT 1000/ACT 21, financial need.

Award: Full tuition and fees   Apply by: March 1

Minority Research Scholars

Aimed at attracting academically talented minority students to the Schools of Science, Engineering, Allied Health, Dentistry (dental hygiene), Nursing, Physical Education or Social Work. The research component is designed not only to acclimate students to a research setting, but also to actively involve them in undergraduate research activities. Research mentors from IUPUI faculty and the corporate sector help the scholar to structure their research program.

Eligibility: Students must meet the academic program's admission requirements, have at least a B grade in all mathematics classes, be an Indiana resident, a U.S. citizen or permanent resident.

Award: Tuition and fees, renewable   Apply by: April 1

For more information:

Dr. Marchusa Huff

IU School of Nursing   (317) 274-8049

Outstanding Freshman Scholars

Awards well-rounded students excelling not only in academics but also in extracurricular activities, leadership abilities and/or community services.

Eligibility: New Incoming students admitted by February 1 st , must be in the top 15% of their high school class with 1200 SAT or 26 ACT.

Award: $3,000 for 4 years   Apply by:February 1

For more information:

Scholarship Office   (317) 274-5516

IUPUI

Indianapolis, IN 46202   www.iupui.edu/~scentral

LANSING COMMUNITY COLLEGE

Student Leadership Academy

The Student Leadership Academy is a unique leadership development experience combining leadership theory with practice in community service settings. Students are exposed to various opportunities to develop a positive sense of community leadership and service.

Academy students participate in the two year leadership curriculum, in addition to regular study. Studies include: Leadership Development; Responsibilities of Leadership; Managing Conflict; Team Building; Initiating Change; Leading by Serving; Empowering and Delegating; Creative Problem Solving/ Decision Making; Ethics; Articulating a Vision and Leading with Goals. Practical experience in planning and implementing a leadership conference, evaluating programs, and selecting candidates is included.

Students also serve on and/or observe community boards and committees with the Lansing School District and Lansing Community College.

Award: $1,310   # Given: 23

Apply by: Early February

For more information:

Lansing Community College   (517) 483-1285

Student Life, Room 2473   www.lansing.cc.mi.us/stulife/

Gannon Vocational Technical Building

Lansing MI 48901-7210

LASELL COLLEGE

Arnow Scholars, Uphams Scholars, Leadership and Lasell Service Awards

        Award: total $130,000   # Given: 37

For more information

        Director of Student Financial Planning   (617) 243-2156
        Lasell College
        1844 Commonwealth Ave
        Newton MA 02166

LESLEY COLLEGE

Lesley Scholars

        Lesley Scholars must show a commitment to working with people and a desire to pursue a career in education, human services, or management. Commitment is shown through work and volunteer experience.

        Award: $2,500   Apply by: March 1

Leadership Scholars

        Awarded to students with strong high school records, and demonstrated commitment and excellence in one or more of the following areas: community service; teaching or working with children; business or management.

        Award: $5,000   # Given: Varies

Presidential Scholar

        For a first year student who reflects the institution's commitment to the development of women athletes by having already demonstrated both academic strength and leadership in her school and community during high school.

        Award: Full tuition   # Given: 1

AHANA Scholars

        To entering freshman who show potential for leadership based on work and/or volunteer experience, a commitment to working with people, and a desire to pursue a career in education, human services and management.

        Award: Full tuition   # Given: 10
        Apply by: March 1   Renewable

For more information:

        Nancy Mehlem, Ed.D., Assoc. Provost   (617) 349-8517
        Lesley College Office of the Provost
        29 Everett Street
        Cambridge, MA. 02138-2790

LORAS COLLEGE

Valder Social Justice Service Award

        Provides awards to juniors entering their senior year at Loras College, who want to demonstrate their commitment and leadership in the field of social justice advocacy, and who will be devoting their summer to service in that field.

        Social justice advocacy projects emphasize leadership development and empowerment. They address the root causes of poverty, racism, and other man-ifestations of powerlessness and discrimination such as: hunger, homelessness, housing discrimination, unemployment, underemployment, employment dis-crimination and exclusion from the political process.

Eligibility: College juniors.

Award: Approximately $3,000   # Given: 2 - 3

For more information:

Nancy M. Zachar   (319) 588-7029

Loras College, MS # 221

1450 Alta Vista

Dubuque, IA 52001-0178

MANCHESTER COLLEGE

Manchester College offers service and non-profit management scholar-ships. A central goal of the College is to nurture "... a dedication to service of oth-ers and an acceptance of the demands of responsible leadership".

Service Scholarships

For students who combine academic promise and substantial service. Minimum 1050 SAT or 23 ACT

Award: $8,000

Non-Profit Leadership Award

For students who have an interest in non-profit management. Minimum 1050 SAT or 23 ACT

Award: $8,000

College Presidential Awards

Given to top students, selected on the basis of academic achievement and promise, commitment to service and demonstrated leadership.

All scholarships are renewable.

Apply (all): By December for priority consideration.

For more information:

Office of Admissions   (800) 852-3648

Manchester College

N. Manchester, IN 46962   www.manchester.edu/intro/admiss/FinAid

MARQUETTE UNIVERSITY

Burke Scholarship

Honors and encourages lifetime development of the humanitarian ethic manifest in a commitment to service. Awarded to academically talented students who exhibit leadership in a manner which reflects exceptional commitment to community. Recipients must complete 450 hours of meaningful service each year, and live on campus for first two years of program.

Eligibility: High school senior with ank at or near the top 10 percent (when applicable), family residency in Wisconsin, ACT composite of 28 or SAT of 1200.

Award: Full-tuition plus $3,000 annual stipend, renewable for 4 years.

Given: 10   Apply: February 1

Ignatius Community Service Scholarship

Awarded to entering students who demonstrate an exceptional commitment to leadership through service to others.

Award: $4,000   # Given: varies

Renewable for 4 years

For more information:

Office of Undergraduate Admissions

Marquette University

Milwaukee, WI 53201-1881   www.marquette.edu/apply@mu/scholarships/

U of Maryland, Baltimore county

The France/Merrick Scholars Program

For socially involved undergraduate students at UMBC. Allows students to focus more fully on community service through UMBC's The Shriver Center.

Eligibility: Incoming freshmen.

Award: $1000+Full tuition, room, board   # Given: 10

Apply by: December 15   Renewable for 4 years

For more information:

Office of Scholarships   (410) 455-3813

U of Maryland, Baltimore County   schl_info@umbc.edu

1000 Hilltop Circle

Baltimore, MD 21250   www.umbc.edu/undergrad/s_additional.html

Maryville College

The Bonner Scholars

Bonner Scholars volunteer in the community 10 hours per week during the academic year, and 240 hours over the summer.

Award: $2,100   Apply by: February 1

Bradford Scholars

The Bradford Scholars teach literacy to adults.

Award: $3,000   # Given: 20

Renewable

The Church and College Scholars

These students do various activities mainly in Presbyterian churches.

Award: $2,000   # Given: 40

Apply by: February 15   Renewable

For more information:

Financial Aid Office

(865) 981-8100

Maryville College   (800) 59-SCOTS

Maryville, TN 37804   finaid@maryvillecollege.edu

www.maryvillecollege.edu/admissions/finaid-scholarships.html

University of Massachusetts

Citizen Scholars Program

This two-year program is for students who wish to serve their community, and become active leaders in the commonwealth. Citizen Scholars are expected to complete a curriculum of 5 community service-learning courses, and attend monthly colloquia. Students must complete a minimum of 60 hours community service in each of the four semesters they are in the program.

Opportunities for an additional summer stipend to support a summer service-based practicum. Preference to students with a demonstrated record of community service and a clear commitment to integrating service with their learning.

Eligibility: Freshman or sophomore with a demonstrated record of prior community service, and a commitment to future community service, 3.2 GPA.

> Award: $1,000 per year for 2 years   # Given: 12
>
> Apply by: March 1

For more information:

> Office of Community Service Learning
> Commonwealth College
> Room 610 Goodell
> UMass
> Amherst, MA 01003-3295   www.comcol.umass.edu/currentstudents/index.asp

McKendree College

McKendree College is looking for students with a demonstrated commitment to community service. McKendree values experiential education and takes seriously its mission of helping students achieve personal growth, an awareness of social responsibility, and an appreciation of the diversity of culture. Courses in which service is an integral part of the learning experience are offered.

> Award: half tuition   # Given: 3
>
> Apply by: February 17

For more information:

> Lyn Huxford, Coordinator   (618) 537-6901
> Center for Public Service   lhuxford@atlas.mckendree.edu
> McKendree College
> Lebanon, IL 62254   www.mckendree.edu/cps/Comm.SeviceScholarshippg.htm

University of Michigan - Flint

Broome, Jr. Scholarship

For African-Americans living in the greater Flint area who have participated in school and/or community service activities. 3.00 GPA.

Croner Memorial Scholarship

Students pursuing studies in Resource Science with a major in physical geography (including geology). MI resident enrolled as full-time. 3.00 GPA.

Hashbarger Scholarship

Women students who have completed at least 84 credit hours, 2.80 GPA, and have demonstrated commitment to community service.

Dr. Douglas Wright Memorial Scholarships

Full-time African-American students, leadership skills, commitment to community service, and promotion of human rights. 3.00 GPA, financial need.

Martin Luther King Junior Community Service Scholarship

For undergraduate students who have actively engaged in service and volunteerism during the past three to five years. 2.8 GPA.

McCree Scholarship

Flint area African-Americans, participated in school/community service. Academic/career goals with an interest in helping others. 3.00 GPA.

McKinnon Scholarship

Genesee County residents who have participated in school and/or community service activities. 3.50 GPA.   Renewable

Lavoy Smith Memorial Scholarship

For Native American and African American students who have demonstrated commitment and contribution to the community. 2.50 GPA.

Lillian and Bruce Wright Memorial Scholarship

For returning adults - students who have been active in the political process at local, state, or national level will be given preference. 3.00 GPA, major or minor in political science, public administration or engineering.

Horace T. Sanders Social Work Scholarship

For undergraduate Social Work majors, part-time or full-time. Min. 3.0 GPA, and completed at least 50 credit hours. Financial need is not considered.

Social Work Leadership Scholarship

For undergraduate Social Work majors, part-time or full-time. Min. 3.0 GPA, and completed at least 55 credit hours. Financial need is not considered.

Student Government Council Service Scholarship

Scholarship intended to recognize those students who demonstrate a commitment to academic, social and volunteer pursuits.

For more information:

Office of Financial Aid   (810) 762-3444
277 University Pavilion   www.flint.umich.edu/departments/finaid
The University of Michigan-Flint
Flint, MI 48502-2186

MILLIKIN UNIVERSITY

Service-Learning Scholarships

Recipients are expected to work 3 hours weekly in support of the Center for Service Learning, and their own individually developed external service-learning project. Criteria for the award include past volunteerism experience, and the ability to communicate with and motivate others.

Award: $2,000   # Given: 2 per freshman class

Apply by: February 28   Renewable for 4 years

For more information:
    Millikin University
    Center for Service Learning
    1184 West Main   (217) 362-6463
    Decatur, IL 62522   www.millikin.edu/servicelearning/criteria.asp

UNIVERSITY OF MINNESOTA

College Of Education & Human Development Student Community Service

Recognizes outstanding, non-paid volunteer service by CEHD students to nonprofit organizations and group. Primary focus is on extracurricular efforts that lead to direct improvement of the welfare of children, adults, youth, and families.

    Award: $1,000   # Given: up to 40
    Apply by: May 1

For more information:
    Student & Professional Services
    College of Education and Human Development   (612)625-1506
    University of Minnesota
    110 Wulling Hall
    178 Pillsbury Drive SE
    Minneapolis, MN 55455   education.umn.edu/SPS/awards/CEHDawards.html

MISSOURI VALLEY COLLEGE

American Humanics Scholarships

For Girl Scouts interested in professional careers in youth or human service agencies. Award includes leadership scholarship and a work-&-learn scholarship.

Eligibility: 2.5 HS GPA, documented leadership roles, involvement in community service, and diversity of activities in personal life.

    Award: $6,500   # Given: 10
    Renewable for 4 years

For more information:
    Dr. Carl T. Gass
    Dean of Human Services
    Missouri Valley College
    Marshall, MO 65340

MONTEREY INSTITUTE

Institute scholarships give special consideration given to who have volunteered with programs such as Amity Institute, ESL Volunteers International, VIA, United Nations Volunteers, World Teach, Peace Corps, or independently.

Eligibility: Entering students (must have completed sophomore year at a community college or other 4 year institution).

    Award: up-to $10,000

For more information:

Monterey Institute of Int'l. Studies	(408) 647-4100
425 Van Buren Street	www.miis.edu
Monterey CA, 93940	

NEW COLLEGE FLORIDA HERITAGE AWARD

Heritage Scholars will be selected for exceptional leadership, activism, service and/or creativity.

Award: $5,000/year for four years   Apply by: February 1

For more information:

www.ncf.edu/Admissions/Documents/ncha.htm

NEW ENGLAND COLLEGE

Leadership and Community Service Scholarships

For HS seniors demonstrating a high degree of involvement in community service or extra-curricular activities during high school. Selection based upon information in student's admission application. New England College awards approximately $100,000 in Leadership and Community Service Scholarships annually.

For more information:

Office of Admissions	(603) 428-2232
New England College	
Henniker, NH 03242-3293	www.nec.edu/admissions/scholarships.html

UNIVERSITY OF NEW HAMPSHIRE

Ruth E. Farrington Forestry

Undergraduates and graduate students in forestry and related fields.

Award: up to one-half in-state tuition

Edward Cass Adams

Students in Wildlife Mgm't./Research or Conservation of Natural Resources.

Gordon L. Byers Scholarship

Students enrolled in the Water Resources Management Program.

Elizabeth Greene Scholarship

Commitment to a career in Environmental Conservation with a sincere interest in public service, academic performance, and financial need.

Nancy Coutu Wildlife Scholarship

Student majoring in wildlife who gives good service to the community.

For more information:

Department of Natural Resources	
College of Life Sciences & Agriculture	(603) 862-1020
215 James Hall	
56 College Road	

NORTHERN ARIZONA UNIVERSITY

Arizona Congress of Parents and Teachers Scholarship

> For students planning on a career in teaching.
>
> Eligibility: Arizona high school graduate, intended enrollment in the NAU Teacher Education Program, academic scholarship and financial need.
>
> Award: $400   # Given: 1

For more information:

> AZ Congress of Parents and Teachers Scholarship Committee
> 2721 North Seventh Avenue
> Phoenix, AZ 85007

Associated Students for Women's Issues Scholarship

> For students with documented involvement in gender issues.
>
> Eligibility: Full-time enrollment, 2.5 GPA.
>
> Award: $400   # Given: 4

For more information:

> Associated Students in Women's Issues Organization
> Northern Arizona University
> PO Box 6003
> Flagstaff, AZ 86011-6003

Bill Morrall Conservation Scholarship

> For students in ecosystem analysis, fish and wildlife management, forestry and range management, conservation journalism or education, environmental pollution, soil conservation, land use planning, energy etc.
>
> Award: $500   Apply by: mid-March

For more information:

> College of Ecosystem Management or College of Arts and Sciences
> www.nau.edu/envsci/Scholarships.html

The Environmental Fund for a Sustainable Future Scholarship

> Provides funding for junior and senior Environmental Sciences majors currently enrolled full-time and in good standing with NAU.
>
> Award: up tp $1,500   Apply by: mid-March

For more information:

> College of Ecosystem Management or College of Arts and Sciences
> www.nau.edu/envsci/Scholarships.html

The Lisa Marie Jones Memorial Scholarship

> Provides funding for junior and senior Environmental Sciences majors currently enrolled full-time and in good standing with NAU. Arizona Resident with financial need and GPA of 2.5 or above
>
> Award: $500   Apply by: mid-March

For more information:

> College of Ecosystem Management or College of Arts and Sciences
> www.nau.edu/envsci/Scholarships.html

Wassaja Scholarship

NAU student committed to serving Native American Communities.

Award: $1,000

For more information:

Institute for Native Americans　　　　　(928) 523-9557

Navajo Engineering & Construction Authority of NM Scholarship

Eligibility: Navajo engineering, business management, education, nursing, or pre-med majors; financial need; and 3.0 minimum cumulative GPA.

Award: $1,000　　　　　　　　　　# Given: 1

Solid Waste Association of North America Scholarship

Promotes the protection of public heath and the environment through sanitary waste collection, the conservation of resources through recycling, the disposal of waste with minimal impact, and the recovery of energy.

Eligibility: Majors in environmental fields of study in the Colleges of Engineering, Arts and Sciences or Ecosystem Science and Management. Recipients must be U.S. Citizens; Arizona residents; have a cumulative 3.0 GPA or above; be juniors or seniors at NAU upon collecting this scholarship; and show a commitment to a career that benefits the environment.

Award: $750　　　　　　　　　Apply by: March 1st

Ben Avery Scholarship

Sponsored by the Arizona Chapter of Soil and Water Conservation Society to assist university juniors and seniors in their pursuit of a degree in a natural resource-related field and assist them to gain practical knowledge regarding land stewardship. The SWCS will also provide scholarship recipients with assistance in obtaining hands-on experience through internships, volunteer programs and employment programs. In addition, the Soil and Water Conservation Society will assist university students in establishing collegiate chapters of the SWCS. The sponsors of the scholarship hope that the recipients will be employed and work to conserve the State of Arizona's Natural Resources.

Eligibility: Arizona resident; enrolled in a 4-year Arizona university as a junior or senior the year the scholarship is awarded; major in natural resource related field (i.e. soil science, range management, wildlife management); minimum 2.5 cum GPA.

Award: $500　　　　　　　　　Apply by: April 15

For more information:

NAU Scholarship Office　　　　　　scholar@nau.edu

www4.nau.edu/finaid/Scholarship/index.htm

NORTH CAROLINA STATE UNIVERSITY

All scholarships below are for Forestry students.

Academic Scholarships

Eligibility: Incoming Freshman: High School GPA of 3.4, SAT of 1150. Current & Transfers Students : GPA of 3.2

Award: $2,500 - $5,000, renewable　　　# Given: 30

Work Scholarships

Recipient must work in a college-owned forest performing management activities. Most recipients are juniors and seniors.

Eligibility: GPA of 2.5

Award: $$16/hr up to $2,400   # Given: 15

Gifford Pinchot Scholars Program

For students with a double major in Forest Management and Humanities or Social Sciences placing forest management in the context of cross-cultural perspectives, global issues, and public policy.

Award: $2,000 - $3,000   # Given: 10

For more information:

Dr. Sarah Warren   stwarren@social.chass.ncsu.edu

Dr. Erin Sills, Department of Forestry   erin_sills@ncsu.edu>

Summer Camp Scholarships

For attending the ten-week NC State Forestry Summer Camp.

Eligibility: Undergraduates enrolled in Department of Forestry with a minimum GPA of 2.5.

Award: $500-$1,000   # Given: 5

For more information contact:

Dr. Richard Braham   Richard_Braham@ncsu.edu

Department of Forestry

NC State University

Campus Box 8002   (919) 515-7568

Raleigh, NC 27695   natural-resources.ncsu.edu/for/studentinfo/scholars.html

NORWICH UNIVERSITY

President's Scholarship

Awarded to one incoming cadet and one civilian student with a record of involvement in extracurricular activities at school, community.

Eligibility: 1200 SAT or 29 on the ACT, 3.0 GPA.

Award: tuition, room and board, renewable

Captain Alden Partridge Scholarship

To cadets who demonstrate leadership qualities in high school, either in clubs, organizations, sports or community service organizations or projects.

Award: $5,000 a year for four years

Admiral George Dewey Scholarship

For cadets who demonstrate outstanding community service.

Award: $3,500 a year for four years

General Grenville M. Dodge Scholarship

Awarded to cadets who have contributed to either school or community through leadership roles or service activities.

Award: $2,000 a year for four years.

Leadership Achievement Scholarship

For civilian students who demonstrate leadership qualities in HS, in clubs, organizations, sports or community service organizations or projects.

Award: $5,000 a year for four years.

Community Service Scholarship

To civilian students who demonstrate outstanding community service.

Award: $3,500 a year for four years.

For more information:

Admissions Office (800) 468-6679

Norwich University

Northfield, VT 05663 www.norwich.edu/admiss/undergraduate/

NOTRE DAME UNIVERSITY

The Center for Social Concerns is a visible sign of the Notre Dames' commitment to social concerns. Central to this process is enhancing spiritual and intellectual awareness about today's complex social realities, calling us all to service and action for a more just and humane world.

James F. Andrews Scholarship Fund/Notre Dame Alumni Clubs

Provides a Social Concerns Tuition Scholarship to each Notre Dame student who participates in a Summer Service Project. ND students have the opportunity to work for and learn from disadvantaged populations across the country and beyond. Students receive 3 credits in Theology.

The Center for Social Concerns seeks, in the words of the Notre Dame mission statement, to "create a sense of human solidarity and concern for the common good that will bear fruit as learning becomes service to justice."

Award: $1,700 # Given: 150+

For more information:

Center for Social Concerns (219-631-5293)

Notre Dame University centerforsocialconcerns.nd.edu/index.htmlc/prgms.html

OBERLIN COLLEGE

Bonner Scholars Program

See the Bonner Scholars Program listing.

For more information:

Director, Bonner Scholar Program (440) 775-8055

Oberlin College

Oberlin, OH

OHIO WESLEYAN UNIVERSITY

Meek Community Service and Leadership Award

Recognize the importance of community service on campus and students who embody a sincere commitment to service learning. Awarded individually according to level of commitment to and involvement with community service.

Eligibility: entering students who complete community service application.

Award: up to $10,000 per year, renewable # Given: 30

Apply by: February 15

For more information:

Community Service Award Co-ord.	800-922-8953, x3020.
Admission Office	owuadmit@cc.owu.edu
Ohio Wesleyan University	admission.owu.edu/merit.html
Delaware, Ohio 43015	

OLIVET COLLEGE

Bonner Scholars Program

See the Bonner Scholars Program listing.

Community Responsibility Scholarship

Olivet College has developed a new academic vision, Education for Individual and Social Responsibility, which promotes a culture of responsibility through participation in community service, volunteerism, and service.

The Program rewards responsibility, community service and civic participation. The greater the involvement, the more responsibility you exhibit, the higher the scholarship award.

For more information:

Office of Student Development & Youth Outreach Services
Olivet College
Olivet, MI 49076   (269) 749-7635
                          www.olivetnet.edu

OTTERBEIN

Community Service Scholarship

Awarded to one first-year or sophomore student who has demonstrated commitment to community service and scholarship during HS or while at Otterbein College. The student will coordinate a community service program while at Otterbein. The award will be decided on the basis of demonstrated commitment to community service, a cumulative GPA of 3.0, ability to coordinate a service project while at Otterbein and leadership potential.

Award: $1,500

For more information:

Admissions Office   (614) 823-1502 or (888) OTTERBEIN
Otterbein College
Westerville, OH 43081   www.otterbein.edu/Admission/Financial_aid/financial_aid.asp

PITZER COLLEGE

Trustee-Community Scholarships

To first-year students in recognition of academic excellence combined with extraordinary commitment to community service; outstanding leadership and/or exceptional talent. Application is an automatic part of the admission process.

For more information:

Admission & Financial Aid
Pitzer College

Plattsburgh SUNY

Community Service Scholarship

Recipients are required to engage in 12 hours of community service per week throughout the academic year. Criteria include demonstration of a commitment to community service and documentation of service experience.

Eligibility: incoming freshman, fall transfers, 2.5 GPA, transfer 2.8 GPA.

Award: $2,500   # Given: 15

Apply by: mid- April

Clinton County Americorps Community Service Scholarship

For freshmen and transfer students with a eye toward helping their community. The students become part-time Americorps members and must complete 15 hours per week of community service in a local agency.

Eligibility: students entering sophomore or junior year.

Award: modest living allowance while serving, health care and child care benefits are available if eligible, end of term $4,725 (part-time members receive $1,000).

For more information:

Office of Service Learning & Leadership   (518) 564-4830

Plattsburgh State University

Plattsburgh, NY 12901   plattsburgh.edu/campuslife/service/cservscholar.cfm

Portland State University

Frank Roberts Community Service Scholarship

Awarded to a PSU graduate student who exemplifies a spirit of public service and commitment to education. Must be in good academic standing, and enrolled for at least 6 credit hours per term. An excellent undergraduate portfolio is required and financial need will be considered.

Award: $2,000 + resident instructional fees, renewable

Apply by: April 15

Kayo Uchida Sato Memorial Scholarship

Eligibility: full-time PSU student; Asian or other ethnic minority majoring in math or the natural sciences, 3.0 GPA and financial need.

Barry Commoner Scholarship

Named for the internationally known environmental scientist, is awarded to a student with an academic career interests in the area of environmental policy or science.

Eligibility: full-time, junior or senior with min. GPA of 3.0, financial need.

Apply by: April 1

Paul Croy Scholarship

Named for a western educator and poet, for a student with academic and career interests in the area of environmental policy and decision-making.

Eligibility: full-time, junior or senior with min. GPA of 3.0, financial need.

Apply by: April 1

Jack S. Schendel Commemorative Scholarship

Awarded to an outstanding undergraduate health education major with a minimum 3.25 GPA.

Award: $1,000, renewable   Apply by: February 15

Portland Teachers Program

For minority students, junior level standing. Committed to completion of the degree and basic teaching certificate at PSU and seek subsequent employment as a teacher in the Portland Public Schools.

Award: tuition waiver

Awards also available in Graduate Schools of Education and Social Work..

For more information:

Office of Academic Affairs
349 Cramer Hall
Portland State University
Portland, OR   www.oaa.pdx.edu/OAADOC/SCHOLARSHIPS/scholarships.html

PROVIDENCE COLLEGE

Feinstein Institute

Demonstrated commitment to and promise in the area of public and community service. Students majoring in Public & Community Service are eligible. College will match some Americorps scholarship awards for incoming students.

For more information:

Feinstein Institute for Public Service

Martin Luther King Jr. Scholarship

Selection is based on academic potential, leadership, community service.

Eligibility: All minority students, financial need.

Southeast Asian Scholarship

Awarded to students with strong high school performance, community service, and demonstrated leadership potential.

Eligibility: Qualified entering freshmen of Southeast Asian descent currently residing in the Greater Providence area, financial need.

For more information:

Providence College   (410) 865-2535
River College and Eaton St.
Providence, RI 02918-0001   www.providence.edu/admiss/pcfasfa.htm#SG

UNIVERSITY OF PUGET SOUND

George J. Matelich Scholarship

Awarded to exceptional students with exceptional drive, discipline and determination to achieve a high measure of success after college, strong moral character and commitment to campus and/or community service through meaningful activities that benefit the larger community.

Eligibility: Faculty nominated undergraduate seniors or juniors who graduate from high schools located in the Pacific Northwest (WA, OR, ID, MT, AK).

Award: $10,000　　　　　　　　　　　# Given: 6

Walter Price Leadership / Community Service Scholarships

To incoming freshman and transfer students on the basis of leadership abilities and community service involvement. Special application required.

Award: $3,000　　　　　　　　　　　# Given: 7

Renewable for three additional years.

For more information:

University of Puget Sound　　　　　　(206) 756-3211
Office of Admission　　　　　　　　　www.ups.edu/financialaid/
1500 N. Warner St.
Tacoma, WA 98416

PURDUE UNIVERSITY

Bartlett Tree Foundation

For students who have completed at least one year of study and demonstrated professional interest in urban forestry/arboriculture.

Award: $2,000　　　　　　　　　　　# Given: 1

Claude M. Gladden Scholarships, Minority Scholarship

Beginning freshmen admitted to Forestry and Natural Resources.

Award: $1,000　　　　　　　　　　　# Given: 3
　　　　$500　　　　　　　　　　　　# Given: 2
　　　　$1,500 - Minority student　　　# Given: 2

For more information:

Forestry and Natural Resources
www.agriculture.purdue.edu/fnr/html/ugrad/scholarships.htm

Botany and Plant Pathology Scholarships

Eligibility: students in Crop Protection & Plant Science.

Award: $500-$1,500　　　　　　　　　# Given:up to 15

For more information:

Department of Botany and Plant Pathology　　botany@purdue.edu
Purdue University　　　　　　　　　　　(765) 494-4614
Lilly Hall of Life Sciences
915 W. State Street
West Lafayette, Indiana 47907-2054　　　www.btny.purdue.edu

ST. JOHN FISHER COLLEGE

Fisher Service Scholarship

Recognizes and rewards high school seniors who demonstrate an ongoing interest in serving the needs of others through community service.

Award: one-third total yearly cost of tuition, fees, and room and board.

Given: 36　　　　　　　　　　　　Renewable for 4 years

For more information:

Admissions Office   (800) 444-4640
St. John Fisher College
3690 East Avenue
Rochester, NY 14618   www.sjfc.edu/prostd/svcsch.asp

SAM HOUSTON STATE UNIVERSITY

Biology And Environmental Science Academic Scholarship
> Eligibility: entering freshmen as well as on-campus students, 3.0 GPA.
>
> Award: $1,000

Wilson-Warner Scholarships
> Awarded to outstanding Biology and Environmental Science majors.
> Eligibility: 3.5 GPA.
>
> Award: $1,500 - $3,000

For more information:
Scholarships   (409) 294-1540
Department of Biological Sciences   bio_klb@shsu.edu
Sam Houston State University
Huntsville, TX 77341-2116   www.shsu.edu/~bio_www/u-schol.html

UNIVERSITY OF SAN FRANCISCO

MAURICIO ROMERO AWARD
> For the graduating senior who demonstrates excellence in both academics and community service.
>
> Award: $1,000

SAN FRANCISCO BAY AREA COMMUNITY SERVICE AWARD
> For the graduating Politics student who demonstrates the most outstanding community service, beyond the call of duty, in the San Francisco Bay Area, during his/her college years.
>
> Award: $1,500

INTERNATIONAL COMMUNITY SERVICE AWARD
> Granted to the graduating Politics student who demonstrates the most outstanding community service, beyond the call of duty, on the national or international level, during his/her college years.
>
> Award: $1,500

For more information:
University of San Francisco
2130 Fulton Street
San Francisco, CA 94117-1080   www.usfca.edu/politics/awards.htm

SEATTLE UNIVERSITY

Sullivan Leadership Awards
> Students are selected on the basis of service, demonstration of leadership, commitment to a vision that is just and for the common good, as well as strong academic achievement.

Sullivan Scholars are welcomed into the community of 24 scholars. Before each school year begins, they travel with the scholars to a lodge in a small town on the Oregon coast, for a four-day leadership retreat.

Leadership candidates must demonstrate leadership through school activities, public service, and community involvement. Social Justice applicants must demonstrate a commitment to justice and the good of others through service to their communities, churches, and/or schools.

Eligibility: 3.5 GPA. U.S. citizen or permanent resident. Freshmen from Alaska, Idaho, Oregon, Montana, Washington.

Award: full tuition, room & board   # Given: 6
Renewable for 4 years

The Thomas J. Bannan Scholarship in Science and Engineering

For juniors, this is a two-year award subject to academic performance demonstrated by maintaining a GPA of 3.0 and active participation in the Bannan Scholar Enrichment Program. This program includes service, scholarly, and social activities, as well as opportunities to compete for one of several Bannan Scholar summer research stipends.

Eligibility: Junior or Senior standing in science and engineering as recognized by Fall Quarter, as a continuing student or new transfer student. Be a full-time major in the School of Science and Engineering for the Fall Quarter. GPA 3.5 or higher for previous college-level work. Record of campus involvement and community service, and a commitment to participate in service as a Bannan Scholar. Both domestic and international students may apply.

For more information:

Office of Undergraduate Admissions   (206) 296-5800
Seattle University   admissions@seattleu.edu.
Seattle, WA 98122   www.seattleu.edu/sullivan/

SMITH COLLEGE

Springfield Scholarship

Awarded to entering students from Springfield, MA on the basis of academic achievement and contributions to school and community.

Award: Full tuition   # Given: 3

For more information:

Smith College
Financial Aid Office
College Hall Rm. 10   (413) 585-2530
Northampton, MA 01063   (800) 221-2579
        www.smith.edu/fao

SONOMA STATE UNIVERSITY

Scholarships for Environmental Studies and Planning majors.

Stocking and Riley Scholarships

Award: $750 - $1,000

Delphine Tague Environmental Studies Scholarship

Prefer students in Energy Management and Design Study Plan.

Award: $1,000

Melissa Lindsay Brown Scholarship

Eligibility: female California high school graduate; ENSP or geology major; career interest in environmental geology.

Award: $1,000

Carlos Asa Call Scholarship

Geography, biology, or ENSP major. Prefer interest in climatology, etc.

Award: $700

Education Scholarships

Can be awarded to ENSP students pursuing environmental education.

George H. and Lucy Cassidy Memorial Scholarship

Female; Plans to teach; Prefer Sonoma Valley and Financial Need.

Award: $1,200

Gertrude D. Cassidy Memorial Scholarship

Female; Plans to teach; Prefer Sonoma Valley and Financial Need.

Award: $1,500

Eligibility for all: attending or have applied for admission to SSU. The application period is late November to February 15.

For more information:

The Scholarship Office   (707) 664-2261
Stevenson Hall, Room 1066   www.sonoma.edu/ensp/scholarships.html
Sonoma State University
Rohnert Park, CA 94928

UNIVERSITY OF SOUTHERN CALIFORNIA

Leo Buscaglia Scholarship for Inner City Teacher Education

Upon completion of degree at USC the student will return to the home high school from which he or she graduated to teach.

Eligibility: graduating senior from the seven local high schools.

Award: full tuition   # Given: 1

For more information:

Dr. Judith Grayson   (213) 740-3476
Director, Teacher Education   grayson@bcf.usc.edu

Environmental Studies Scholarships For Excellence

Resume should include, among other things, a list of honors, awards, and scholarships received (if any), a list of extra curricular activities, and whether you have been involved in a research project with a professor.

Eligibility: Preference given to those students who are pursuing a course of study directly related to the natural environment. 3.30 GPA.

Hugo R. Santora Scholarship For Foreign Students

Preference given to international students pursuing study directly related to the natural environment and intending to return to their homeland.

Eligibility: foreign students, overall GPA of 3.30

For more information:

Environmental Studies Program   (213) 740-7770
Hancock Building, Room 232   cwis.usc.edu
University of Southern California   environ@rcf.usc.edu
Los Angeles, CA 90089   www.usc.edu/dept/LAS/enviro/envscholarship3.htm

The Norman Topping Student Aid Fund

The Topping Student Aid Fund is the only student-funded financial assistance program of its kind in the nation. Established by two USC students in 1970, the fund assists primarily local area, low income students. These students must also demonstrate a high level of community involvement and academic potential. Topping Scholars are required to volunteer 20 hours per semester to a USC community organization or organization of their choice. These community service commitments have included: summer camp counseling for inner city youth; tutoring students in the neighborhood; counseling at substance abuse clinics and federal prisons; assisting at local hospital emergency rooms.

For more information:

Norman Topping Student Aid Fund   (213) 740-7575 (Voice)
Leadership, Service & Scholars   (213) 740-0139 (FAX)
Division of Student Affairs   www.usc.edu/student-affairs/ntsaf
University of Southern California   ntsaf@mizar.usc.edu
Student Union 202G
Los Angeles, CA 90089-0890

> *Sentiment without action is the ruin of the soul.*
> Edward Abbey

SOUTHWEST MISSOURI STATE UNIVERSITY

Multicultural Leadership Scholarship

For incoming students who have demonstrated leadership through involvement in various school and civic organizations. Historically under-represented minorities are strongly encouraged to apply.

Eligibility: HS seniors rank in top-half of class, admitted to SMSU.

Award: required student fees (in-state) for the academic year

Apply by: February 1   Renewable for 4 years

For more information:

Minority Student Services   www.smsu.edu/minority/

Pepsi-Cola Public Affairs Scholarship

Awarded to students with a demonstrated record of service, leadership and qualities consistent with the goals of the public affairs mission. Award seeks to produce citizens of enhanced character, more sensitive to needs of the community, more competent and committed in their ability to contribute to society.

Eligibility: Minimum of 45 hours completed at SMSU. 3.25 GPA.

Award: $1,000   # Given: 5

Apply by: April

Boyce/Wall Street Journal Public Affairs Award

Awarded to a SMSU student who has a demonstrated record of service, leadership and qualities consistent with the goals of the public affairs mission.

Eligibility: minimum of 60 hours at SMSU, demonstrated record of service, leadership, and qualities consistent with public affairs mission.

Award: $1,000   # Given: 1

Apply by: March 1

For more information:

Financial Aid Office	(417) 836-5000
SMSU	www.smsu.edu
901 S. National	
Springfield, MO 65804	publicaffairs.smsu.edu

STANFORD UNIVERSITY

Hass Public Service Summer Fellowships

Support to explore public service, and support to develop and implement innovative, collaborative service projects that address community needs.

Eligibility: Proposals for projects in the U. S. or international by undergrads preferred, graduating seniors/graduate students considered.

Award: to $3,00   # Given: 10-15

Tom Ford Fellowship in Philanthropy

Intends to bring more young people into philanthropic work by providing graduating seniors the opportunity to work with a mentor at a U.S. foundation. Recipients placed in a foundation appropriate to their interests and experience.

Award: $27,500   # Given: 2-3

Apply by: February 1

Dr. and Mrs. C. J. Huang Teaching Fellowship

Jointly administered by the Haas Center and VIA, this program provides the opportunity for a student to teach in a rural setting in China for 1-2 years. recipients; graduating seniors, graduate students preferred. Undergrads and recent graduates may also apply.

Award: airfare, health insurance, travel to VIA annual China conference and service project funding

Given: 1-2   Apply by: February 3

CFSV John Gardner Fellowship in Philanthropy

Community Foundation Silicon Valley offers this opportunity for undergraduate students to explore ways to build community through philanthropy. Recipients spend 10 weeks, full-time during the summer at Community Foundation Silicon Valley and its supporting foundations in San Jose, CA.

Award: $3,500   # Given: 2

Apply by: February 10

Education and Youth Development Summer Fellowship, Fellowship in Interfaith

Community Ministry, African Service Fellowship, Fellowship in Public Interest Law, Urban Summer Fellowships, China Teaching Fellowship and others also available.

For more information:

Haas Center for Public Service   haas-fmp.stanford.edu/default.htm

STERLING COLLEGE

AmeriCorps and VISTA Matching Scholarships

Sterling has enjoyed a lasting relationship with a variety of Service and Conservation Corps programs in Vermont. Sterling supports AmeriCorps and VISTA volunteers by continuing to offer a matching educational award.

Award: to $3650   # Given: Varies

Merit based scholarships are directed towards those individuals who have done something outstanding in their life (ie. community service, academic achievement, volunteer opportunities, etc).

For more information:

Financial Aid Coordinator   (802) 648-3591
Sterling College   www.sterling.edu
Craftsbury Common, VT 05827

DONALD A. STRAUSS SCHOLARSHIP

Award scholarships to Junior class level students at preselected 4 year California colleges or universities who have demonstrated an interest in public service, have outstanding leadership potential, have developed and can demonstrate effective communication skills, and wish to 'make a difference' in local, regional, or national communities.

Eligibility: Nominated by the President or Chancellor or their designee of each eligible 4 year California institution (see list below).

Award: $10,000   # Given: 14

Apply by: see individual school deadlines below

Participating Universities/Colleges and Contacts

CALIFORNIA INSTITUTE OF TECHNOLOGY
Lauren Stolper, Director - Fellowships Advising and Study Abroad
lstolper@caltech.edu   (626) 395-2150   Apply by: February 1

HARVEY MUDD COLLEGE
Amanda Pilcher, Director - Foundation Relations
amanda_pilcher@HMC.Edu   (909) 621-8350   Apply by: February 7

LOYOLA MARYMOUNT UNIVERSITY
Rosie Pulido, Financial Aid/Scholarship Counselor - Financial Aid Office
rpulido@lmu.edu   (310) 338-7848   Apply by:21

OCCIDENTAL COLLEGE
John Bak, Director - Corporate, Foundation and Government Relations
jbak@oxy.edu   (323) 259-2641   Apply by: February 12

SCRIPPS - THE WOMENS COLLEGE - CLAREMONT
Amy Marcus-Newhall, Associate Dean of the Faculty
amarcusn@ScrippsCollege.edu   (909) 607-3244   Apply by: February 5

HAAS CENTER FOR PUBLIC SERVICE, STANFORD UNIVERSITY
  Karyn Bechtel - Fellowship Programs Coordinator
  KBechtel@stanford.edu   650) 725-7408   Apply by: February 3
U C BERKELEY
  Alicia Hayes -- Interim Coordinator
  scholarships@learning.berkeley.edu   (510) 643-6929   Apply by: February 18
U C DAVIS
  Carrie Devine, Coordinator - Prestigious National Scholarships & Fellowships
  cldevine@ucdavis.edu   (530) 752-3223   Apply by: January 31
U C IRVINE
  Audrey DeVore, Associate Director - Honors Program
  adevore@uci.edu   (949) 824-7765   Apply by: February 12
U C LOS ANGELES
  Angela Deaver Campbell, Director - Scholarship Resource Center
  adeaver@college.ucla.edu   (310) 206-1795   Apply by: February 21
U C RIVERSIDE
  Mary Coronado, Scholarship Coordinator - Financial Aid Office
  mary.coronado@ucr.edu   (909) 787-7243   Apply by: February 24
U C SAN DIEGO
  Becky Obayashi Scholarship Coordinator - Student Financial Services
  robayashi@ucsd.edu   (858) 534-1067   Apply by: February 3
U C SANTA BARBARA
  Christine Iriart, Coordinator - Special Programs
  ciriart@ltsc.ucsb.edu   (805) 893-2319   Apply by: February 14
U C SANTA CRUZ
  Lynda Goff, Provost and Dean - Undergraduate Education
  goff@cats.ucsc.edu   (831) 459-4908   Apply by: January 29
For more information:
  The Donald A. Strauss Scholarship Foundation
  201 Shipyard Way, Cabin E   (949) 723-0459
  Newport Beach, CA 92663   www.straussfoundation.org/

SWARTHMORE COLLEGE

John W. Nason Community Service Fellowship

The Swarthmore Foundation awards this fellowship to students who wish to conduct off-campus community service projects related to their academic program prior to graduation.

Past recipients have worked with children in urban and tribal communities; created a community literacy project; worked on homesteading, construction, and farming projects; and interned with public interest organizations.

Award: $125 per week

Lang Open Competition Opportunity Grant

All Swarthmore students are eligible to apply for this scholarship to plan or carry out an innovative social action project.

Award: up to $10,000 for project   # Given: 2

up to $1,000 for feasibility study   # Given: 2

For more information:

Patricia James   (610) 328-7320
Office of Community-based Service and Learning
Swarthmore College   pjames1@swarthmore.edu
Swarthmore, PA 19081-1397
www.swarthmore.edu/students/civic/index.html

VANDERBILT UNIVERSITY

Ingram Scholarship Program

An innovative effort to prepare students for responsible careers as well as for a lifetime of useful contributions to the well-being of others. Ingram Scholars participate in community service projects for about 20 hours per month and at least one undergraduate summer. They attend a summer program to develop research and community-building skills.

Eligibility: graduating high school seniors admitted to Vanderbilt.

Award: 50% tuition, stipends of $3,000 for summer projects.

Renewable for 4 years   Apply by: January 3

For more information:

Admissions Office   (615) 322-2561
Vanderbilt University   www.vanderbilt.edu
Nashville, TN 37203-1700

VIRGINIA TECH UNIVERSITY

Service Scholars

Service Scholars are experienced service-learners who provide leadership and coordination for one of the Service-Learning Centers key partnership or program areas. It is a scholarship-with-responsibility -- a scholarship that recognizes a students outstanding work and provides them with some resources to continue that work. A typical Service Scholar position involves ten hours of work each week or 100 hours over the course of a semester.

Service Scholars assist the students involved in a designated program area with training and orientation, getting started, communicating with their site supervisor, reflecting on their service throughout the semester, and fulfilling their service-learning project.

Eligibility: record of service-learning and community service, well-organized, comfortable interacting with individuals and small groups, and good at communicating with diverse groups of people.

Award: $500 per semester

For more information:

The Service-Learning Center   (540)231-6964
202 Major Williams Hall (0168)   utprosim@vt.edu
Blacksburg, VA 24061   www.majbill.vt.edu/SL/

WABASH COLLEGE

Multicultural Scholarships

For students of color who have contributed to their communities and who demonstrate high academic achievement.

Award: $50,000 over 4 years

Apply by: March 1

For more information:

Admissions Office
Wasbash College
P.O. Box 352
Crawfordsville, IN 47933

(800) 345-5385
www.wabash.edu/admis

WARREN WILSON COLLEGE

Service Leadership Scholarships

Warren Wilson College provides an education combining study, work, and service in a setting that promotes wisdom and understanding, spiritual growth, and contribution to the common good. Recipients must demonstrate exceptional leadership skills within the community and volunteer activity.

Award: $1,500
Renewable up to 4 years

Given: 2

For more information:

Office of Admissions
Warren Wilson College
P.O. Box 9000
Asheville, NC 28815-9000

(800) 934-3536
www.warrenwilson.edu

UNIVERSITY OF WASHINGTON

Edward E. Carlson Student Leadership Award

Promotes community service and recognizes student leaders in public service who demonstrate a strong commitment to public service, provide outstanding leadership in the community, and show promise of continued creative civic participation.

S. Sterling Munro Public Service Scholarship

Providing outstanding undergraduates with an opportunity to explore a career in the public sector, learn practical skills, and realize their potential for service and leadership in the community by designing and conducting a service project or enhancing a public service initiative in which they already participate.

Award: $3830 to $5750

Given: 2 - 4

Gates Endowment for Students--Leadership Development Grant

These grants free students from obligations which compete for time and energy they could direct to achieving larger goals.

For more information:

Carlson Leadership & Public Service Center
University of Washington
Box 353760

(206) 616-2885
leader@u.washington.edu

Seattle, WA 98195-3760   depts.washington.edu/leader/index.html

Martin and Ann Jugum Scholarship in Labor Studies

Eligibility: commitment to labor; high academic aptitude; preferably a child of the labor movement or a current activist in the labor movement.

Industrial Relations Research Association Scholarship

Students pursuing a profession in labor and/or labor management.

For more information:

Harry Bridges Center for Labor Studies   (206) 543-7946
U of W. Box 353530   pcls@u.washington.edu
Seattle, WA 98195-3530   depts.washington.edu/pcls/index.php

WASHINGTON STATE UNIVERSITY

Alumni / Foundation Leadership Scholarships

HS seniors involved in leadership in school and/or community activities. Eligibility: 3.3 GPA.

The Alumni Leadership Award - Branch Campus

To branch campus students with outstanding leadership demonstrated through school, work, community, church, or family commitments.
Eligibility: 2.5 GPA.

For more information:

Lewis Alumni Centre   (509) 335-2586
www.finaid.wsu.edu/scholar/AlumAwds.htm

WESLEYAN UNIVERSITY

Davenport Study Grant

Support summer research in public affairs for sophomores and juniors.

Wesleyan Black Alumni Council Undergrad Summer Stipend

$1,500 summer stipend for an African-American student for a summer research project related to African-American concerns.

For more information:

Career Planning Center   www.wesleyan.edu
Wesleyan University   crc@wesleyan.edu
Middletown, CT 06457

WESTERN WASHINGTON UNIVERSITY

Minority Achievement Program Scholarship

Recognizes academic achievement, community service and leadership.
Eligibility: Asian, Black, Chicano/Latino, & American Indian students.

Award: $2,000   # Given: 90
Apply by: March 1

For more information:

Office of Admissions   (360) 650-3471
Scholarship Center, WWU   www.finaid.wwu.edu/scholarships/index.php
Old Main 200

Bellingham, WA 98225

WHEATON COLLEGE

Community Scholars

Recognizes strong academic performance and a demonstrated commitment to leadership and community service. Community Scholars are designated in the admission process in spring of their application year. Stipend is spread over sophomore and junior years.

Wheaton Fellowships

Students develop a placement in a service setting, compose a persuasive proposal and supporting documents, which are judged by service-learning experts.

For more information:

Filene Center for Work and Service-Learning   (508) 286-3798
Wheaton College   www.wheatonma.edu/Filene
Norton, MA 02766

WILSON COLLEGE

Curran Scholars Program

Girl Scout Gold Award recipients may apply for the Curran Scholars Program for students with a history of service to community and/or church. Recipients will complete 260 hours of volunteer service per academic year.

Awards range from $4,000 to the full amount that the student would have received from need-based work-study and student loan programs.

Award: $4,000+   Renewable

For more information:

Susan Olson   (717) 264-4141, ext. 307 or
Office of Admissions   (800) 421-8402
Wilson College   www.wilson.edu
1015 Philadelphia Avenue
Chambersburg, PA 17201-1285

UNIVERSITY OF WISCONSIN AT MADISON

Holstrom Undergraduate Research Fellowships

Provides support for collaborative research between undergraduate students and faculty for research specifically on environmental issues.

Eligibility: junior standing at UW Madison at the time of application.

For more information:

Provost's Office   (608)262-1304
Room 150 Bascom Hall   www.wisc.edu/cbe/research/funding.html
UW Madison
Madison, WI

WITTENBERG UNIVERSITY

Key Club International Scholarship

Selection is based upon acceptance to Wittenberg University, academic achievement, commitment to community service, involvement in Key Club, and extracurricular activities.

Award: $5,000 – $9,000, renewable   # Given: Unlimited
Apply by: February 15

For more information:

Assistant Dean of Admission   800/677-7558, extension 6320
Wittenberg University
PO Box 720
Springfield, OH 45501   www.Wittenberg.edu

XAVIER UNIVERSITY

Benjamin D. Urmston Family Peace Studies Scholarship

Incoming freshman with demonstrated academic excellence and involved in activities showing a commitment to peace and justice.

Award: $1,000   # Given: 1
Apply by: March 20

For more information:

Peace and Justice Programs   (513) 745-3046
Xavier University   www.xu.edu/peace_justice/peace_studies/scholarships.htm
Cincinnatti, OH 45207-5311

YALE

President's Public Service Fellowship

The President's Public Service Fellowship provides support for eight weeks of summer work in New Haven nonprofit and municipal agencies.

Eligibility: Yale undergraduate, graduate, and professional students.

Award: $3,600 to $6,000   # Given: 30-40
Apply by: January 27

For more information:

Yale Office of New Haven Affairs   www.yale.edu/ppsf/index.html
433 Temple St.
New Haven, CT 06520

MAKING A DIFFERENCE SCHOLARSHIPS

◆ ◆ ◆

HEALTH

I shall pass through this world but once. Any good therefore that I can do or any kindness that I can show to any human being, let me do it now. Let me not defer or neglect it, for I shall not pass this way again.

Mahatma Gandhi

AMBUCS Scholarships For Therapists

The objective of "Scholarships for Therapists" is to enhance direct therapy services to people with disabilities by providing financial assistance to students for professional trainings in the following fields of clinical therapy: Occupational Therapy, Physical Therapy, Speech Language Pathology, Hearing Audiology.

Eligibility: US citizen, financial need, junior/senior in a bachelor's degree program, or a graduate program leading to a master's or doctoral degree.

Award: $500 - $1,500   # Given: varies
    $6,000 for 2 years   # Given: 1

Apply by: April 15

For more information send a #10 self-addressed, postage paid envelope or apply on website.

AMBUCS   (336) 869-2166
3315 North Main St.   ambucs@ambucs.com
High Point, NC 27265   www.ambucs.com

American College Of Nurse-Midwives Foundation

Basic Midwifery Scholarships and Varney Participant Award

Eligibility: student in good standing enrolled in an ACNM accredited basic midwifery education program; have completed at least one academic or clinical semester/ quarter, or one clinical module; and be a current member of the American College of Nurse-Midwives.

Ortho-McNeil Pharmaceutical/A.C.N.M. Graduate Fellowship

Eligibility: certified nurse-midwife or a certified midwife; current member of the American College of Nurse-Midwives; graduate student in good standing actively enrolled in a doctoral or post-doctoral education program.

Award: Not stated   Apply by: early March

For more information:

Scholarship Coordinator   (202) 728-9865
American College of Nurse-Midwives   info@acnm.org
818 Connecticut Ave. NW, Suite 900   www.midwife.org/edu/scholarships.cfm
Washington, DC 20006

ACOG/Ortho-McNeil History Fellowship

The American College of Obstetricians and Gynecologists and Ortho-McNeil Pharmaceutical Corporation jointly sponsors one fellowship in the History of American Obstetrics and Gynecology each year. ACOG Junior Fellows and Fellows are encouraged to apply. The recipient of the fellowship spends one month in the Washington DC area working full-time to complete their specific historical research project.

Award: $5,000   Apply by: 1 October 2003

For more information:

Debra Scarborough, MLS AHIP
History Library/Archives   www.acog.org
The American College of Obstetricians and Gynecologists

409 Twelfth Street SW
Washington DC 20024-2588

(202) 863-2578
history@acog.org

AMERICAN DENTAL HYGIENISTS ASSOCIATION

ADHA Institute Scholarship Program

For students in the Baccalaureate or Graduate Degree categories who demonstrate strong potential in public health or community dental health.

Eligibility: enrollment in a dental hygiene program.

Apply by: June 1

Rosie Wall RDH Community Spirit Grant

Two grants for hygienists who are involved in a specific community health or research project. One recipient will be from the state of Hawaii, while the other will be chosen from the rest of the 50 states.

Award: $1,000

Apply by: February 28

For more information:

ADHA Institute
444 North Michigan Avenue, Suite 3400
Chicago, IL 60611

(800) 735-4916
institute@adha.net
www.adha.org/institute/Scholarship/

CRITICAL CARE NURSES

Educational Advancement Scholarships

Advances the art and science of critical-care nursing and promotes nursing professionalism. Supports students completing a generic baccalaureate nursing program, and AACN members who are registered nurses completing a baccalaureate or graduate degree program in nursing. The baccalaureate applicant also describes contributions to critical-care nursing, which include work, community and profession-related activities.

Eligibility: continuously enrolled in a baccalaureate program accredited by National League for Nursing or a graduate program.

For more information:

Educational Advancement Scholarship
American Association of Critical Care Nurses
101 Columbia
Aliso Viejo, CA 92656-1491

(800) 899-2226
www.aacn.org

BETTY FORD CENTER

Summer Institute for Medical Students/Chemical Dependency

An opportunity for medical students to gain a greater understanding and insight into chemical dependency, and the recovery process. Students participate in the Inpatient Program of the Family Program where they will spend five-days gaining first hand knowledge of treatment and recovery issues.

Award: Tuition, support materials, lodging, on-campus meals, travel stipend

For more information:

Betty Ford Center Training Dep't.

(760) 773-4108

39000 Bob Hope Drive   (800) 854-9211
Rancho Mirage, CA 92270   www.bettyfordcenter.org

GEORGIA COUNTRY DOCTOR SCHOLARSHIP

For medical students promising to practice in a Georgia board-approved town of 15,000 or less population. Georgia residents qualify for funding to obtain primary care medical degrees such as Internal Medicine, General Surgery, OB-GYN, Pediatrics and Family Practice.

Award: $10,000 annually for 4 years.   Apply by: May 1

For more information:

The State Medical Education Board of Georgia   404/352-6476
Scholarship Program
Two Northside 75, N. W. Suite 220
Atlanta, Georgia 30318-7701

HARVARD MINORITY HEALTH POLICY

The Commonwealth Fund / Harvard University Fellowship

Prepares minority physicians for leadership positions in minority health policy; to improve the capacity of the health care system to address the needs of minority and disadvantaged populations; to create a network of minority physician-leaders capable of advancing in the public, nonprofit, and academic sectors.

The fellowship program prepares participants to meet these challenges through a one-year, full-time program of rigorous academic training, leading to a master's degree in public health, and instruction in leadership skills. Fellows are taught to identify, analyze, quantify, and develop solutions to public health problems through instruction in financial and organizational management, communications, politics, economics, and ethics.

Eligibility: U.S. citizen physicians who have completed residency. Additional experience beyond residency, such as Chief Residency, is preferred.

Apply by: early January   # Given: 5

For more information:

Minority Faculty Development Program   617-432-2313
Harvard Medical School   mfdp_cfhuf@hms.harvard.edu
164 Longwood Avenue, Rm. 210
Boston, MA 02115   www.mfdp.med.harvard.edu

HAZEL CORBIN MIDWIFERY GRANT

Provide research support to one student who demonstrates academic excellence, and a commitment to evidence-based midwifery care research.

Eligibility: enrolled in a midwifery education program that is accredited by the American College of Nurse-Midwives with supervised research.

Award: $5,000   Apply by: August 1

For more information:

Maternity Center Association Foundation Inc.   (212) 369-7300

Attn: Public Relations
48 E. 92nd St.   info@maternitywise.org
New York, NY 10128-1397   www.maternitywise.org/mca/grants

INDIAN HEALTH SERVICE

IHS provides comprehensive health care to American Indians and Native Alaskans. Scholarships are for studies including: medicine, nursing, nurse-midwifery, social work, chemical dependency, health education, mental health, community health, physicians assistant programs. There is also a loan repayment program for persons in a wide range of health studies who promise to serve in a designated ISHS Retention/,Recruitment Priority site.

Eligibility: students of Native American or Alaska Native descent.

For more information:

Indian Health Service   (301) 443-6197
Scholarship Program
801 Thompson Avenue, Suite 120
Rockville MD 20852   www.ihs.gov

MICHIGAN STATE UNIVERSITY / OSTEOPATHY

The majority of MSU College of Medicine scholarships include community service or a commitment to primary care medicine as a criteria for consideration. There are many more scholarships available than are listed here.

Margaret Aguwa, DO Endowed Scholarship

Eligibility: Only students in their first year of osteopathic medical school and in good academic standing at the end of Fall Semester, preference for under-represented minorities.

Award: minimum $1,000   Apply by: March 1

Blue Care Network of Michigan Scholarship in Honor of Pedro Rivera, D.O.

Eligibility: Incoming or first, second or third year students with financial need. Preference shall be given: Latino students or students who have a demonstrated background serving the Latino community in the United States; students who intend to pursue family practice or are primary care oriented; students who are Michigan residents; students who intend to practice medicine in an underserved community.

Award: minimum $1,000   Apply by: March 1

Dell Endowed Scholarship

Preference given to students entering third or fourth year of medical school, with financial need and commitment to community service

Award: $1,400   Apply by: January 15

International Health Enrichment Fund

Provides funds to pay for food, lodging and travel for as many students as possible each year who want to travel to third world countries and work with supervising physicians as part of their medical school experience.

Eligibility: Students in their first, second or third year of osteopathic medical school. "DO Care" participants shall receive first priority, followed by other international experiences offered by the COM.

Amount: Variable   Apply by: March 1

For more information:

Scholarship Committee   www.com.msu.edu
MSU College of Osteopathic Medicine   517/353-8799

MIGRANT HEALTH CARE

Brings physician assistant, nurse practitioner and nurse-midwife students into rural areas for a four-month fellowship in a sponsored, supervised clinical practice. Funded by the Bureau of Primary Health Care, the fellowship program aims to increase each fellow's cultural sensitivity and understanding of migrant health care issues. Fellowship also provides participants with an awareness of the demographic, economic and environmental health issues that affect migrant and seasonal farmworkers. Fellowship opportunities are created through cooperative efforts between academic clinical training programs and migrant health centers.

For more information:

NRHA Migrant Health Care Fellowship   mail@NRHArural.org
One West Armour Blvd., Suite 203   www.nrharural.org/
Kansas City, MO 64111

NATIONAL HEALTH SERVICE CORPS

Service-conditioned scholarships for full-time students of allopathic and osteopathic medicine, dentistry, nurse practitioner, nurse midwifery, and primary care physician assistants. Each year of support incurs 1 year of service, with a two-year minimum service obligation providing full-time primary health services in federally-designated Health Professional Shortage Areas.

There is also a loan repayment program.

Eligibility: U.S. citizen enrolled, or accepted in a accredited U.S. school.

Award: Tuition, fees, monthly stipend for books, equipment etc.

Apply by: End March

For more information:

NHSC Scholarship Program   (800)638-0824
nhsc@hrsa.gov

nhsc.bhpr.hrsa.gov/get_involved/students.html

NATIONAL MEDICAL FELLOWSHIPS

Wyeth-Ayerst Laboratories Prizes in Women's Health

For female minority medical students. This award recognizes the outstanding talents and future potential of a graduating female student who will practice or conduct research in the field of women's health.

Award: $5,000   # Given: 2

Apply By: March 14, 2003

Ralph W. Ellison Prize

For underrepresented minority applicants with demonstrated outstanding academic achievement, leadership, and community service.

Eligibility: Graduating minority medical student (African-Americans; mainland Puerto Ricans; Mexican-Americans; and Native Americans).

Award: $500   By nomination

Apply by: Mid March

California Community Service Scholarship Program (CSSP)

Exposes students to issues affecting the health status of medically under-served communities in California by involving Scholars in research or community-based clinical training. The goal of the program is to encourage Scholars to establish community-based primary care practices in California.

The California Community Service Scholarships will be awarded on the basis of demonstrated commitment to practice in California, interest in community-based primary care or research, satisfactory academic performance, financial need, and leadership. Eligibility is limited to rising third-year or fourth-year students attending California medical schools.

Bay Area Community Service Scholarships:

Eligibility: California residents enrolled at the following schools in the Bay Area: the University of California Davis School of Medicine, the University of San Francisco School of Medicine, or Stanford Medical School. Candidates for these scholarships may participate in elective rotations of either six or twelve weeks duration at an approved community health center in the Bay Area. Students choosing six- week rotations are expected to participate in a clinical project at their designated site; those choosing 12-week rotations must plan and implement a clinical project at their site.

Award: $7,500 for 6-8 weeks

$15,000 for 12weeks

California Community Service Scholarships:

Eligibility: students enrolled at any medical school in California. Candidates must complete six-week clinical rotations only at approved community health centers in California and are expected to participate in clinical project.

Award $7,500

Fellowship Program in AIDS Care

This program is a joint initiative of NMF and the University of California, San Francisco AIDS Research Institute in response to the severity of the HIV/AIDS epidemic in medically underserved communities.

The goals of the Fellowship Program in AIDS Care are: to increase the number of physicians involved in HIV/AIDS clinical care and research; to train new physicians-including those entering clinical areas not usually linked to AIDS care-to adapt quickly to the changing issues of HIV/AIDS in medical practice; and to create an ongoing communications network for minority physicians to address the complexities of HIV/AIDS care.

The fellowship program consists of a four-week, multidisciplinary training program in HIV/AIDS clinical care and research for up to eight medical students selected in a national competition.

Award: $7,000   # Given: 8
W.K. Kellogg Foundation Fellowship in Health Policy Research

The program develops a cadre of health policy researchers with expertise in the area of program evaluation and measurement. The program awards fellowships to talented minority men or women enrolled in graduate programs in public health, health policy or social policy leading to the doctorate (Ph.D., Dr.P.H., or Sc.D.). The fellowship will provide the opportunity to complete advanced training in research methodology, including quantitative and qualitative methods for measuring the outcomes of health care provided by community-based programs and health care organizations in underserved communities.

Eligibility: Must be admitted to the following schools : Heller Graduate School of Brandeis University, Mailman School of Public Health at Columbia University, Harvard School of Public Health, Johns Hopkins School of Hygiene and Public Health, RAND Graduate School, UCLA School of Public Health, University of Michigan School of Public Health

Award: tuition, fees and a partial living stipend for up to five years.

For more information:

National Medical Fellowships, Inc.	(212).483.8880
5 Hanover Square, 15th Floor	www.nmf-online.org
New York, NY 10004	info@nmfonline.org

NATIONAL STUDENT NURSES' ASSOCIATION

Scholarships for academic achievement, financial need, and involvement in nursing student organizations and community activities related to health care.

Eligibility: Enrolled in state-approved schools of nursing or pre-nursing in associate degree, baccalaureate, diploma, generic doctorate, and generic master's programs. Not for graduate study unless a first degree in nursing.

Award: $1,000 - $2,500   Apply by: January 30,

For more information send a stamped (57¢ postage) self-addressed business size envelope to:

Foundation of the NSNA	
45 Main Street, Suite 606,	nsna@nsna.org
Brooklyn, NY 11201 718-210-0705	www.nsna.org

NATIVE HAWAIIAN HEALTH PROFESSIONS

Assists Hawaiian students who are enrolled or accepted for enrollment in selected accredited health professions training programs. Applicants selected on the basis of: work experience, academic record, demonstrated interest in providing primary care service, experience with Hawaiian culture, financial need

Upon completion of training, scholarship recipients must commit to full-time service equivalent to the number of years for which they received scholarship assistance (minimum of 2 years, maximum of 4). Program participants fulfill their service obligations at sites in the state of Hawaii serving Native Hawaiians, or in federally designated primary health care sites.

Eligibility: Hawaii resident or Native Hawaiian, eligible for appointment as a Federal employee in the U.S. Public Health Service, financial need.

Award: Tuition, books, supplies, stipend of $736/month for twelve months. Funding available for 2 - 4 years.

For more information:

Kamehameha Schools Bishop Estate	(808) 842-8218
Financial Aid Department	
1887 Makuakane Street	finaid@ksbe.edu
Honolulu, HI 96817-1887	www.ksbe.edu

or

Native Hawaiian Health Care Program, Division of Programs for Special Populations

Bureau of Primary Health Care	301/594-4476
4350 East-West Highway, 9th Floor	
Bethesda, MD 20814	bphc.hrsa.gov/programs/HawaiianProgramInfo.htm

NEW YORK STATE DEPARTMENT OF HEALTH
PRIMARY CARE SERVICE CORPS

For individuals studying to become physician assistants, nurse practitioners or midwives. Recipients fulfill a service obligation by providing primary care full-time in an underserved area, or in a facility serving high-need populations in New York State. Recipients work for 18 months for each full-time award, and 9 months for each part-time award with a minimum service obligation of 18 months.

Eligibility: NY resident enrolled, accepted or applied for study in an approved graduate course of study within 24 months of completion of professional training full-time, or within 48 months of completing on part-time basis. Upon completion, must be eligible to practice in NY.

Award: To $15,000 for full time study $7,500 for part-time study

For more information:

NY State Department of Health	(518) 473 7019
Bureau of Health Resources Development	
Primary Care Service Corps	
Empire State Plaza/ Corning Tower, Room 1602	
Albany, NY 12237-0053	

NEW YORK STATE REGENTS HEALTH CARE
SCHOLARSHIPS IN MEDICINE AND DENTISTRY

Awarded to students enrolled in approved medical and dental schools in New York State. Award recipients must promise in writing to practice in a geographic area or facility in NY, certified by the Regents as having a physician or dentist shortage, 12 months for each annual payment received. A minimum of 24 months is required even if an individual receives only one annual payment.

Eligibility: NY resident, economically disadvantaged and/or a member of a minority group historically underrepresented in medicine or dentistry; or graduate of state-sponsored EOP, HEOP, SEEK or College Discovery opportunity programs.

Award: $10,000, renewable   Apply by: May 1

For mor information:

University of the State of New York   (518) 486-1319
The State Education Department
Office of Equity and Access
Bureau of Higher Education Opportunity Programs
VATEA Scholarships, Room 1071, EBA
Albany, NY 12234   www.highered.nysed.gov/kiap/scholarships/rhc.htm

NC SCHOLARSHIP-LOANS FOR HEALTH, SCIENCE AND MATH

For those who work full-time for one calendar year in designated "health shortage" facilities. For each school year a loan was received, the borrower will have his/her loans "forgiven" through approved service to the state.

Eligibility: North Carolina resident; a 3rd, 4th or 5th year student in an approved undergraduate program, or unconditionally accepted into a graduate level program, financial need.

Award: $5,000 - baccalaureate - per year; 3 year maximum

$6,500 - masters - per year; 2 year maximum

$8,500 - health professional - per year; 4 year maximum

Apply by: June 1

For more information:

Student Loan Program   (919) 571-4182
N.C. State Education Assistance Authority
P.O. Box 20549
3824 Barrett Drive, Suite 304
Raleigh, North Carolina 27619   www.cfnc.org/paying/loan/career/career_hsm.jsp

RMHC/UNCF HEALTH AND MEDICAL SCHOLARS PROGRAM

This program of Ronald McDonald House Charities and The United Negro College Fund (UNCF) offers scholarships to support the next generation of doctors, nurses, and healthcare professionals from the African American community. The program is part of RMHC's commitment to create, find and support programs that directly improve the health and well being of children worldwide.

Eligibility: Students must be full-time sophomore college students pursuing full-time degrees in premedical, health care and health science fields at UNCF member institutions. For a listing of the colleges/universities, view the UNCF web site, www.uncf.org

Award: two-year full-tuition scholarships   # Given: 10

For more information:

Cindy Nair   (703) 205-3489
UNCF/The College Fund
8260 Willow Oaks Corporate Drive
Fairfax, VA 22031   www.rmhc.com/mis/scholarships_uncf/index.html

The Albert Schweitzer Fellowship

Grow into your ideals, so that life can never rob you of them.

Albert Schweitzer

Furnishes direct assistance to the Hospital in Lambaréné, where an internationally- supported staff provides health care. The Fellowship selects more than 50 senior medical students from New England medical schools to serve for three months in Lambaréné as Albert Schweitzer Fellows.

Provides service opportunities for aspiring health professionals, who undertake projects worthy of emulation locally and nationally. Programs are rooted in Dr. Schweitzer's belief that there is a vast untapped reservoir of idealism in our communities that, if nurtured, honored, and provided with specific opportunities for action, can become a powerful resource in combatting the tragic problems of those without adequate health care.

Different state programs vary in eligibility (undergraduate and/or graduate schools), and fields of study (health only, or health, law, environment etc.)

Award: All Schweitzer Fellowships are $2,000 and include a number of activities for fellows to support these students: 200 hours Direct Service; attending Monthly Meetings; participation in a Symposium Series; mentoring from fellowship alumni.

Baltimore Schweitzer Fellows Program

Fellows have come from several of the health professional schools at University of Maryland, Johns Hopkins University, and the College of Notre Dame. Fellows work with an existing community agency.

Eligibility: Baltimore area students enrolled in a degree program in health and human-service fields including schools of medicine, public health, nursing, social work, dentistry, pharmacy and law as well as such disciplines as education, health care administration, and counseling psychology.

Apply By: March 5   # Given: 15

For more information:

Lee Bone, RN, MPH, Program Director

Baltimore Schweitzer Fellows Program   (410) 955-6887

624 N. Broadway, Room 610   www.schweitzerfellowship.org/baltimore.htm

Baltimore, Maryland   21205   bone@jhsph.edu

Boston Schweitzer Fellows Program

An interdisciplinary program focused on service, leadership development, and reflection. Past Fellows have been students in such fields as public health, nursing, occupational therapy, acupuncture, optometry, dentistry, health education, pharmacy, medicine, veterinary medicine, social work, and law.

Eligibility: Students from Boston and Worcester area schools who are obtaining professional degrees in health-related fields

Apply by: January 15   # Given: 28

For further information:

Boston Schweitzer Fellows Program   617-667-3115

c/o The Albert Schweitzer Fellowship

330 Brookline Avenue, Libby 330   www.schweitzerfellowship.org/boston.htm

Boston, MA 02215   info@schweitzerfellowship.org

North Carolina Albert Schweitzer Fellows Program

Crossing boundaries that often separate our professional schools from our communities, and isolate different professional health disciplines from each other, this program unites a diverse range of health professional students, faculty, and community-based providers who share a commitment to public service. Applications addressing rural problems will be given special consideration.

Eligibility: Enrolled in a NC degree-granting program in a health professional field (medical, nursing, public health, social work).

Apply by: Mid February   # Given: 19

For more information:

Barbara Heffner, Program Coordinator   (704) 892-4850
No. Carolina Schweitzer Fellows   beheffner@hotmail.com
P.O. Box 1636   www.schweitzerfellowship.org/nc.htm
Davidson, NC 28036

New Hamsphire - Vermont Schweitzer Fellows Program

The Schweitzer Fellowship -- in collaboration with Dartmouth Medical School, the University of Vermont College of Medicine, and the Vermont Law School -- provides service opportunities for aspiring professionals in health, law, and the environment. Crossing boundaries that often separate our professional schools from our communities, and isolate different professional disciplines from each other, this program unites a diverse range of students, faculty, and community-based workers who share a commitment to public service.

Eligibility: enrolled in a VT or NH degree-granting program in medicine, law, public health, nursing, social work, education, health care administration, counseling, psychology and other disciplines broadly related to health care.

Apply by: February 15

For more information:

Becky Torrey, Program Coordinator   rebecca.b.torrey@dartmouth.edu
New Hampshire/Vermont Schweitzer Fellows Program
10 Sausville Road   (603) 643-1479
Etna, NH 03750   www.schweitzerfellowship.org/nh_vt.htm

Chicago Schweitzer Urban Fellows Program

In collaboration with the Health and Medicine Policy Research Group, provides service opportunities and support for aspiring health professionals who seek to help those currently underserved by our health care system. Fellows tackle health issues such as HIV/AIDS, asthma, chronic and other infectious diseases, teen pregnancy, substance abuse, homelessness, violence, and literacy.

Eligibility: Students of graduate level health professional schools, including medicine, nursing, public health, social work, optometry, osteopathy, pharmacy, physical therapy, podiatry, law, biological sciences, psychology, etc...

Apply by: April 15   # Given: 20

For more information:

Kristin LaHurd, MPH, Program Director   312-372-4292
Chicago Area Schweitzer Fellows Program
Health and Medicine Policy Research Group

29 E. Madison Street, Suite 602   kristin@hmprg.org

Chicago, IL 60602   www.schweitzerfellowship.org/us_programs.htm

The Pittsburgh Schweitzer Fellows Program

Sponsored in collaboration with the Southwest Pennsylvania AHEC, the goal is to support health professional students in providing direct service that addresses the health needs of underserved individuals and communities in rural or urban areas of the United States. Fellows contribute to the Resource Guide for Community Service Opportunities in Southwestern Pennsylvania.

Eligibility: professional undergraduate students (such as those in baccalaureate nursing programs) or graduate students enrolled in a health or health-related program in Pittsburgh and southwestern Pennsylvania.

For more information:

Pittsburgh Schweitzer Fellows Program , c/o Southwest PA AHEC

Lexington Technology Park

400 North Lexington Avenue   www.schweitzerfellowship.org/us_programs.htm

Pittsburgh, PA 15208   (412)247-0185

UTAH RURAL PHYSICIAN LOAN REPAYMENT PROGRAM

For students in accredited medical schools with a strong commitment to rural health care. Students must exhibit strong academic standards in undergraduate studies. There is an incurred obligation of one year full-time primary health care service in a rural area of Utah for each year of award.

Eligibility: commitment to serve in a rural medically-underserved area of Utah upon completion of postgraduate training. For each postgraduate year served in a Utah rural area, a percentage of educational loans are repaid.

For more information:

Utah Department of Health

Bureau of Local and Rural Health

P.O. Box 16990

Salt Lake City, UT 84116-0990   health.utah.gov/primary_care/scholarloanmenu.html

WASHINGTON RURAL PHYSICIAN, PHARMACIST & MIDWIFE

For students agreeing to serve for three-five years as a primary care physician in a rural shortage area of the state of Washington. Applicants are selected based upon, but not limited to, academic standing, prior experience in medically underserved or rural shortage areas, academic/ humanitarian achievements and letters of recommendation.

Eligibility: accepted into or currently enrolled in an accredited program and continues to make satisfactory progress.

Award: $25,000-$35,000/year

For more information:

State of Washington   (206) 753-5902

Higher Education Coordinating Board

917 Lakeridge Way

Olympia, WA 98505   www.doh.wa.gov/hsqa/ocrh/slrp/facts.htm

MAKING A
DIFFERENCE
SCHOLARSHIPS

GRADUATE
&
POST-GRADUATE
FELLOWSHIPS

*From what we get, we can make a living;
what we give, however, makes a life.*
Arthur Ashe

The Who Cares Fellowships Guide

By Darcy Lockman

Want to advance your career? Feeling isolated and burned out? A fellowship can change your life.

During one nine-month period Amy Field worked in the media, on a political campaign, in the government, and with a labor union, a business, and a nonprofit. No, she's not the biggest flake you've ever heard of: She's a former Coro fellow. The Coro Fellows Program is a full-time graduate-level program that matches its fellows with leaders of public affairs organizations for six short internships. One of the oldest and most prestigious fellowships, it strives to produce effective community leaders.

The Coro fellowship is just one of many programs that allow nonprofit types to check out different areas of public affairs, trade ideas with fellow do-gooders, take classes in relevant fields, or just take a much-needed breather. Fellowships can remove you from your day-to-day life and remind you what spawned your interest in nonprofit work in the first place, they offer new ideas and fresh plans to implement in your own organization.

Field, who currently recruits fellows for Coro, chose to pursue a fellowship after college because she wasn't sure where she wanted to go in the nonprofit sector. "I was introduced to an entirely new set of options," she says. "I didn't know how to find out what I was good at. Through the fellowship, I did a different internship every month. It was an exploration and discovery of what's out there in public affairs. As someone who wants to make a difference, I was allowed to figure out what ways there are to do that."

A fellowship can give you the necessary experience to make a difference effectively. "It's difficult to find a public interest job," explains Gia Lee, a Georgetown University Women's Law and Public Policy fellow, "especially doing litigation, straight out of law school. Public interest organizations don't have the time or resources to train new lawyers, and litigation takes a lot of training so they want people with experience. It's a valuable proposition for the recent grad because the organization invests a great deal in you in terms of training. It works out well for them, too, because they don't have to pay for your services—your fellowship does that."

Not, it should be added, very well. Where Lee's classmates graduated into corporate firms whose salaries begin just under six figures, public interest law fellows typically earn in the mid-30s. Like other fellows, of course, Lee is not in this for the money. She has always been interested in women's and civil rights. This year-long fellowship will give her the opportunity to become something of an expert on both.

Lee is anxious about still having to find a public interest job at the end of year. She shouldn't be. When Field's fellowship finished, she received four job offers without lifting a resumé—demonstrating that the primary benefit of a fellowship is the contacts that you make. Current fellows and alums throughout the nonprofit sector claim that out of all the fellowship perks—seminars, retreats, professional training, cash, etc.—the contacts that they make have the most lasting impact on their work.

Kellogg National Leadership Program fellow Tony Defeill explains: "I founded a nonprofit a few years ago with a lot of involvement from others, but I was the one that stuck around for the long haul. I felt like I was out there on my own. I didn't have mentors or a fellowship of peers to nurture and support what I do. Now I have that. Through my interactions with these people, I'm challenged to think differently. I learn to work with people in a way that can affect change in a different manner than I was familiar with before."

"The notion of a peer support group is significant," notes Henry Izumizaki, executive director of San Francisco Bay Area Eureka Communities, an organization that brings together the executive directors of community-based organizations to improve their leadership skills. "Nonprofit folks tend to be competitive instead of supportive because they're going after the same funding sources, looking for the right staffs. They need to build trusting relationships to overcome this, because they can learn so much from each other. A fellowship offers an avenue for doing this."

"If I'm having trouble with a certain situation," says Saundra Bryant, Eureka fellow and executive director of All People's Christian Center, "I can call one of my Eureka fellows and ask how they've handled it. A couple of us are even joining forces to work on a collaborative project."

Through the people that fellows meet as well as the experiences that they have, fellowships also offer a singular opportunity for growth—both professionally and personally. Many programs, such as the Kellogg Foundation, fund their fellows' interests in subjects that are only tangential to their areas of concentration. They'll pay for you to take guitar lessons, for example, or yoga classes if you believe that it will somehow enhance your personal or professional life. Says Defeill, "All of it makes you better at the work you do, and if the work you do is improving the world then fellowships improve the world." However, fellowships may not improve your marriage: Defeill reports that married fellows often complain of outgrowing their mates.

Fellowships are undergoing some changes themselves. Programs like Kellogg and Eureka have started to wonder whether their fellows are contributing to the goals that the fellowships exist to advance. "Even after years of lots of money going in," explains Izumizaki, "there was no overt or clear outcome required. So none was evaluated. People are looking at that and wondering, hmm, what happened here?" Kellogg has hired someone to find out.

Although future fellows may find more pressure to produce solid results, they'll also find a more activist-friendly funding environment. Douglas Maguire, the director of the Fund for Social Entrepreneurs, says that "there's a move toward increased flexibility on the part of funders to meet the real time needs of tomorrow's community leaders, rather than have the community leaders jump through a series of hoops to meet the cycles of foundations. We're moving towards a more customer-driven system."

Fellowship programs are figuring out other ways to help their fellows better. They recognize that the greatest benefit that they can provide is professional contacts. Following the example of fellowships from other professions, like law and medicine, many nonprofit fellowship programs are working to put together tight alumni networks, by hiring people to assemble rosters and make former fellows accessible to one another. They're looking at professional programs like the Georgetown University Women's Law and Public Policy Fellowship, which introduces its lawyer fellows to top civil-rights attorneys and makes sure that they attend prestigious legal events—like a moot court at the Supreme Court or a dinner to celebrate the anniversary of Roe v. Wade—for ways to open similar doors for their fellows. "Many of the programs have been around," says Maguire. "There's now a base of people who've been through these programs and we want to tap the asset that's been created."

In the end, though, it's not who you know but who you are. Although all of the people interviewed for this story would choose to do their fellowships again if given the chance, "there's no one-to-one relationship between success of a fellowship and success of a person," says Izumizaki. "A fellowship is a tool, and the people who know how to use the tool kit will be the most successful."

Reprinted from Who Cares Magazine, Summer 1998.

AEF Summer Fellowships

The Asian Pacific American Bar Association Educational Fund assists law students to obtain internship positions with a public interest organization that benefits either the Asian Pacific American community or the metropolitan Washington, D. C. community-at-large. Public interest organizations include government agencies, entities and establishments, and other non-profit organizations or entities serving the public interest. The internship must be unpaid (except for nominal payment for such items as transportation), be for no less than ten weeks or a total of 400 hours, in metropolitan Washington, D.C.

Award: Approx. $3,000   # Given: Approx. 4
Apply by:April 12
For more information:
AEF   www.aef-apaba.org
P.O. Box 2209
Washington, D.C. 20013-2209

Air & Waste Management

For students training for careers in air pollution control or waste management. Criteria for selection include academic achievement, and professional and community contribution.

Eligibility: full time graduate students.

Award: $17,000   Apply by: early December
For more information:
AWMA   (800)270-3444,
One Gateway Center, Third Floor   www.awma.org
Pittsburgh, PA 15222

American Ass'n. for the Advancement of Science

NIH Science Policy Fellowships

Fellows spend one year at the National Institutes of Health (NIH) in NIH's Office of the Director or in one of the Institutes and Centers. Fellows will learn about the analysis, development, and implementation of policies that affect the conduct of medical research.

Eligibility: A PhD or an equivalent doctoral-level degree by the application deadline in any physical, biological, or social science, any field of engineering, or any relevant interdisciplinary field. Federal employees not eligible.

Stipend: $58,000-$74,000 +health insurance and relocation allowance
Given: 6   Apply by: mid January

Global Security

Fellows will spend one year, working to bring public health and medical expertise to bear on issues relating to biological weapons, bioterrorism nonproliferation and federal-response planning efforts. The fellowship is designed to facilitate a multifaceted, cross-disciplinary approach to the issue of biological threats, by bringing biomedical and public health experts together with experts from intelligence, arms control and law enforcement communities.

Eligibility: MD, DVM, or a PhD in the biological sciences, public health, or a related field by the application deadline. Federal employees are not eligible for the fellowships. All applicants must be U.S. citizens.

Stipend: $58,000 + health insurance, relocation and professional travel allowances.

\# Given: 1   Apply by: early January

Roger Revelle Fellowship in Global Stewardship

Fellow will work for one year in a domestic or international environmental policy area within the Congress, a relevant executive branch agency, or elsewhere in the policy community.

Eligibility: Must have a PhD or an equivalent doctoral-level degree by the application deadline in any physical, biological, or social science, any field of engineering, or any relevant interdisciplinary field. Individuals with a master's degree in engineering and at least six years of post-degree professional experience may apply. Applicants must be U.S. citizens. Federal employees are not eligible.

Stipend: $58,000 + health insurance, relocation and professional travel allowances.

\# Given: 1   Apply by: early January

NSF Science and Engineering Fellowship Program

Fellows spend one year at the National Science Foundation (NSF), learning how NSF funds science, while providing scientific, engineering, and educational input on issues relating to NSF's mission to support fundamental science and engineering research and education.

Eligibility: Must have a PhD or an equivalent doctoral-level degree by the application deadline in any physical, biological, or social science, any field of engineering, or any relevant interdisciplinary field. Individuals with a master's degree in engineering and at least three years of post-degree professional experience may apply. Applicants must be U.S. citizens. Federal employees are not eligible.

Stipend: $58,000-$74,000 + health insurance and relocation allowance

\# Given: 3   Apply by: mid January

Congressional Science & Engineering Fellowship

Fellows spend one year on Capitol Hill working with Members of Congress or congressional committees as special assistants in legislative and policy areas requiring scientific and technical input.

Eligibility: Must have a PhD or an equivalent doctoral-level degree by the application deadline in any physical, biological, or social science, any field of engineering, or any relevant interdisciplinary field. Individuals with a master's degree in engineering and at least three years of post-degree professional experience may apply. Applicants must be U.S. citizens. Federal employees are not eligible.

Stipend: $58,000 + health insurance and relocation allowance

\# Given: 2   Apply by: early January

Science, Engineering & Diplomacy Fellowship

Fellows work in international affairs on scientific and technical subjects for one year -- either in foreign policy at the U.S. Department of State, or in international development for the US Agency for International Development.

Eligibility: Must have a PhD or an equivalent doctoral-level degree by the application deadline in any physical, biological, or social science, any field of engineering, or any relevant interdisciplinary field. Individuals with a master's degree in engineering and at least three years of post-degree professional experience may apply. Applicants must be U.S. citizens. Federal employees are not eligible.

Stipend: $58,000-$71,000 +health insurance and relocationallowance

Given: 15+   Apply by: mid January

Risk Policy Fellowships in Health, Safety and the Environment

Fellows work for one year at either the US Dep't. of Agriculture or the Food and Drug Administration, providing scientific and technical input on issues relating to human health, economic and environmental aspects of risk assessment or risk management.

Eligibility: Must have a PhD or an equivalent doctoral-level degree by the application deadline in any physical, biological, or social science, any field of engineering, or any relevant interdisciplinary field. Individuals with a master's degree in engineering and at least three years of post-degree professional experience may apply. Applicants must be U.S. citizens. Federal employees are not eligible. Risk modelers and individuals with a DVM, MD, or a PhD in the natural sciences or economics are especially encouraged to apply.

Stipend: $58,000 + health insurance, relocation and professional travel allowances.

Given: 5   Apply by: early January

EPA Environmental Science & Engineering Fellowship

Fellows work for one year at the U.S. Environmental Protection Agency in Washington, DC, on an array of projects relating to science, policy, the environment and risk assessment.

Eligibility: Must have a PhD or an equivalent doctoral-level degree by the application deadline in any physical, biological, or social science, any field of engineering, or any relevant interdisciplinary field. Individuals with a master's degree in engineering and at least three years of post-degree professional experience may apply. Applicants must be U.S. citizens. Federal employees are not eligible.

Stipend: $58,000 + health insurance, relocation and professional travel allowances.

Given: 10   Apply by: early January

For more information:

AAAS Fellowship Programs   (202) 326-6700
1200 New York Ave., NW   science_policy@aaas.org
Washington, DC 20005   www.aaas.org

AMERICAN ASSOCIATION OF UNIVERSITY WOMEN

The AAUW is committed to expanding educational opportunities for women, working to forge a more equitable environment and future for women of all races, creeds, ages and nationalities.

American Fellowships

Women doctoral candidates completing dissertations or scholars seeking funds for postdoctoral research leave. One-year postdoctoral research leave fellowships, dissertation fellowships, and summer/short-term research publication grants are offered. U.S citizens or permanent residents only.

> Award: $30,000 - postdoctoral research leave
>> $20,000 - dissertation
>> $6,000 - summer/short-term research publication grant

> Apply by: November 15

Community Action Grants

These grants provide seed money to individual women and AAUW branches for innovative programs or nondegree research projects that promote education and equity for women and girls within the United States or its territories.

University Scholar-in-Residence Award

Colleges and universities may apply for funding for the University Scholar-in-Residence award to support a woman scholar to undertake and disseminate research on gender and equity for women and girls. Institutions may use the funds to bring a qualified scholar to the institution for a fixed period or to designate a scholar currently at the institution.

> Stipend: $50,000   Proposals due: October 15

Eleanor Roosevelt Teacher Fellowships

Awarded to women K-12 public school teachers who develop innovative curriculum projects designed to encourage girls' interest and achievement in math, science, and/or technology.

Eligibility: must be U.S. citizens or permanent residents who have taught for at least three years and are committed to teaching beyond fellowship year.

> Award: $5,000 - $10,000 plus participation in Teacher Institute

> # Given: 25   Apply by: early January

International Fellowships

For full-time graduate or postgraduate study or research in the U.S. awarded to women who are not U.S. citizens or permanent residents. Supplemental grants support a community action project in the fellow's home country. Post-Fellowship Supplemental Community Action Grants available.

> Award: $18,000-$30,000   # Given:58

> Apply by: January 15

Selected Professions Fellowships

Awarded to women in the final year of graduate study in designated fields where women's participation has been low, and to engineering doctoral candidates. Special consideration is given to applicants who show professional promise in innovative or neglected areas of research and/or who practice in areas of public interest. Fellowships in Business Administration, Law and Medicine (M.D., D.O.) degree programs are restricted to women of color to increase participation and access in these historically underrepresented fields.

Eligibility: Women who intend to pursue a full-time course of study at accredited institutions during the fellowship year in one of the designated degree programs where women's participation traditionally has been low (see list on website). Applicants must be U.S. citizens or permanent residents.

> Award: $5,000 - $12,000 - Master's and First Professional Awards

$20,000 - Engineering Dissertation Awards

For more information:

AAUW Educational Foundation
1111 Sixteenth St. N.W.
Washington, DC   20036

(202)728-7602
foundation@aauw.org
www.aauw.org

ABA LEGAL OPPORTUNITY SCHOLARSHIP FUND

Provides financial assistance to ensure that racial and ethnic minority students have the opportunity to attend law school for three years. Evaluation criteria include whether an applicant is a member of a racial and/or ethnic minority that has been underrepresented in the legal profession and participation in community service activities. Many law schools have matching programs for this fund, listed on the web site.

Eligibility: entering first-year law student with a minimum GPA of 2.5, financial need and a citizen or permanent resident of the U.S.

Award: $5,000, renewable   Apply by: February 28

For more information:

Fund for Justice and Education
750 N. Lake Shore Drive
Chicago, IL 60611

(312)988-5415

www.abanet.org/fje/losfpage.html

AMERICAN GEOLOGICAL INSTITUTE

See undergraduate listings.

AMS GRADUATE FELLOWSHIPS

AMS Graduate Fellowship in the History of Science

Awarded to a student wishing to complete a dissertation on the history of the atmospheric, or related oceanic or hydrologic sciences. The award will support one year of dissertation research and can be used to support research at a location away from the student's institution.

Eligibility: graduate student in good standing.

Stipend: $15000   Apply by: mid-February

AMS/Industry/Government Graduate Fellowships

Sponsored by leading high-technology firms and government agencies and are designed to attract promising young scientists to prepare for careers in the meteorological, oceanic, and hydrologic fields.

Eligibility: Students entering their first year of graduate study. Candidates currently studying chemistry, computer sciences, engineering, environmental sciences, mathematics, and physics who intend to pursue careers in the atmospheric, oceanic, or hydrologic sciences are also encouraged to apply.

Stipend: $15000   Apply by: mid-February.

For more information:

Education Program
American Meteorological Society

202-737-1043

1120 G Street, NW, Suite 800   amsedu@dc.ametsoc.org
Washington, DC 20005   www.ametsoc.org/AMS/amsedu/scholfeldocs/

AMERICAN MUSEUM OF NATURAL HISTORY

International Graduate Student Fellowship Program at the Museum's Center for
Biodiversity and Conservation

An opportunity for non U.S. citizens to study a diversified curriculum in
biodiversity, conservation, systematics, and public policy. Students can
create a graduate program bringing an interdisciplinary mix of skills and experience to bear on the environmental problems of their countries.

Students are part of a joint Museum-university program offering the Ph.D.
degree. Under the direction of a Museum curator, or other staff member, students
will attend classes at both the Museum and their chosen university.

Applicants should first contact the Office of Grants and Fellowships at the
Museum to discuss their interests, background, and eligibility for the Program.
Students must simultaneously apply to the Museum AND to one of 4 cooperat-
ing universities depending on field of study. Joint programs are with Columbia
University, providing students opportunities in vertebrate and invertebrate pale-
ontology, astrophysics, earth and planetary sciences, and evolutionary biology;
Cornell University in entomology; City University of New York in the
Evolutionary Biology Program; Yale University in molecular biology/systematics.
Contact the university to request application forms for the Ph.D. program in the
appropriate field of study, and to ascertain the deadline date.

Eligibility: Both U.S. citizens and non U.S. citizens are eligible to apply.
Applicants must have a bachelor's degree and be able to fulfill university admission requirements

Award: Travel assistance, stipend (12 months) and tuition, renewable for four years.

Apply by: November 30 to the Museum, Universities have their own dates.

For more information:
Office of Grants and Fellowships
American Museum of Natural History   grants@amnh.org
New York, NY 10024-5192 research.amnh.org/biodiversity/center/programs/grad.html

AMERICAN OCCUPATIONAL THERAPY FOUNDATION

See undergraduate listings.

AMERICAN PLANNING ASSOCIATION SCHOLARSHIPS

The following American Planning Association national and state awards
are made to students currently enrolled in degree programs in Planning or a
closely related field, as described below. Awards made to students enrolled in an
approved Planning Accreditation Board (PAB) college or university.

National Awards

APA Planning Fellowships

Eligibilty: 1st and 2nd year graduate Planning students (African-American,
Hispanic, or Native American) who are citizens of the United States .

160   Graduate & Post-Graduate

Awards:$1,000 -$5,000   Apply by: April 30

Charles Abrams Scholarship

Eligibilty: U.S. citizens who are enrolled, or have been accepted for enrollment at the graduate planning programs of Columbia, Harvard, MIT, the New School for Social Research, or the University of Pennsylvania.

Award: $2,000   Apply by: April 30

For more information:

Kriss Blank   kblank@planning.org

American Planning Association

122 S. Michigan Ave. Suite 1600

Chicago, IL 60603   www.planning.org/institutions/scholarship.htm

State Awards

Arizona APA Chapter

Eligibilty: Arizona State University students in undergraduate and graduate planning programs, University of Arizona students in the Graduate Planning Program , Northern Arizona University students in Graduate Planning Program.

Award: $2,000   #Given: 4

For more information contact Ron Short, AICP, at 480-595-1930.

California APA Chapter

Eligibility: students entering their final year of a of an undergraduate or master's degree program in California: Cal Poly Pomona; Cal Poly San Luis Obispo; San Jose State University; the University of California campuses at Berkeley, Irvine, and Los Angeles; and the University of Southern California. Criteria include financial need and increasing diversity in the profession.

Award: $400-$2,500   #Given: over 6

For more information:

Paul Wack   pwack@calpoly.edu

City and Regional Planning Department   (805) 756-1315

San Luis Obispo, CA 93406   www.californiaplanningfoundation.org

Connecticut APA Chapter

Diana Donald Scholarship for graduate students in a planning or related field. Applicants must be either Connecticut residents or attending a Connecticut school. Criteria includes financial need.

Award: $1,000   # Given: 1

Sam Pine Scholarship for undergraduates in planning, architecture, or related fields. Selection criteria include financial need, then scholarship.

Award: $2,000   # Given: 1

For more information:

Connecticut Chapter President, Dan Tuba   datuba@aol.com

Ohio APA Chapter (Ohio Planning Conference)

Eligibility: US citizen resident of, and graduate of a high school in one of the following Ohio counties: Cuyahoga, Geauga, Lake, Lorain, Medina, Portage or Summit. Must be enrolled as a full-time undergraduate student or enrolled or officially accepted for enrollment as a full-time graduate student.

Award: $1,000   Apply by: May 15

For more information:

Kristin Hopkins   kris@dbhartt.com

Scholarship Committee Chairperson   216-696-0400

Texas APA Chapter

Eligibility: Planning students in the three AICP accredited planning schools in the state: Texas A&M, The University of Texas at Austin, and The University of Texas at Arlington. The planning programs' faculty heads or their financial assistance staff determine the recipients of the scholarships. Out-of-state students, including foreign students, who receive a $1,000 scholarship are then eligible to pay in-state tuition, which can amount to a savings of $7,000 to $8,000 per student.

Award: $2,000   #Given:9

For more information: contact the chair of the university planning programs listed above.

American Sociological Association

Community Action Research Initiative

To encourage sociologists to undertake community action projects that bring social science knowledge, methods, and expertise to bear in addressing community-identified issues and concerns. Grant applications are encouraged from sociologists seeking to work with community organizations, local public interest groups, or community action projects.

Sociologists are expected to work in relevant community organizations. The proposed work can include such activities as needs assessments; empirical research relevant to community activities or action planning; the design and/or implementation of evaluation studies; or analytic review of the social science literature related to a policy issue or problem. Innovative placements and plans are encouraged. Program seeks to link sociologists with community action groups and to use sociological research to advance the goals of those groups.

Eligibility: sociologists in academic settings, research institutions, private and non-profit organizations, and government. Advanced graduate students are eligible, but funding cannot be used to support doctoral dissertation research.

Award: $1,000 - $2,500   # Given: 4

Apply by: February 1

Minority Fellowship Program

Supports the development and training of minority sociologists in mental health. Funded by a grant from the National Institute of Mental Health (NIMH), the MFP seeks to attract talented minority students interested in mental health issues and to facilitate their placement, work, and success in graduate programs throughout the U.S.

Eligibility: Seniors in colleges or universities, students in master only programs who have been accepted or are applying to doctoral programs, or students in the early stages of their doctoral program in sociology departments which have strong mental health research programs. Must be one of the following racial/ethnic groups: Blacks/African Americans, Latinos/as, American Indians or Alaskan Natives, and Asians, or Pacific Islanders. Fellows must be citizens, noncitizen nationals or residents of the U.S.

Award: annual stipend of $16,500 plus additional arrangements for the payment of tuition will be made with universities or departments. Funding may be extended for up to three years. Beyond the first year, recipients are obligated to engage in research on mental health and mental illness and/or teaching for a period equal to the length of time they receive the award.

Teaching Enhancement Fund

These grants are intended to support projects that extend the quality of teaching of sociology in the United States and Canada. Projects that will be considered should serve as seed-projects that will continue to have an impact in months and years to come and be systemic in impact.

Eligibility: an individual, a department, a program, or a committee of a state/regional association. Individuals must be a member of ASA.

Award: up to $1000   # Given: 1-2

Apply by: February 1

For more information:

ASA Minority Affairs Program   minority.affairs@asanet.org

or Spivack Community Action Research Initiative

American Sociological Association   www.asanet.org/student/funding.html

1307 New York Avenue NW, Suite 700

Washington, DC 20005-4701

AMERICAN WATER WORKS ASSOCIATION

Abel Wolman Fellowship

Supports promising students in pursuing advanced training and research in the field of water supply and treatment. Doctoral fellowship providing up to two years of support is awarded each year to the most outstanding student. Selection based on the quality of the applicant's academic record, the significance of proposed research to water supply and treatment, and the potential to do high quality research.

Eligibility: Anticipating completing a Ph.D. within two years of the award, citizenship or permanent residence in Canada, Mexico or the U.S.

Stipend: up to $20,000, renewable   Apply by: January 15

AWWA Academic Achievement Awards

The Academic Achievement Award encourages academic excellence by recognizing contributions to the field of public water supply. All Masters theses and doctoral dissertations that are relevant to the water supply industry are eligible. The manuscript must reflect the work of a single author and be submitted during the competition year in which it was submitted for the degree.

Award: $1,500-$3,000   # Given: 4

Apply by: October 1

Larson Aquatic Research Support

The Larson Aquatic Research Support scholarship provides support for doctoral and Masters students interested in careers in the fields of corrosion control, treatment and distribution of domestic and industrial water supplies, aquatic chemistry, and/or environmental chemistry.

Award: $5,000 - $7,000   Apply by: January 15

Holly Cornell Scholarship

Sponsored by CH2M Hill, encourages and supports outstanding female and/or minority Masters students in pursuit of advanced training in the field of water supply and treatment.

Award: $5,000   Apply by: January 15

Thomas R. Camp Scholarship

Sponsored by Camp Dresser and McKee, Inc., the Thomas R. Camp Scholarship provides support to outstanding students doing applied research in the drinking water field. It is awarded to doctoral students in even years and Masters students in odd years.

Award: $5,000   Apply by: January 15

For more information:

Scholarship Coordinator   (303) 347-6206
American Water Works Association   acarabetta@awwa.org
6666 W. Quincy Avenue
Denver, CO 80235   www.awwa.org/About/scholars/

ARIZONA HYDROLOGICAL SOCIETY

AHS Scholarship

Scholarships to encourage students in hydrology, hydrogeology, and other water resources related fields at any Arizona university or college.

Eligibility: a graduate student fitting the above category.

Award: $1,500   # Given: 3
Apply by: June 30

CAP Scholarship Announcement

The Central Arizona Project Award is for papers on water research that focus specifically on water issues that affect central and Southern Arizona and the Colorado River. Papers can focus on legal, economic, political, environmental, or water management issues, as well as any other issue that might be of interest to CAP or Arizona water users.

Eligibility: students at any college or university in the State of Arizona. Papers should represent the student's original, unpublished research.

Award: $1,000   # Given: 1

Winners will also be invited to present their research at the Arizona Hydrological Society's annual symposium, expenses paid.

Apply to: submit a one page abstract electronically to vcampo@cap-az.com.

Deadline: May 23, 2003

For more information:

U.S. Geological Survey   (928) 556-7142
2255 N. Gemini Drive, Bldg. 3
Flagstaff, AZ 86001   www.azhydrosoc.org

Arkansas Environmental Federation

See Undergraduate listing.

Asian Pacific American Institute for Congressional Studies

Daniel K. Inouye Fellowship Program

The Fellowship is designed to provide a unique opportunity to an outstanding graduate student who has a commitment to the Asian American and Pacific Islander communities, and who plans to pursue a career in public service. The fellow will spend nine months in Washington, D.C., in the Congressional office of the Chair of the Asian Pacific American Caucus (CAPAC).

Anheuser-Busch/Frank Horton Fellowship

The Fellowship is designed to provide a unique opportunity to an outstanding graduate student who has a commitment to the Asian American and Pacific Islander communities, and who plans to pursue a public policy career. The fellow will spend nine months in Washington, D.C., either in the office of a Congressional member, a Congressional committee or a federal agency.

Eligibility: For both Fellowships, must have a Bachelor's degree and a 3.3 GPA. U.S. citizen or legal permanent resident.

Award: $15,000 and medical insurance.

Apply by: Early February

For more information:

APAICS
1001 Connecticut Ave., NW Suite 835
Washington, D.C. 20036

(202) 296-9200
apaics@apaics.org
www.apaics.org

Association to Unite the Democracies

Grant program for studies in the area of peace and conflict resolution, especially through world federalism and international integration. Awards for a thesis or dissertation relating to international integration and federalism; coursework that places major weight on international integration and federalism; or an independent project relating to international integration and federalism.

For more information:

Frank Educational Fund c/o AUD
502 H. St. SW
Washington, D. C. 20024-2726

atunite@aol.com
(202)347-9465
www.unionnow.org

Atlantic Fellowships in Public Policy

Provides an opportunity for outstanding US mid-career professionals to study and gain practical experience in a wide variety of public policy areas in the United Kingdom, as well as a firsthand introduction to the European Union.

Atlantic Fellowships have three goals: to enable US public policy experts to conduct policy research in the UK and benefit from British ideas and best practice; to improve the theory and practice of public policy in the UK and the US; and to create a transatlantic network of public policy experts and practitioners concerned with society's most pressing needs and encourage ongoing collaboration and exchange.

Where possible, Fellows are expected to obtain paid leave. The basic award is not intended to match Fellows' US salaries. Allowances are enhanced for those Fellows unable to obtain paid leave. Other allowances include: Travel to and from the UK, Institutional fees, Family stipend, Monthly local travel allowances for baggage, travel in the UK and setting-up. Fellows staying in the UK for longer than 6 months are entitled to free medical care .

Eligibility: mid-career professionals active in public, business or philanthropic sectors; exceptional personal and intellectual qualities; professional achievement; U.S. citizens, at least five years experience in their professions. Successful candidates likely to be in late twenties to early forties.

Apply by: Mid-December   # Given: 10

For more information:
Atlantic Fellowships
The British Council, Cultural Department   (202) 588-7844
The British Embassy
3100 Massachusetts Avenue, NW   Atlantic.Fellow@us.britishcouncil.org
Washington DC, 20008-3600   www.britishcouncil-usa.org/learning/policy/atlantics.shtml

ATLANTIC SALMON FEDERATION

ASF Olin Fellowships

Offered annually to individuals seeking to improve their knowledge or skills in advanced fields, while looking for solutions to current problems in Atlantic salmon biology, management and conservation. The Fellowships may be applied toward a wide range of endeavors including salmon management, graduate study, and research. Applicants need not be enrolled in a degree program.

Eligibility: Legal residents of the United States or Canada.

Award: $1,000 - $3,000   Apply by: March 15

Crabtree Internship

For individuals interested in obtaining experience in salmon conservation involving research and development, usually requiring field work. Applicants for the award will have had some formal training, and/or experience, in areas related to conservation and will be expected to be interested in pursuing, or continuing in, a career where such expertise will be useful. Both students, and those already in the work force, are eligible to apply. The work period will typically be three months, usually, but not necessarily, during the summer period.

Award: $5,000   Apply by: March 15

For more information:
Atlantic Salmon Federation
P.O. Box 5200
St. Andrews, N.B. EOG 2XO
Canada   www.asf.ca

Ian Axford Fellowships in Public Policy

Gives outstanding American professionals the opportunity to study, travel, and gain practical experience in public policy in New Zealand, including first-hand knowledge of economic, social and political reforms, and management of the government sector.

The program seeks to reinforce NZ/US links by enabling Americans of high ability and leadership potential to come to New Zealand to gain experience, build contacts in the field of public policy development, and improve the practice of public policy in the US and New Zealand by the cross-fertilization of ideas and experience in the two countries.

Six-to nine-month Fellowships are offered in any area of public policy such as education and training; local government and urban affairs; youth and families; workplace issues; environment; science and technology; welfare reform; health care; crime prevention; community development; policy relating to indigenous peoples; public sector reform; tax policy and transportation.

Eligibility: US citizens with at least five years professional experience. Recipients are likely to be in their late twenties to early forties.

Stipend: NZ$500-NZ$4,000/ month depending on whether fellow able to obtain full paid leave; family and other allowances.

Apply by: March 15   # Given: 2

For more information:

Peter Sawires   ps@cmwf.org

The Commonwealth Fund   (212)606.3851

One East 75th Street

New York, NY 10021-2692   www.cmwf.org

Bat Conservation International

See Undergraduate listing: www.batcon.org/schol/schol.html

Harry A. Blackmun (Law) Scholarship

Honors law students who combine high academic achievement and dedication to public service.

Apply by: June 15

For more information:

Harry A. Blackmun Scholarship Fdn.   (410) 685-3813

118 West Mulberry Street

Baltimore, MD 21201

Blinks Research Fellowship Program at Friday Harbor Laboratories

Brings together enthusiastic fellows with the remarkable biological resources and scientific minds at a marine science research facility. In keeping with the University of Washington's policy of encouraging cultural diversity in its student body, the program seeks students of diverse backgrounds and interests to participate in a six to ten week summer research project in the marine sciences. By linking fellows with marine scientists, fellows learn both the process and the substance of scientific research. As the research progresses, fellows will be encouraged to become semi-independent collaborators. The experience will expose fellows to the life and work of a marine science research laboratory.

The Setting: Friday Harbor Labs is University of Washington's marine science field research station. Located north of Puget Sound in the San Juan Islands, FHL takes advantage of a remarkable diversity of marine habitats and organisms. Research at FHL emphasizes marine invertebrate zoology, phycology, fisheries science, conservation biology, molecular biology, oceanography and other scientific disciplines.

Eligibility: students who are entering their senior year of college/university, or post-baccalaureate, or graduate students.

Award: room, board, round trip travel + $750/month stipend.

Apply by: March 1   # Given: 3-5

For more information:

Friday Harbor Laboratories   206-616-0708
620 University Rd.
Friday Harbor, WA. 98250

Boston Consortium on Gender, Security and Human Rights Fellows Program

The Boston Consortium, a working group of five academic centers in the greater Boston area, was created to change the political and academic understanding of the security field so that the dynamics of gender become salient at all points in the conflict process, from prevention through post-conflict reconstruction. By knitting together theoretical insights and accumulated experience from the fields of gender studies, international security, negotiation, and human rights, the Consortium aims to create a cadre of top-level, motivated intellectuals and practitioners who will share the best of what is known at the intersection of these disciplines. The program, to be initiated in September 2003, will be comprised of five or more Fellows, with each fellow affiliated with one of the five participating centers:

Center for Human Rights & Conflict Resolution (CHRCR), Fletcher School of Law and Diplomacy, Tufts University

Carr Center for Human Rights Policy, John F. Kennedy School of Government, Harvard University

Center for Gender in Organizations (CGO), Simmons Graduate College of Management

Peace and Justice Program, Wellesley College

Women and Public Policy Program, John F. Kennedy School of Government, Harvard University

For more information:

California Adolescent Nutrition and Fitness

The mission of the California Adolescent Nutrition and Fitness (CANFit) Program is to engage communities, and build their capacity to improve the nutritional status and physical fitness of California's low-income multi-ethnic youth 10-14 years of age. Graduate scholarships are available for African American, American Indian/Alaska Native, Asian/Pacific Islander or Latino/Hispanic students expressing financial need to study nutrition, physical education, or culinary arts in the state of California.

The application essay for 2003 is entitled, "The junk food industry often targets urban youth, negatively impacting their nutrition and health. What steps can the average adult take on a personal, community, and national level to combat these negative influences?"

Eligibility: Enrollment in an approved masters level or doctoral graduate (12-15 units of graduate course work completed with a 3.0 or better cumulative GPA) program in Nutrition, Public Health Nutrition, or Physical Education; or American Dietetic Association Approved Pre-professional Practice Program at an accredited university in California. Financial need, minority student affiliation.

Award: $1,500   # Given: 5-10

Apply by: March 31

For more information:

CANFit   (800) 200-3131

2140 Shattuck Avenue, Suite 610   www.canfit.org

Berkeley CA 94704   info@canfit.org

CA Association of Black Social Workers

See undergraduate listings.

California Teachers Association

See undergraduate listings.   www.cta.org/InsideCTA/TrainingHR/Scholarship

California Teachers Association

Martin Luther King Jr Memorial Scholarship

For ethnic minority persons obtaining degree credentials for teaching-related careers in public education.

Eligibility: Hispanic, Asian, American Indian, Alaskan Native, Pacific Islander and African American. CA resident. Active members of CTA, their dependent children, or ethnic minority active members of Student CTA.

Award: $250 - $2,000   # Given: Varies

Apply by: March 15

For more information:

Scholarship Coordinator   (650) 697-1400

CTA - Human Rights Dept

Graduate & Post-Graduate   169

PO Box 921
Burlingame, CA 94011

California Water Environment Association

Kirt Brooks Scholarship

For individuals attending a graduate school or technical trade school, with major related to wastewater industry.

Eligibility: Masters or Ph.D. goals, public administration, engineering, etc., related to water pollution control industry. CWEA membership.

Award: $250-$1,000   Apply by: February 1

For more information:

California Water Environment Ass'n.   (510) 382-7800
7677 Oakport Street, Suite 525
Oakland, CA 94621-1935   www.cwea.org/

Carnegie Endowment for International Peace

Carnegie Junior Fellows work for one year as research assistants to the Endowment's senior associates working on the Carnegie Endowment's projects such as non-proliferation, democracy building, international economics, China-related issues and Russian/Eurasian studies. Junior Fellows have the opportunity to conduct research for books, co-author journal articles and policy papers, participate in meetings with high-level officials and organize briefings attended by scholars, activists, journalists and government officials.

Eligibility: graduating seniors or students who have completed their bachelor's degree within the past academic year; must be nominated by one of 200 participating colleges and eligible to work in the United States.

Given: 10   Apply by: January 15

For more information:

Carnegie Endowment for Int'l. Peace   (202) 939-2221
2400 N Street NW, Suite 700   jrfellowinfo@ceip.org
Washington, DC 20037   www.ceip.org

Central States Water Association

Wrc Travel Fellowship

For a study tour in England of the research and development facilities of the Water Research Centre and a treatment facility. Applicant must be a degreed engineer with at least three years experience in capital works or operations, working on collections systems, wastewater treatment, or other areas within the environmental water quality engineering and be between the age of 25 and 35.

Award: $3,300

For more information:

Dwayne E. Nelson   (612) 296-7383

Robert A. Canham Scholarship

For a post-baccalaureate student in the environmental field.

Eligibility: member of Water Environment Federation, academic and practical experience in the environmental field. Accepted into a graduate program.

Award: $2,500

For more information:

Charles A. Hansen   (847) 303-0363
Central States Water Environment Association
2480 Amy Lane
Aurora, IL 60596-4202   www.cswea.org

WINSTON CHURCHILL SCHOLARSHIP

Demonstrated concern for the critical problems of society is one of the criteria for selection of students wanting to study engineering, mathematics, or natural science at Churchill College, Cambridge University, England.

Scholars may choose to enroll in master of philosophy programs in anatomy, biological anthropology, botany, chemistry, environment and development, pathology, physiology, polar studies, or zoology; post-graduate study in anatomy, botany, engineering, pathology, and physiology.

Eligibility: U. S. citizen between the ages of 19 and 26 enrolled in one of the institutions participating in the scholarship competition. Upon taking up a Churchill Scholarship, scholar must hold a bachelor's degree or its equivalent from a U. S. college or university, and may not have attained a doctorate.

Award: Tuition & fees, $25,000 to $27,000

Apply by: Early November   # Given: 11

For more information:

Contact Churchill Representative in your Graduate Fellowship Office during Spring Quarter of the year prior to the application deadline.

Winston Churchill Foundation   (212) 879-3480
P.O. Box 1240, Gracie Station   churchillf@aol.com
New York, NY 10028   www.thechurchillscholarships.com

COLORADO TRUST FELLOWS - REGIS UNIVERSITY

Designed to prepare Coloradans as future managers of nonprofit organizations. Graduate students receive support to attend the Master of Non-profit Management program at Regis University. The project has three components: academic training in nonprofit management; an internship with a nonprofit organization; and interactive training with business, government and community leaders.

Eligibility: demonstrated leadership potential, ready to contribute towards the health and well-being of Colorado residents.

Given: 12

For more information:

The Colorado Trust   303-837-1200,
Jean Merrick   jean@coloradotrust.org
                                           www.coloradotrust.org
Regis University   303-458-4336

Paul Alexander, Chair, Master of Nonprofit Management

www.Regis.edu

Concern/America

Concern/America is an international development and refugee aid organization. Volunteer professionals -- in the fields of public health, nutrition, health education, sanitation and community organizing work -- to assist impoverished communities and refugees in developing countries in their efforts to improve their living conditions. Volunteers serve for a minimum of two years in projects in Mexico, El Salvador, Guatemala, Honduras, Nicaragua, Guinea and Mozambique.

Eligibility: Degree/experience in public health, medicine, nutrition, nursing, agriculture, community development, education, or appropriate technology; Fluency in Spanish (except for the projects in Africa) or ability to learn Spanish at own expense; At least 21 years of age; Work experience abroad desirable.

Benefits: room and board, transportation, health insurance, monthly stipend, repatriation allowance..

For more information:

Concern/America   (800)266-2376
PO Box 1790   www.concernamerica.org
Santa Ana, CA 92702

CONGRESSIONAL HISPANIC CAUCUS INSTITUTE

Public Policy Fellowship Program

Every year, the nine-month Fellowship Program (late August to late May) offers up to 21 promising Latinos from across the country the opportunity to gain hands-on experience at the national level in the public policy area of their choice (General Public Policy Fellowship). Fellows have the opportunity to work in such areas as international affairs, economic development, education policy, housing, or local government. CHCI also aims to develop leaders in areas of public health administration (Edward Roybal Public Health Fellowship), telecommunications (Telecommunications Fellowship),corporate-public interest (Corporate Fellow), and financial services (Financial Services Fellowship). These specialized fellowships are open only to individuals with a graduate degree.

Eligibility: U.S. citizens and permanent residents of Hispanic background. 3.0 GPA; recent college graduate or currently enrolled grad student.

Award: $2,061-$2,500 + medical coverage and transportation.

Scholarship Awards

For Latino students who have a history of performing public service-oriented activities in their communities and who plan to continue contributing in the future. Leadership is valued above GPA.

Eligibility: Acceptance into an accredited community college, four-year university, or a graduate/professional program; financial need; U.S. citizenship or legal permanent residency.

Award: $5,000 to attend a four-year or graduate-level academic institution
$1,500 to attend a two-year community college.

For more information:

Congressional Hispanic Caucus Inst.   (800) 392-3532
504 C Street, N.E.
Washington DC 20002   www.chci.org/chciyouth/index.html

CONGRESSIONAL FELLOWSHIPS ON WOMEN/PUBLIC POLICY

Women's Research and Education Institute awards annual fellowships to a select number of graduate students with a proven commitment to equity for women. WREI Fellows gain practical policy making experience and graduate credit as they work as Congressional legislative aides in Washington, D.C.

The WREI Fellowship program is designed to encourage: more effective participation by women in the formulation of policy options; promote activities that encourage the translation of research into policy; raise awareness that national and international issues concerning women are interdependent; better understanding of how policies affect women and men differently; greater appreciation of the fact that issues often defined as "women's issues" are really of equal importance to men.

Eligibility: enrolled in, or have recently completed, a graduate or professional-degree program at an accredited institution in the U. S.

Award: stipends for tuition and living expenses

Apply by: mid-June

For more information:

WREI Congressional Fellowship Program
Women's Research and Education Institute
1750 New York Avenue, NW, Suite 350
Washington, DC 20006   www.wrei.org/fellowships/index.htm

CONNECTICUT FOREST AND PARK ASSOCIATION

See Undergraduate listing: www.ctwoodlands.org

CONSERVATION FEDERATION OF MISSOURI

Charles P. Bell Scholarships

For studies related to conservation.

Eligibility: Enrolled in a field of study related to management of natural resources, specifically fish, wildlife, forest, soil, and water. Applicants must be Missouri residents, and those applicants enrolled in Missouri schools will be given preference.

Award: $600   # Given: 1

Apply by: January 15

For more information:

Bell Scholarships   (314) 634-2322
728 W. Main St.   confedmo@socket.net
Jefferson City, MO 65101   www.confedmo.com/scholarships.asp

Council on Int'l Educational Exchange

The U.S. Department of Education has awarded CIEE funding under the Fulbright-Hays Group Projects Abroad Program to provide financial assistance to students who are participating in the Chinese language programs offered by the CIEE Centers at Peking University, East China Normal University (Shanghai), Nanjing University, and National Chengchi University (Taipei).

Eligibility: U.S. citizen or U.S. permanent resident enrolled in an institution of higher learning who plans a teaching career in modern foreign languages or area studies, completed 2 years of college-level Mandarin Chinese language training at the beginning of the program or the equivalent. Equivalency may be based on a language professor's evaluation or a language proficiency exam score.

Award: $500 - $4,000.

Apply by: Summer, Fall, and Academic Year Programs is April 15
Spring programs is November 15

For more information:

Council on International Educational Exchange   1-800-40-STUDY
205 E. 42nd St.   www.ciee.org/council_isp_scholarships.cfm
New York, NY 10001   scholarships@ciee.org

Creative Responses to Homelessness

A one-year opportunity for college graduates interested in learning about the not-for-profit sector, and creative responses to homelessness and poverty. Fellows work on special projects related to the development and management of Common Ground's programs.

Common Ground seeks recent college graduates who are motivated, creative, hard-working, and open to new experiences. Although we do take into consideration previous work in a social service related field, our primary concern is that the candidate have an interest in our work.

Fellows receive seminars and training on issues related to homelessness and poverty, and exposure to all aspects of Common Ground's work.

Stipend: $10,000 +housing and benefits   Apply by: mid-April

For more information:

Common Ground Community HDFC   (212) 389-9323
505 Eighth Avenue
New York, NY 10018   www.commonground.org/employment/index.asp

Soros Justice Fellowships

Support individuals working to restore fairness and discretion to the U.S. criminal justice system on a range of issues, including juvenile justice, sentencing reform, higher education in prison, the death penalty, drug policy, indigent defense, re-entry of prisoners into communities, immigrants' rights, and civil liberties.

Soros Justice Media Fellowship

A one-year program that funds journalists working in print, photography, radio, and documentary film to improve the quality of media coverage of incarceration and criminal justice issues.

The Soros Justice Postgraduate Fellowship

A two-year program that funds lawyers, advocates, activists, and former prisoners to support national criminal justice reform.

The Soros Justice Senior Fellowship

A one-year program that supports activists, academics, and community leaders to raise the level of national discussion and scholarship and prompt policy debate on issues of incarceration and criminal justice.

Eligibility: Final year of graduate study, or within six years of graduation in the fields of law, public health, economics, social work, or other areas related to criminal justice.

Stipend: $35,000 to $98,200, health benefits, support for graduate education debt.

Given: 20+

Soros Justice Student Fellowship

Provided to students at NYU School of Law. Includes summer internships in criminal justice agencies. Requires a binding commitment to work in the field of criminal justice for at least three years beyond graduation.

Award: full tuition, stipend for summer internship

Apply by: October 1

For more information:

Miriam Porter   (212) 548-0146
Program Officer for Fellowships   www.soros.org/crime/
Soros Foundation
New York, NY

DEMONSTRATION OF ENERGY-EFFICIENT DEVELOPMENTS

See undergraduate listings.

DISL GRADUATE FELLOWSHIPS

The Dauphin Island Sea Lab has a strong history of success in providing funding for it's graduate students. Student stipend support is available through both university and DISL fellowships, university and DISL-funded teaching assistantships, and extramurally-funded research assistantships. Over the past several years, over 95% of students have been fully-funded. At many schools, funded students in good academic standing are also provided with tuition fellowships that cover 100% of tuition costs.

Eligibilty: students from a DISL member-school basing their graduate program at the DISL. Of these, one fellowship is reserved for an in-coming student while the other two are open to both in-coming and returning students.

Award: $10,560 for incoming MS students

$11,040 for MS students with an approved prospectus

$13,000 for incoming Ph.D. students

$14,000 for Ph.D. students who have been admitted to candidacy.

Given: 3   Apply by: April 15

For more information:

University Programs Registrar, Sally Brennan

REU Research Fellowships   (251) 861-7502

Dauphin Island Sea Lab   www.disl.org

101 Bienville Blvd.   sbrennan@disl.org

Dauphin Island, AL 36528   univ-prog.disl.org/graduate.html

Thomas Dolan, IV Conservation Fellowship

This graduate student fellowship offers a stipend for three months of directed research related to the Philadelphia Zoo's One With Nature program priorities.

Stipend: $5,000   Apply by: April 15t

For more information:

215-243-5309   www.phillyzoo.org/at/work/internships_conserv.asp

Frederick Douglass Institute for African and African-American Studies

University of Rochester

Historical and contemporary dissertations and research on the economy, society, politics, and culture of Africa and its diaspora are welcomed. Projects on the human and technological aspects of energy development and agriculture in Africa are also welcomed.

Support is for fellows writing their dissertation. Fellows will work with Institute director and organize a colloquium. For postdoctoral candidates, fellowships support the completion of a research project. Postdoctoral fellows will have departmental affiliation and teach one course and conduct a seminar during the year. All fellowships are residential.

Eligibility: predoctoral students

Award: Predoctoral - $15,000

Postdoctoral - $35,000

Graduate - tuition plus $10,000 - $12,000 stipend

Apply by: January 30

For more information:

Assoc. Director for Research & Curriculum

Frederick Douglass Institute for African & African-American Studies

University of Rochester   www.rochester.edu/College/AAS/newaas/

302 Morey Hall   fdi@troi.cc.rochester.edu.

Rochester, NY 14627   (716) 275-7235

Du Bois-Mandela-Rodney Fellowship

University of Michigan, Ann Arbor

Supports scholars of high ability engaged in postdoctoral work on the Afro-American, African, and Caribbean experiences of men and women of color.

The Center seeks applications from scholars in the humanities and social sciences whose work addresses key issues in understanding the connections between culture, society, and the state in Africa and which questions the assumptions inherited by the field of African studies from its colonial and anti-colonial past. The Center is interested, for example, in research on: ways in which colonial and anti-colonial conceptions about African culture were used to explain social, political, and economic change.

Eligibility: must have a Ph.D. and be no more than five years beyond the completion of their degree.

Stipend: $36,000   Apply by: November 30

For more information:

Du Bois-Mandela-Rodney Fellowship   (313) 764-5513
Center for Afro-American & African Studies   caasinformation@umich.edu
505 S. State St.4700 Haven
www.umich.edu/~iinet/caas/fellowships.html
University of Michigan Ann Arbor, MI 48109-1092

DUCKS UNLIMITED'S INSTITUTE FOR WETLAND AND WATERFOWL RESEARCH

The purposes of this fellowship is to assist in the development of talented young professionals who are dedicated to furthering the conservation of wetlands and wetland wildlife, and to advance scientific understanding of the biology of waterfowl and wetlands in North America.

Eligibility: graduate students enrolled at any North American University.

Award: up to $7,000   # Given 1
Apply by: November 15

For more information:

Dr. Michael G. Anderson, Canadian Director
Institute for Wetland and Waterfowl Research
Ducks Unlimited Canada   (204) 467-3231
P.O. Box 1160
Stonewall, MB Canada R0C2Z0   m_anderson@ducks.ca

DORIS DUKE CONSERVATION FELLOWSHIP PROGRAM

Supports outstanding graduate students enrolled in master's degree programs at some of the nation's leading environmental schools. In addition to tuition support, the program also provides stipends for internships at nonprofit organizations and loan repayment for fellows who pursue nonprofit or public sector careers after graduation.

The fellowship program awards graduate students in conservation programs at Duke University, the University of Michigan, the University of Montana, the University of Wisconsin and Yale University.

For more information:

fdncenter.org/grantmaker/dorisduke/index.html

Earthjustice Legal Defense

The Rick Sutherland Fellowship enables socio-economically disadvantaged lawyers, with otherwise insufficient financial means, to engage in public interest litigation that would benefit the environment through employment with a non-profit organization. The fellowship is a two year grant to help pay student loans while working for a nonprofit.

Eligibility: lawyers who have graduated from law school within three years of the anticipated employment date, have significant outstanding student loans, and have obtained or accepted an offer of employment from a 501 C (3) or (4) organization.

Award: To $12,000 (two years)   Apply by: September 30

For more information:

Earthjustice
426 17th Street, 6th Floor
Oakland, CA 94612-2820   www.earthjustice.org/about/education/Sutherland.html

East-West Center, Honolulu, Hawai'i

Graduate Degree Fellowship Programs for degree study at the University of Hawai'i in a variety of fields related to the politics, international cooperation, economic and social changes, and environment of the region. These fellowships are available to individuals interested in participating in the educational and research programs of the East-West Center while pursuing graduate degree study at the University of Hawai'i. Fellowships for both master's (24 month) and doctoral (48 month) degrees are available. Center scholarships are given for degree study at the University of Hawai'i and participation in the Center's international and intercultural programs.

Apply by: November 1

The Asia Pacific Leadership Program

One-year certificate program designed to develop the knowledge and leadership potential of people committed to addressing the issues of the region through regional cooperation. Scholarship support available.

Apply by: February 15

For more information:

EWC-UHM Scholarship Office, Education Program
East-West Center   808/944-7735
1601 East-West Road   ewcuhm@eastwestcenter.org
Honolulu, HI 96848-1601   www.eastwestcenter.org

Eisenhower/ Roberts Graduate Fellowships

Supports study and education dealing with the role of government in a free society, with the relationship between international and domestic issues, and improved understanding of world affairs. Research topics relating directly to President Eisenhower, his administration, and issues of major concern to him will command special attention. Areas of study include government, history, economics, business administration, and international affairs.

Eligibility: advanced stage of doctoral candidacies, preferably at the point of preparing their dissertations. Less advanced graduate students or persons who've recently earned their doctorates will also be considered.

Award: $7,000 - $10,000   Apply by: Mid February

For more information:

Contact your graduate fellowship coordinator.

The Eisenhower Institute

915 15th Street, NW, 8th floor   (202)628.4444

Washington, DC 20005   www.eisenhowerinstitute.org

EL POMAR FELLOWSHIP

El Pomar Fellowship in Community Service

A two year fellowship program in community service. Recipient receives intensive professional development training to prepare for leadership roles in the nonprofit world. Responsibilities include grant making and community outreach programs. Ideal applicant will have strong leadership skills and capability, interest in public/ community service, strong verbal and writing skills, initiative. Must be willing to travel throughout Colorado.

Eligibility: BS or BA degree and a Colorado connection: be a state resident, have attended an in-state college/university, or have immediate family who are residents or past residents.

Apply by: early February

For more information:

El Pomar Foundation   (800)554-7711

10 Lake Circle   fellowship@elpomar.org

Colorado Springs, CO 80906   www.elpomar.org

ENVIRONMENTAL FELLOWSHIP & LEADERSHIP PROGRAM

Switzer Environmental Fellowship Program

To highly qualified individuals, with a strong commitment to the applied side of science, who plan graduate studies in California or New England.

Award: $13,000

Environmental Leadership Grants Program

Furthers the Foundation's leadership development goals and improves the effectiveness of environmental organizations in California and New England. The purpose is to facilitate the entry of Switzer Fellows into the public sector and to give nonprofit organizations greater access to technical and scientific expertise.

For more information:

Switzer Fellowship Network   www.switzernetwork.org/

ENVIRONMENTAL LAW ESSAY CONTEST

Roscoe Hogan Environmental Law Essay Contest

Each entry must be submitted through a faculty adviser. Students, through their faculty advisor, must file the "Intent-to-Enter" form indicating their intent to submit an essay for national judging. Entrants from Fall and Spring semester classes must submit the form by fax or mail by early February.

Eligibility: any student currently enrolled in an accredited American law school may submit a legal essay on the topic.

For students enrolling in International Service Learning master's program.

Award: $5,000   # Given: 1

Apply by: early February

For more information:

Hogan Environmental Law Essay Contest	(202) 965-0355 fax
1050 31st Street, NW	
Washington, D.C. 20007	www.roscoepound.org

ENVIRONMENTAL MANAGEMENT

Bridgestone/Firestone, Vanderbilt University

To support study in Environmental Management Ph.D. program for a term of three years.

Award: tuition, fees, monthly stipend   # Given: 1 - 2

Apply by: March 15

For more information:

VCEMS	(615) 332-8004
1207 18th Avenue South	vcems@ctvax.vanderbilt.edu
Nashville, TN 37212	www.vanderbilt.edu/vcems/bridgestone.html

ENVIRONMENTAL PROTECTION AGENCY

Minority Academic Institutions (MAI) Fellowships

The purpose of the fellowship program is to encourage promising students to obtain advanced degrees and pursue careers in environmentally related fields. This goal is consistent with the mission of EPA, which is to protect human health and to safeguard the natural environment – air, water, and land – upon which life depends. This program will benefit both the public and private sectors, which will need a steady stream of well-trained environmental specialists if our society is to meet the environmental challenges of the future.

Eligibility: Citizens of the U.S. or its territories or possessions, or permanent residents. Resident aliens must include their green card number in their pre-application. Enrollment in a fully accredited four-year U.S. Minority Academic Institution (See list on web site), masters or doctoral degree program in an environmentally related field of specialization. Students who have completed more than one year in the master's program or four years in the doctoral program are not eligible. Students enrolled in a master's program may apply for a doctoral fellowship.

Award: $34,000 annual stipend plus authorized expenses, tuition and fees

Given: 25   Apply by: November 18

For more information:

ETS FELLOWSHIP AND INTERNSHIP PROGRAMS

The ETS (Education Testing Service) Awards Programs are designed to provide scholars and students, at various stages of their careers, opportunities to carry out independent research under the guidance of ETS senior researchers in a variety of fields, e.g., policy research, psychometrics, psychology, teaching, statistics, minority issues, and alternate forms of assessment. The goals of these programs are to provide research opportunities to scholars who either hold a doctoral degree or are enrolled in a doctoral program, and to increase the number of women and minority professionals in the field of educational research.

Summer Program in Research for Graduate Students.

Selected interns who participate in the summer program conduct research on a specific ETS project or program, chosen by the applicant, under the guidance of a senior staff member. Interns also attend twice-weekly seminars and workshops. Applicants must have completed one full year of academic coursework toward their Ph.D. or Ed.D. on or before June 1 of the award year.

Award: 2 months. Stipend: $4,000. Limited round-trip travel expenses.

Apply by: February 1

www.ets.org/research/fellowships/feloosum.html

Postdoctoral Fellowship Program

Up to three individuals will be selected as fellows, and invited to conduct independent research described in a proposal submitted as part of the application process. Candidates must hold a doctoral degree.

Award: 1 year Stipend of $38,000 and limited relocation expense reimbursement.

Apply by: February 1

www.ets.org/research/fellowships/feloo-post.html

Harold Gulliksen Psychometric Research Fellowship Program.

Open to both national and international applicants who are enrolled in a doctoral program and have completed at least two years of full-time study toward their Ph.D. During the academic year, fellows will study at their universities and participate in a research project under the supervision of an academic mentor and in consultation with an ETS scientist. During the summer, fellows will be invited to participate in the ETS Summer Program in Research for, working under the guidance of an ETS researcher in Princeton.

Award: One academic year of funding to the fellow's university to pay each fellow a stipend of $15,000 ($1,500/month for 10 months). The university will also receive an educational allowance of $7,500 to defray tuition, fees, and work study commitments.

Apply by: early December

Sylvia Taylor Johnson Minority Fellowship in Educational Measurement.

A fellow will be selected to conduct independent research, described in a proposal submitted as part of the application process.

Eligibility: U.S. Citizens who received doctoral degree within past 10 years.

Award: 1 year Stipend set in relation to the successful applicant's compensation at the home institution. Limited relocation expenses will be reimbursed.

Apply by: January 10

For more information:

Educational Testing Service
MS-10R
Princeton, NJ 08541-0001.

609-734-5949 or 609-734-1806
www.ets.org/research/fellowships.html

ENTOMOLOGICAL SOCIETY OF AMERICA

Joseph H. Camin Fellowship

The award supports graduate students attend the Acarology Summer Program at Ohio State University or an equivalent institution where they can obtain training in the systematics of acarines. Made annually, the value of the fellowship depends on interest earned from the endowment.

Stanley Beck Fellowship

Assists needy students in entomology and related disciplines at a college or university in the United States, Mexico or Canada. The is based on physical limitations or economic, minority, or environmental conditions. This fellowship was established as a tribute to Stanley D. Beck, a notable scientist who pursued his profession despite the effects of a debilitating disease.

Award: varies each year   Apply by: September 1

Normand R. Dubois Memorial Scholarship

To encourage research by graduate students directed toward the use of biologically based technologies to protect and preserve forests in an environmentally acceptable manner.

Eligibility: candidate for a master's or doctoral degree at an accredited university. Must be nominated.

Award: $1,500   Apply by: July 1

For more information:

Entomological Society of America
9301 Annapolis Road
Lanham, MD 20706-3115

(301) 731-4535
www.entsoc.org

EQUAL JUSTICE WORKS FELLOWSHIP

These two-year fellowships are for public interest lawyers who work in conjunction with host nonprofit organizations to launch projects that serve low-income and other needy communities. As the nation's largest postgraduate, public service, legal fellowship program, the Equal Justice Works Fellowships Program has put scores of lawyers to work on some of the nation's greatest challenges, such as homelessness, access to health care, consumer rights, domestic violence, community development, discrimination in housing and employment, workers' rights, and children's health and welfare issues.

Because the goal is to create new public interest positions, Equal Justice Works Fellowships are not used to fund general staff attorney positions within existing organizations. Instead, they should provide fellows with the opportunity to exercise leadership on a discrete project. Project proposals may be generated by individuals, organizations or both.

Eligibility: third-year law students or graduates from a law school that is an Equal Justice Works member (see web site for a list).

Award: Salary and loan repayment assistance, benefits, a national training program.

Apply by: Individuals Mid September, Organizations end October

For more information

Equal Justice Works Fellowships Program Assistant

Equal Justice Works	www.equaljusticeworks.org
2120 L Street, NW Suite 450	(202)429-9766 or (202).466.3686
Washington, DC 20037-1541	fellowships@equaljusticeworks.org

THE EXPLORERS CLUB® EXPLORATION FUND

In support of exploration and field research, made primarily to graduate students. Expeditions aided will be for scientific purposes, in accordance with the Club's stated objective, "to broaden our knowledge of the universe".

Award: up to $5,000   Apply by: January 31

For more information:

The Explorers Club	(212) 628-8383
46 East 70th Street	office@explorers.org.
New York, NY 10021	www.explorers.org

THE FINANCIAL WOMEN'S ASSOCIATION OF SAN FRANCISCO

To encourage leadership and provide opportunities for Bay Area women in the field of finance.

Eligibility: Female students in finance or related field enrolled during the fall semester at an accredited Bay Area college or university, minimum GPA of 3.4. Financial need and community involvement and leadership considered.

Award: $10,000   # Given: 6

Apply by: February 28

For more information:

FWA Scholarship Committee	(415) 333-9045
PO Box 26143 Gateway Station	www.fwasf.org
San Francisco, CA 94126	info@fwasf.org

FULBRIGHT

The Fulbright Program is designed to "increase mutual understanding between the people of the United States and the people of other countries". Grants are awarded to American students, teachers, and scholars to study, teach, lecture, and conduct research abroad and to foreign nationals to engage in like activities in the United States. Recipients will have superior academic or professional qualifications and potential, along with the ability and willingness to share ideas and experiences with people of diverse cultures. Pre-Doctoral Fellowships are offered to American and foreign graduate students and graduating seniors. For more information:

College students should contact their campus representative.

Council for Int'l. Exchange of Scholars (202) 686-4000
3007 Tilden Street, NW Suite 5M scholars@cies.iie.org
Washington, DC 20008-3009 www.cies.org

Fulbright Indo-American Environmental Leadership Program FIAELP

FIAELP is designed for mid-level environmental professionals in the private sector, or with government or non-governmental organizations (NGOs). The program combines 8-12 week practical fellowships in India with opportunities for networking with Indian counterpart organizations. The selected individuals will be placed at Indian public, private or non-governmental organizations, including academic institutions and research centers.

Eligibility: Preferably have a Master's degree (or higher) in a relevant discipline, at least five years of relevant professional experience, US citizen.

Award: travel, stipend, professional allowance, and health insurance.

Given: 15   Apply by: October 1

For more information:

IIE Environmental Exchange Division 202-326-7769
1400 K St., NW
Suite 650
Washington, DC 20005 /www.iie.org/dc/

GARDEN CLUB OF AMERICA

Interchange Fellowship in Horticulture and Landscape Design

Fosters British-American relations through the interchange of scholars in fields related to horticulture. Program allows a student from the U.S. to undertake a work/study program in the United Kingdom. Appropriate fields of study include horticulture, botany, landscape architecture and environmental studies.

Eligibility: college graduates who have earned a BA or BS degree. Because of a 26 year-old age limit on student travel vouchers in Great Britain and Europe, it is strongly advised that   applicant be 26 or younger. Finalists will be requested to attend an interview at their own expense with time and place determined annually.

Award: Tuition, travel, room & board, expenses, personal allowance.

Apply by: November 15

For more information send self-addressed stamped envelope to:

Scholarship Committee (212) 753-8287
The Garden Club of America www.gcamerica.org/scholarships.htm
14 E. 60th St. csutton@gcamerica.org
New York, NY 10022-1614

Katharine M. Grosscup Scholarships

To encourage the study of horticulture and related fields.

Eligibility: college juniors, seniors or graduate students at the masters degree level, preferably from IN, KY, MI, OH, PA and WV. Personal interview in

Cleveland is required of all finalists.

> Award: To $3,000   # Given: 2+
>
> Apply by: February 1

For more information:

> Grosscup Scholarship Committee   Fax: (216) 721-2056 No phone calls.
>
> Cleveland Botanical Garden   www.gcamerica.org/scholarships.htm
>
> 11030 East Boulevard
>
> Cleveland, OH 44106

GCA Fellowship in Ecological Restoration

Supports study and research in ecological restoration.Study should conform to the Society of Ecological Restoration's definition:"The process of assisting the recovery and management of ecological integrity (which) includes a critical range of variability in biodiversity, ecological processes and structures, regional and historical context and sustainable cultural practices"

> Eligibility: graduate students pursuing an advanced degree.
>
> Award: $8000   # Given: 1
>
> Apply by: January 15

For more information

> Gregory D. Armstrong, Director   (608) 262-2746
>
> University of Wisconsin-Madison Arboretum www.gcamerica.org/scholarships.htm
>
> 1207 Seminole Highway   wiscinfo.doit.wisc.edu/arboretum/
>
> Madison, WI 53711   gdarmstr@facstaff.wisc.edu

Francis M. Peacock Scholarship for Native Bird Habitat

For study of U.S. winter or summer habitat for threatened or endangered native birds. Opportunity to pursue real habitat-related issues that eventually benefit bird species and lend useful information for management decisions.

> Eligibility: college seniors and graduate students
>
> Award: $4,000   # Given: 1
>
> Apply by: January 15

For more information:

> Scott Sutcliffe   Fax: (607) 254-2415 No phone calls.
>
> Cornell Lab of Ornithology   lh17@cornell.edu
>
> 159 Sapsucker Woods Road   www.gcamerica.org/scholarships.htm
>
> Ithaca, NY 14850   lbirdsource.cornell.edu

GCA Award in Coastal Wetlands Studies

Supports young scientists in their field work and research in coastal wetlands (defined as those tidal or nontidal wetlands found in the coastal states, including those of the Great Lakes).

> Eligibility: graduate students in coastal wetlands science.
>
> Award: $5000   # Given: 1
>
> Apply by:mid-February

For more information:

> Carl Hershner, Ph.D., Chair, Center for Coastal Resources Management
>
> Virginia Institute of Marine Science   (804) 684-7380
>
> P O Box 1346   www.gcamerica.org/scholarships.htm

Gloucester Point, VA 23062-1346   carl@vims.edu

Carherine H. Beattie Fellowship

Research grants through the Center for Plant Conservation. Preference to projects focusing on the endangered flora of the Carolinas and southeastern U.S.

Award: up to $4000   # Given:1

Apply by: December 31

For more information:

Manager of Conservation Programs, Center for Plant Conservation

Missouri Botanical Garden   (314) 577-945

PO Box 299   cpc@mobot.org

St. Louis, MO 63166-0299   www.mobot.org/cpc/beattie.html

GCA Awards in Tropical Botany

Eligibility: Ph.D. candidates for field study in tropical botany..

Award: $5500   # Given: 2

Apply by:December 31

For more information:

Attn: GCA Awards in Tropical Botany   (202) 778-9632

Education for Nature Program   nadia.cureton@wwfus.org

World Wildlife Fund   www.gcamerica.org/scholarships.htm

1250 24th Street, NW

Washington, DC 20037

JOHN GARDNER FELLOWSHIP

Stanford University and the University of California, Berkeley

Encourages outstanding students to consider careers of public service. Fellowships give graduates opportunities to invest their talent, energy and training in public service. They are provided with an assignment in a government or non-profit agency. Each Fellow will have a mentor to help with professional growth and development. Past assignments have included drafting legislation in a Congressional office; working on health and environmental issues in an advocacy organization or a foundation; or working with a city school superintendent, on a Mayor's staff or in a Governor's office.

Eligibility: Graduating seniors at Stanford University and UC Berkeley, with a commitment to public and voluntary sector service, U.S. citizen.

Stipend: $25,000 (ten months) + travel and other related expenses.

Given: 3 from each campus   Apply by: early February

For more information:

Stanford:	U.C. Berkeley:
Haas Center for Public Service	Institute of Governmental Studies
558 Salvatierra Walkway	111 Moses Hall
Stanford University	University of California
Stanford, CA 94305	Berkeley, CA 94720
(650) 725-2870	(510) 643-8533
	www.igs.berkeley.edu/programs/gardner/

haas-fmp.stanford.edu/opportunities/oppo_felw/oppo_felw_gardner.html

GENDER AND GLOBALIZATION IN ASIA AND THE PACIFIC

This program seeks to answer the question, what is meant by globalization, and how are women active in, and acted upon by, the processes involved in globalization? Under the auspices of the Office for Women's Research and the Women's Studies Program at the University of Hawai`i, research themes include: women and economic transformation; women's health globally; migration/refugees/diaspora movements and communities; militarism and global violence; domestic violence and victimization; gender, race and representation; global connections of indigenous peoples; and reparation movements and interracial justice.

Eligibility: Scholars with a doctoral degree from Asia/Pacific regions or from any nation interested in studying gender issues related to Asia and the Pacific.

For more information:

Women's Studies Program((808) 956-7464
University of Hawai'i
2424 Maile Way, SSB 722
Honolulu, HI 96822   www2.soc.hawaii.edu/ws/index.html

GLOBAL PUBLIC SERVICE LAW PROJECT

Supports Global Public Service Scholars who visit New York University each year, to practically assist them in their difficult and often groundbreaking work making change in the legal structure and wider culture of their societies. The curricular and extra-curricular work allows the student-lawyers to learn from each other and to trade practical strategies across borders, and supports graduates to work for up to one year at a law-related public interest organization of their choosing upon graduation. Through the Global Public Service Law Project, NYU hopes to help local activist lawyers in their work, while also feeding the emerging phenomenon of cross-border public interest lawyering.

Scholars choose an area of specialization from the following: political and civil rights; social justice and economic rights; criminal justice; international public service law and practice; or institutional, practical, and managerial issues in public interest law practice.

Eligibility: Lawyers who will have at least two years of post-graduate public service work experience. At least ten scholars will be non-U.S. citizens or permanent residents and will receive a full tuition waiver, travel, and stipend. United States citizens and permanent residents are not eligible for a Global Public Service Scholarship, but they may be considered for partial scholarships on a case by case basis.

For more information:

Global Public Service Law Project   (212)998-6428
NYU School of Law

NYU School of Law
110 W. Third Street, Second Floor
New York, NY 10012

law.gpslp@nyu.edu
www.law.nyu.edu/globallawschool/gpslp.html

HANKE - COMMUNITY ASSOCIATIONS

For students working on topics related to community associations. Eligible fields of study include law, economics, sociology, and urban planning or other disciplines. Studies must relate to community associations generally, and to topic of the candidate's proposed community associations research project.

Eligibility: enrollment in a master's, doctoral, or law program.

Award: $2,000

For more information:

CAI Research Foundation
225 Reinekers Lane, Suite 300
Alexandria, VA 22314

(703) 548-8600

www.cairf.org/schol/hanke.html

HARVARD PUBLIC INTEREST LAW

Kaufman Postgraduate Fellowships honor graduating students and recent alumni/ae of Harvard Law School who embody the spirit of public interest lawyering. Kaufman Fellowships provide partial support for one to two years of public interest work.

The committee seeks fellows who show potential to become outstanding public service lawyers. Public interest work is broadly defined as encompassing all law-related work that serves a distinctly public purpose and involves a significant financial sacrifice. Examples include: poverty law in legal service organizations, public interest nonprofit organizations, public defender or criminal prosecutor associations, int'l. development organizations, or government agencies.

Eligibility: graduating students and recent alumni/ae of Harvard Law.

Award: $3,000-$7,000

Given: 20-25

Apply by: Early March

For more information:

The Kaufman Fellowship Committee
Office of Public Interest Advising
Harvard Law School, Pound Hall 328
Cambridge, MA 02138

pia@law.harvard.edu
(617) 495-3108

www.law.harvard.edu/Students/opia/

HAWAII COMMUNITY FOUNDATION

Offers a number of different scholarships for students in Hawaii of good moral character who show potential for filling a community need, and who demonstrate intent to return to, or stay in Hawaii to work.

For more information:

Hawaii Community Foundation
900 Fort St. Mall, Suite 1300
Honolulu, HI 96813

www.hawaiicommunityfoundation.org

HAWKINSON FOUNDATION FOR PEACE AND JUSTICE

See Undergraduate listing.

HEARST MINORITY/PHILANTHROPIC/NON-PROFIT

Philanthropic Studies or Nonprofit Management, IUPUI

Provides members of minority groups the opportunity to engage in the study and practical application of philanthropy, while pursuing an M.A. in Philanthropic Studies or M.P.A. in Nonprofit Management. The Philanthropic Studies program focuses on the history, culture and values of philanthropy. The M.P.A. is designed for persons employed in nonprofit agencies, and those seeking management careers in the nonprofit sector.

The Fellowship is a 10-month appointment. Hearst Fellows devote time to both formal study and the practice of philanthropy. Fellows study under the tutelage of a faculty mentor in a special field of interest (e.g. management, history, social work) and interact with top scholars and leaders in the philanthropic and nonprofit world.

Eligibility: Members of groups traditionally under-represented in organized philanthropy; recent graduates, scholars, active volunteers or nonprofit practitioners. Admitted to the Philanthropic Studies or the Nonprofit Management program. Demonstrated interest in and commitment to the philanthropic tradition. Involvement in the voluntary sector is extremely helpful.

Stipend: $15,000 for housing and living expenses. Tuition is waived.

Apply by: February 1

For more information:

Hearst Minority Fellowship Program
Indiana Univ. Center on Philanthropy
550 West North Street, Suite 301
Indianapolis, IN 46202-3162

(317) 274-4200
www.philanthropy.iupui.edu/hearst.htm

TERESA HEINZ SCHOLARS FOR ENVIRONMENTAL RESEARCH

Provides doctoral dissertation and master's thesis or project enhancement support for research on emerging environmental problems. Research must have public policy relevance that increases society's understanding of environmental problems and their solutions.

Eligibility: Doctoral Dissertation Support - Candidates for doctoral degree who will have fulfilled all pre-dissertation requirements by May   including approval of the dissertation prospectus, and expect to submit a completed dissertation by May, 2002. Enrolled in a doctoral degree program at Carnegie Mellon, Cornell, Harvard, Penn State, Princeton, Stanford or Yale University.

Master's Thesis Support: Candidates for the master's degree. Enrolled in a graduate program of one of the universities listed above, as well as Florida A&M University or Texas A&M University at Corpus Christi.

Award: $10,000 Doctoral
$5,000   Masters

Given: 8
Given: 8

Apply by: Early February
For more information:

Heinz Scholars for Enviro. Research	(412) 497-5775
3200 CNG Tower	scholars@heinz.org
Pittsburgh, PA 15222	www.hfp.heinz.org/scholars/

HELLER SCHOOL FOR SOCIAL POLICY & MANAGEMENT

Feldman Graduate Fellowship In Sustainable Development

Combining Study in the U.S. and Fieldwork in a Rainforest Conservation Site in a Developing Country, the Fellowship for the Master of Arts in Sustainable International Development will be awarded to an early to mid-career planner interested in integrated conservation and development. The Fellow joins SID graduate students from over 30 countries for an interdisciplinary study of development and project management emphasizing poverty reduction, gender, human rights, and biodiversity conservation. The Feldman Fellow will concentrate on integrated conservation and development and work in a conservation site during the second year of the Master's degree program.

Award: full tuition, fees, airfare and living expenses for the year-in-residence at Brandeis, and airfare and subsistence allowance for the second year fieldwork.

Apply by: January 31

For more information:

sidfeldman@brandeis.edu

Poverty Alleviation and Sustainable Communities in the Greater Mississippi Delta

This graduate scholarship combines a Year-in-Residence at Brandeis University with Second Year Fieldwork in the Delta. The scholar will join early to mid-career professionals from over 40 countries for an interdisciplinary study of development and social change emphasizing poverty reduction, gender, human rights, environmental conservation, and project planning and management.

Eligibility: residents of Mississippi, Louisiana, Arkansas, Tennessee, Kentucky, Missouri, and Illinois, or candidates with a demonstrated commitment to the development of the Delta Region. Graduates of Historically Black Colleges and Universities and women are especially encouraged to apply.

Apply by: March 15   Award: full tuition

How to apply: Letters of nomination may be faxed or sent as email attachments in MS Word format to sdsouth@brandeis.edu.

For more information:

Sustainable Development Master's Program	781-736-2770
Brandeis University	sdsouth@brandeis.edu
Waltham, Massachusetts 02454-9110	heller.brandeis.edu/sid

HUDSON RIVER FOUNDATION

Tibor T. Polgar Fellowship

In cooperation with the New York State Department of Environmental Conservation, the fellowship provides a summertime grant and research funds for students to conduct research on the tidal Hudson estuary from the Federal

Dam at Troy, New York, to New York Harbor. The objective is to gather important information on all aspects of the River, and to train students in conducting estuarine studies and public policy research.

Eligibility: undergraduate and graduate students. Must be sponsored by a primary advisor who is willing to commit sufficient time for supervision of the research and to attend at least one meeting to review the progress of the research. Advisors will receive a stipend of $500.

Award: $3,800   # Given: 8

Apply by: mid February

Hudson River Graduate Fellowships

For advanced graduate students conducting research on the Hudson River system. Applicants must be enrolled in an accredited doctoral or master's program, and must have a thesis research plan approved by the student's institution or department.

Award: Doctoral-$15,000 stipend+ incidentals research budget up to $1,000.

Masters-$15,000 stipend+ incidentals research budget up to $1,000.

Given: up to 6   Apply by: mid April

For more information:

Polgar Fellowship Committee

Hudson River Foundation   info@hudsonriver.org

40 West 20th Street, 9th Floor   www.hudsonriver.org

New York, NY 10011   (212)-924-8290

THE INSTITUTE FOR WOMEN'S POLICY RESEARCH

IWPR works primarily on issues related to equal opportunity and economic and social justice for women. Fellowships assist in professional development of students and graduates interested in economic justice for women.

The Mariam K. Chamberlain Fellowship Program

Research Fellows work as a general research assistant on a variety of research projects and reports. Research tasks may include reviewing literature; collecting, checking and analyzing data; gathering information; and preparing reports and report graphics. Attending relevant Congressional briefings, policy seminars and meetings is also an integral part of the fellowship program.

Eligibility: bachelor's degree in a social science discipline, statistics, or women's studies. Graduate work is desirable but not required.

Award: $1,600 + health insurance and a public transportation stipend.

Apply by: mid-February

For more information

Fellowship Coordinator

Institute for Women's Policy Research   www.iwpr.org

1400 20th St. NW, Suite 104

Washington, D.C. 20036

IWPR/GW Fellowship in Women's Public Policy Research

The recipient of this fellowship will participate in research at the Institute for Women's Policy Research during the fellowship year, while enrolled as a full-time graduate student at The George Washington University. IWPR's current research program includes poverty and welfare, family and work, child care, employment and earnings, health and violence, and indicators of women's status. Specific research projects will be mutually agreed upon by IWPR, the fellow's advisor, and the fellow.

Eligibility: Students enrolled in or applying to any of the graduate programs at The George Washington University are eligible to apply.

Award: $10,000 + 18 hours tuition credit at George Washington Univ.

Apply by: early March

For more information:

IWPR Fellowship

Women's Studies Program Office

2201 G Street NW, Funger Hall, Suite 506-I,

Washington, DC 20052   www.iwpr.org/

International Peace Scholarship Fund

Provides grants-in-aid for women from other countries for graduate study in the United States and Canada. Applicant must commit to return to her own country upon completion of her degree program.

Eligibility: women qualified for admission to full time graduate study, working toward a graduate degree in US or Canada.

Award: To $6,000   Apply by: January 31

For more information:

P.E.O. International Peace Scholarship Fund

P.E.O. Sisterhood Executive Office   (515) 255-3153

3700 Grand Avenue

Des Moines, Iowa 50312   peointernational.org

Joint Japan/ World Bank

Supports graduate studies (either Masters or Doctoral) for nationals of World Bank member countries in subjects related to development such as economics, business, planning, also health, population, agriculture, environment and natural resource management, civil engineering, education. Scholars study in well-known Universities in any World Bank member country, except their own.

For more information:

Joint Japan/ World Bank Grad. Scholarship   (202) 473-6849

700, 18th St. NW, Room M-4107

Washington, DC 20433   www.worldbank.org/wbi/scholarships/index.html

Kentucky Environmental Protection

See Undergraduate listing.

Beatrice Krauss Fellowship Competition

This fellowship is intended to assist graduate students in Botany.
Eligibility: graduate students majoring in Botany, financial need.

Award: $500 - $3,000.

Apply by :October 1

For more information:

www.botany.hawaii.edu/botany/krauss10.htm

LAND ECONOMICS

For graduate study in land economics, architecture, law, geography, urban planning, landscape architecture, environmental planning, civil engineering, government, public administration, real estate, or urban studies.

Eligibility: graduate student in the United States, Canada, or Great Britain.

Award: $3,000   Renewable

Apply by: Late March

For more information:

Lambda Alpha International	(312) 201-0101
104 South Michigan Ave. Suite 1500	lai@lai.org
Chicago, IL 60603	www.LAI.org

LAND STEWARDSHIP FOR CONSERVATION PROFESSIONALS

Atlantic Center for the Environment conducts a four-week fellowship program on land conservation and stewardship for conservation professionals from countries in the Caribbean and Latin America, introducing participants to conservation issues in the northeastern United States and eastern Canada, and enabling them to begin a dialogue with their North American counterparts. Its broad goals are to provide training and professional development for conservation leaders from the Caribbean and Latin America, promote an exchange of ideas and innovations in the area of landscape conservation and stewardship, and strengthen the capacity of NGOs in both regions to conserve natural areas.

Eligibility: leaders, staff, or volunteers with a NGO involved in biodiversity conservation, landscape conservation, sustainable agriculture, sustainable forestry, or rural community development. Proficiency in English.

Given: 8   Apply by: early March

For more information:

Atlantic Center for the Environment	(978) 356-0038
Brent Mitchell, Director, Stewardship Program	brentmitchell@qlf.org
QuebecLabrador Foundation	
55 South Main Street	
Ipswich, MA 01938	www.qlf.org

ANNA SOBOL LEVY FELLOWSHIPS

Enables American students to attend Hebrew University of Jerusalem for one year as graduate-level visiting students in the fields of armed services, diplomatic corps, government, public service or related professions.

Eligibility: recent college graduates and current graduate students.

Award: $5,000 for a tutorial, and additional funds for dorm housing.

Apply by: March 1

For more information:

The Hebrew University	(800) 404-8622
Coordinator of Graduate Academic Affairs	(212) 472-2288
11 East 69th St	hebrewu@hebrewu.com
New York, NY 10021	overseas.huji.ac.il/grad_anna_sobol.asp

LINK FOUNDATION ENERGY FELLOWSHIP

Two year fellowship fosters energy research; enhances theoretical and practical knowledge and application of energy research.

Eligibility: U.S. citizens or residents working toward a Ph.D in the fields of science and engineering.

Award: $25,000/year   Apply by: December 1

For more information:

Link Foundation Energy Fellowship Program	(603) 646-2674
Dr. Lee Lynd, Administrator	www.linkenergy.org
Thayer School of Engineering	
Dartmouth College	
Hanover, NH 03755	

Sentiment without action is the ruin of the soul.
Edward Abbey

LOUISIANA WATER ENVIRONMENT ASSOCIATION

See Undergraduate listing.

MACARTHUR CONSORTIUM FELLOWSHIPS IN INTERNATIONAL PEACE AND COOPERATION

Provides fellowships and research assistantships for Ph.D. candidates working on the following dimensions of world society: war and institutions of violence including civil wars and regional conflict and cooperation in an international context; globalization; society and the ecosphere; identity and social power. The Consortium is comprised of Stanford, University of Minnesota, and the University of Wisconsin.

For more information:

cisac.stanford.edu	www.icgc.umn.edu

MACARTHUR FELLOWS PROGRAM

Awards unrestricted fellowships to talented individuals who have shown extraordinary originality and dedication in their creative pursuits and a marked capacity for self-direction. The purpose of the Program is to enable recipients to exercise their own creative instincts for the benefit of human society.

Recipients may be writers, scientists, artists, social scientists, humanists, teachers, activists, or workers in other fields, with or without institutional affiliations. They may use their fellowship to advance their expertise, engage in interdisciplinary work, or, if they wish, to change fields or alter the direction of their careers. Although nominees are reviewed for their achievements, the fellowship is not a reward for past accomplishment, but rather an investment in a person's originality, insight, and potential.

The Foundation does not require or expect specific products or reports from Fellows, and does not evaluate recipients' creativity during the term of the fellowship. The Fellowship is a "no strings attached" award in support of people, not projects.

Eligibility: The Program does not accept applications or unsolicited nomination. Nominees must be either residents or citizens of the United States.

Stipend: $500,000 paid out in equal quarterly installments over five years.

For more information:

macfellows@macfound.org   www.macfound.org

George Perkins Marsh Conservation Fellowship

Provides a partial tuition waiver to one or more M.S.E.L. or LL.M. candidates each year. Proposals for both Research and Teaching Fellowships are considered. The Environmental Law Center welcomes proposals which advance the cause of environmental stewardship.

For more information:

Vermont Law School

P.O. Box 96, Chelsea Street

South Royalton, VT 05068   www.vermontlaw.edu/community/elc/elcllmmar.cfm

Robert S. McNamara Fellowship

For a Master's degree in Public Policy at The Woodrow Wilson School of Public and International Affairs, Princeton University.

Eligibility: Mid-career professionals from all World Bank borrowing member countries who meet the M.P.P. program's normal eligibility requirements.

Award: full tuition fellowship, a travel allowance, and a stipend for living expenses

For more information:

Master's Degree in Public Policy   (609) 258-4836

Robertson Hall, Princeton University   mpp@wws.princeton.edu

Princeton, NJ 08544-1013   www.wws.princeton.edu/degree/mpp.html

Mellon Fellowships in Humanistic Studies

Seeks to attract exceptionally promising students preparing for careers in teaching and scholarship in humanistic studies, by providing top-level, competitive, portable awards -- contributing thereby to the continuity of teaching and research of the highest order in America's colleges and universities. The Mellon Fellowships seek to identify and encourage persons who are committed to teaching and have a broad vision of learning.

Eligibility: any college senior or recent graduate who has not yet begun graduate study; U.S. citizen or permanent resident; applying to a program leading to the Ph.D. in a humanistic field. High GPA and GRE scores.

Award: $17,500. plus tuition and fees   # Given: 85

Apply by: mid-December (request application by early December)

For more information:

Woodrow Wilson Nat'l. Fellowship Fdn.   (609) 452-7007

Mellon Fellowships   www.woodrow.org/mellon

CN 5329   mellon@woodrow.org

Princeton, NJ 08543-5329

MEXICAN AMERICAN LEGAL DEFENSE/EDUCATIONAL FUND

An annual scholarship for entering, or enrolled law school students with a demonstrated commitment to work with the Latino community.

Eligibility: financial need and academic achievement.

Award: $2,000 - $6,000

For more information:

MALDEF   (213) 629-2512

Law School Scholarship Program

634 Spring Street, 11th Fl.

Los Angeles, CA 90014   www.MALDEF.org/education/scholarships.htm

MISSOURI BOTANICAL GARDEN

Beattie Fellowship for Conservation Horticulture

To promote conservation of rare and endangered flora in the U.S. Fellowship will compensate work done by graduate student at a botanical garden jointly serving the program of the Center for Plant Conservation and the student's curricular studies in biology, horticulture or a related field.

Eligibility: Graduate students with an interest in rare plant conservation. Preference given to students whose projects focus on the endangered flora of the Carolinas and the southeastern U.S.

Award: $1,000 - $4,000   Apply by: December 31

For more information:

Center for Plant Conservation   (314) 577-9452

www.mobot.org/cpc/beattie.html

Chatham Fellowship in Medical Botany

To protect and preserve knowledge about the medicinal use of plants by providing research support in the field of ethnobotany.

Eligibility: Ph.D. candidates and recent Ph.D.graduates (last five years).

Award: $4,000   Apply by: January 15

For more information:

Dr. James S. Miller   (314) 577-9503

Missouri Botanical Garden   james.miller@mobot.org

PO Box 299
St. Louis, MO 63166-0299   www.mobot.org/MOBOT/Research/jobs.shtml

The Nation Institute

Puffin/Nation Prize for Creative Citizenship

The Puffin Foundation Ltd. and the Nation Institute are the mutual sponsors of an annual award given to an individual who has challenged the status quo through distinctive, courageous, imaginative and socially responsible work of significance. Candidates are to be found in a broad range of occupations and pursuits, including academia, journalism, public health, literature, art, the environmental sciences, labor and the humanities.

Award: $100,000

I.F. Stone Award

Seeks to encourage young journalists to engage in the sort of independent investigative journalism exemplified by the late I.F. Stone, who combined progressive politics, investigative zeal and a compulsion to speak truth to power with a steadfast commitment to human rights and the exposure of injustice. Each year a panel selects the work of one student journalist and awards the winner with a cash prize. Prize-winning pieces have explored a corporate cover-up of toxic waste dumping, police brutality and educational grants for prisoners.

Robert Masur Fellowship in Civil Liberties

Each year the Masur Fellowship is awarded to a law student pursuing significant activities during the summer in the area of civil rights and civil liberties. The Fellowship includes a modest honorarium.

For more information:

The Nation Institute   www.nationinstitute.org
33 Irving Place, 8th Floor   (212) 209-5400
New York, NY 10003   instinfo@nationinstitute.org

National Council of State Garden Clubs

See undergraduate listings.

National Estuarine Research Reserve

The Graduate Research Fellowship Program offers qualified master's and doctoral students the opportunity to address scientific questions of local, regional and national significance. The result is high-quality research focused on improving coastal management issues.

All GRF projects must be conducted in a National Estuarine Research Reserve and enhance the scientific understanding of the reserve's ecosystem. While graduate research fellows receive hands-on experience, reserve managers and coastal decision makers receive vital ecological data. Some research projects have focused on natural versus human impacts on estuaries, nonpoint source pollution, invasive species and habitat restoration science.

Eligibility: masters and doctoral candidates.

Award: $17,500   Apply by: November 1

For more information:

    Erica Seiden,   (301)713-3155 ext. 172

    NOAA/Estuarine Reserves Division

    1305 East-West Highway, N/ORM5, SSMC4, 11616

    Floor, Silver Spring, MD 20910   erica.seiden@noaa.gov

    Attn: NERRS GRF.   www.ocrm.nos.noaa.gov/nerr/fellow.html

National Network for Environmental Management Studies Fellowships

The EPA's NNEMS program is a comprehensive fellowship program that provides students an opportunity to participate in a fellowship project that is directly related to their field of study. Each year, the NNEMS program offers approximately 50 to 60 research projects, developed and sponsored by EPA Headquarters in Washington, D.C. and in EPA's ten regional offices throughout the U.S. The projects are specifically narrow in scope, allowing students to complete the research project while working full-time at EPA during the summer or part-time during the school year. Recipients of NNEMS fellowships receive a stipend based on the student's level of education and the project.

Eligibility: Enrolled graduate or undergraduate student.

For more information:

    NNEMS Program   (800)358-8769

    US EPA (1704A)

    1200 Pennsylvania Ave, NW

    Washington, DC 20460   www.epa.gov/epapages/epahome/intern.htm

National Pathfinders Scholarship

See undergraduate listings.

National Sea Grant Federal Fellows

Dean John A. Knauss Marine Policy Fellowships

The Knauss Marine Policy Fellowship provides a unique educational experience to students who have an interest in ocean, coastal, and Great Lakes resources and in the national policy decisions affecting those resources. The program matches highly qualified graduate students with hosts in the legislative branch, the executive branch, or appropriate associations/ institutions located in the Washington, D.C. area for a one-year paid fellowship beginning February 1.

Past offices hosting Fellows include the Senate Commerce, Science, and Transportation Committee; House Committee on Resources; EPA; National Oceanic and Atmospheric Administration; and U.S. Fish and Wildlife Service.

Eligibility: graduate or professional degree students in a marine or aquatic-related field at a U.S. accredited institution of higher education. Individuals who have held a fellowship in the Washington, D.C. area the year prior to the Knauss/Sea Grant Fellowship competition are disqualified.

Stipend: $38,000   # Given: 30

Apply by: Early April   Apply to: local Sea Grant Program

For more information:

Nikola "Kola" Garber   nikola.garber@noaa.gov

Knauss Sea Grant Fellows Program Manager

National Sea Grant College Program   301-713-2431 ext. 124

1315 East-West Highway, R/SG, Room 11718

Silver Spring, MD 20910   www.nsgo.seagrant.org/funding.html

NATIONAL SECURITY EDUCATION PROGRAM

See Undergraduate listing.

NATIONAL URBAN FELLOWS

A full-time graduate program comprised of academic course work and field experience, leading to a MPA from the School of Public Affairs, City University of NY. For talented mid-career individuals committed to the solution of urban and rural problems. The program prepares Fellows for leadership roles in public policy and administration in government agencies and not-for-profit organizations. Academic component is followed by a nine-month "hands-on" mentorship.

Eligibility: U.S. citizen, women or minority, 3-5 years of experience in a managerial or administrative capacity.

Apply by: end February

For more information:

National Urban Fellows   (212)349-6200

59 John Street, Suite 310

New York, NY 10038   www.nuf.org

NATIONAL WILDLIFE FEDERATION ENVIRONMENTAL CONSERVATION FELLOWSHIP

Fellowships are offered to graduate students in fields relating to wildlife, natural resource management, and protection of environmental quality.

Eligibility: Applicants must be citizens of the United States, Canada or the Republic of Mexico.

Award: up to $10,000   Apply by: July 15

For more information:

National Wildlife Federation   (202) 797-6800

Environmental Conservation Fellowship Program.

1412 - 16th Street N.W.

Washington, DC 0036-2266   www.nwf.org/careergateway/fellowshowto.cfm

NATIVE AMERICAN ECONOMIC DEVELOPMENT SCHOLARSHIP

For Native American graduate students in the areas of law, business and planning, who are committed to economic development in Native American communities. The program is a joint venture between UNM's School of Law,

Anderson Schools of Management, and the School of Architecture and Planning.

The aim is to build an interdisciplinary community of Native American professional students who understand the issues of economic development facing Native peoples, and are preparing to become leaders in Native communities.

Eligibility: enrollment in an American Indian tribe, recognition as an Alaska Native by an Alaska Native government, or status as a Native Hawaiian; experience and background in Indian Country or other Native communities, commitment to economic development in Native communities; and potential for leadership in Indian Country or other Native communities.

Award: $5,000, renewable   # Given: 6
Apply by: May 1
For more information:
Susan Mitchell   (505) 277-0572
Director of Admissions   (800) 326-6580
UNM School of Law
Albuquerque, NM   lawschool.unm.edu/finances/aid/lawschool.htm

NEW JERSEY SCHOOL OF CONSERVATION

Fellowship provides field teaching opportunities and course work leading to a Master of Arts Degree in Environmental Studies with a concentration in Environmental Education. Appropriate studies include natural sciences, social sciences, humanities, and outdoor pursuits.

Eligibility: BA degree with a concentration in elementary or secondary education, natural sciences, social studies or related disciplines. 3.0 GPA.

Award: Room, board, $500 stipend, tuition for required courses.
Apply by: January 15
For more information:
Dr. John Kirk, Director and Professor of Environmental Studies
New Jersey School of Conservation   (201) 948-4646
Montclair State University
1 Wapalanne Road
Branchville, NJ 07826   csam.montclair.edu/njsoc/Assistantship.htm

NEW YORK CITY URBAN FELLOWS PROGRAM

A nine-month fellowship combining work in Mayoral offices and City agencies with an intensive seminar component studying key issues facing city government. Fellows become instrumental in the policy planning, long-term research efforts, direct service delivery and day-to-day problem solving responsibilities of the office. Persons interested a career in urban government are encouraged to apply regardless of academic major or previous fields of training.

Eligibility: Graduated college within last 2 years.

Stipend: $25,000 and health insurance   Apply by: Mid January
For more information:
NYC Urban Fellows Program   (212) 669-3695
NYC Department of Citywide Administrative Services

1 Centre Street, Rm 2425
New York, NY 10007   www.nyc.gov/html/dcas/html/urbanfellows.html

Non-Profit Sector Research

William Randolph Hearst Endowed Scholarship for Minority Students

The Nonprofit Sector Research Fund, a grantmaking program of The Aspen Institute in Washington, D.C., offers the William Randolph Hearst Endowed Scholarship in conjunction with a summer internship program open to members of minority groups based on need and academic excellence. Both graduate and undergraduate students are eligible for the award. Through this scholarship program, the Fund seeks to introduce a diverse group of students to issues relating to philanthropy, voluntarism, and nonprofit organizations. Recipients may arrange with their colleges or universities to receive academic credit..

Eligibility: graduate or undergraduate student, financial need, available to attend The Aspen Institute in Washington, D.C. for 10-12 weeks in the summer.

Award: $2,800-$4,200   Apply by: March 15

For more information:

Nonprofit Sector Research Fund   (202) 736-5800
The Aspen Institute   nsrf@aspeninstitute.org
One Dupont Circle, NW, Suite 700
Washington, DC 20036   www.nonprofitresearch.org

Northern Arizona University

See Undergraduate listing.

Park People

See Undergraduate listing.

University of Peace, Costa Rica

The Department for Gender and Peace Studies' Master of Arts Degree in Gender and Peace Building has been designed to address the interaction between Gender and Peace Building when discussing topics such as: The Study of Peace and Nonviolent Transformation of Conflict; Cultures and Cultural Transformation: from a Culture of War to a Culture of Peace; Strategies of Inclusion and Exclusion: Diverse Human Groups; Peace Processes: Conflict Analysis, Resolution and Transformation; Gender Analysis of the Environment and Sustainable Development

With the support of the Government of Finland, a limited number of scholarships are available to students who demonstrate financial need along with superior academic skills and experience within the field of Gender.

For more information:

www.upeace.org   <acadmin@upeace.org>.

Peace Scholar Dissertation Fellowships

Peace Scholars are outstanding doctoral students, from anywhere in the world, who are enrolled in American universities and conducting dissertation research on international peace and conflict management. Peace Scholars are based at their universities or in appropriate field research sites.

Award: $17,000   # Given: 20

Apply by: November 1

For more information:

United States Institute of Peace   (202) 457-1700

Jennings Randolph Program for Int'l. Peace   TTY: (202) 457-1719

1200 17th Street NW, Suite 200   www.usip.org/jrprogram/scholars.html

Washington, DC 20036-3011   jrprogram@usip.org

POPULATION FELLOWS

University Of Michigan offers two professional fellowships to individuals with a recent master's or doctoral degree in areas related to population/repro-ductive health or population-environment. These two year fellowships take place overseas and involve providing technical assistance to organizations in the devel-oping world. Population Fellows are placed with organizations working to improve family planning and reproductive health programs in the developing world. Population-Environment Fellows work on projects that combine assis-tance for threatened environments with attention to the population dynamics and reproductive health needs of the communities living within them.

The Fellowships are service oriented, and are not traditional research fel-lowships. Fellows are expected to provide technical assistance to their host orga-nization in areas that encompass population and environment issues; research activities, if any, must be applied. The program provides training and interna-tional experience in population/environment field work; technical assistance and furthers the development of integrated approaches to population, health, and envi-ronment activities.

The program's notion of population includes areas such as population pol-icy, family planning, demography, and reproductive health among others. For environment, program includes areas such as natural resource management, resource policy, conservation, and environmental health.

Eligibility: graduate degree in relevant field of study; US citizen or perma-nent resident. Work, academic or volunteer experience, in both population and environment. Early career professionals, from 0-5 years experience.

Award: professional-level stipend and benefits

Apply by: November 1, April 1

For more information:

The Population Fellows Programs   (734) 763-9456

U. of Michigan   michiganfellows@umich.edu

1214 South University, 2nd Floor

Ann Arbor, MI 48104-2548   www.sph.umich.edu/pfps

Public Interest Law Fellows Program

Columbia University's Public Interest Law Initiative (PILI) and The Open Society Justice Initiative (formerly the Constitutional and Legal Policy Institute), sponsor five lawyers from Central and Eastern Europe, Russia, Central Asia and the Caucasus ("the region") for two years of study and practical work experience. One slot in the program is specifically designated for women's rights advocates, one slot for disability rights advocates, and one slot for a Roma rights advocate, with the two remaining slots undesignated.

The Fellows will reside a total of one year in the US, consisting of one semester of study at Columbia University and two three-month internships. Fellows will return to their home countries after the first year, where they will spend at least one year working with their nominating NGO on human rights/public interest advocacy on a non-profit basis in such areas as providing legal services, strategic litigation, campaigning for reform, and human rights training/education.

Eligibility: a minimum of two years relevant work experience outside of law school. Preference will be given to applicants under 35 years of age. Minorities, especially Roma, are strongly encouraged to apply.

Award: travel, stipend for up to 12 months, a textbook allowance, and medical insurance for a year while in the US, local salary during the second year that is equal to an amount determined to be similar to equivalent work by the nominating NGO.

Apply by: March 15   # Given: 5

For more information:

Fellowship Program Manager   212-851-1060
435 W. 116th St, Mailcode 3525
New York, New York   www.pili.org

Public Interest Pioneers

The Stern Family Fund supports policy oriented government and corporate accountability projects. In an era of renewed concentration of political and economic power, the Fund is committed to aiding citizens striving to guarantee the responsiveness of public and private institutions.

The Fund supports systemic reform efforts that attack the root causes of societal problems rather than providing direct services to individuals and communities in an attempt to alleviate the symptoms of these problems; projects that strive for a more equitable distribution of political and economic power; and action-oriented projects with the potential for significant impact.

The Fund provides large seed grants to spark the creation of a new organization or development of projects which take an existing organization(s) in new directions. The Fund searches for individuals with meaningful experience who are prepared to launch innovative government and corporate accountability projects. In contrast to entry-level fellowship programs, the Pioneer program seeks individuals who have a solid record of accomplishment in their careers or life work, and are willing to devote themselves full-time to the proposed endeavor.

Grant: $50,000 - $100,000   # Given: 1 - 2

Renewable   Apply by: early January

All initial inquiries and proposals must be submitted in writing. Questions and letters of introduction may be sent by mail, e-mail or fax, but proposals must be submitted by mail.

For more information:

The Stern Family Fund   (703) 527-6692

P.O. Box 1590   sternfund@starpower.net

Arlington, VA 22210-0890   www.sternfund.org

PUBLIC SERVICE SCHOLARSHIP

See undergraduate listing.

RADCLIFFE INSTITUTES FOR ADVANCED STUDY

The Fellowship Program is a scholarly community where individuals pursue advanced work across a wide range of academic disciplines, professions, or creative arts. Radcliffe Institute fellowships are designed to support scholars, scientists, artists, and writers of exceptional promise and demonstrated accomplishment, who wish to pursue work in academic and professional fields and in the creative arts. The Radcliffe Institute sustains a continuing commitment to the study of women, gender, and society.

Applicants whose projects draw on the resources of the Institute's Schlesinger Library on the History of Women (the country's foremost archive in women's history) or the Henry A. Murray Research Center (a national archive of social science data on human development and social change) are looked on favorably, but such a focus is not a requisite for applying.

Eligibility: Scholars, scientists, artists, or writers in any field who have completed a doctorate or appropriate terminal degree at least two years prior to appointment, or comparable professional achievement in the area of the proposed project Creative writers and visual artists must meet specific eligibility criteria. Women and men from any country are encouraged to apply.

Award: up to $50,000   Apply by: October 1

For more information:

Radcliffe Institute Fellowships Office   (617) 496-1324

34 Concord Avenue   www.radcliffe.edu

Cambridge, MA, 02138   fellowships@radcliffe.edu

RHODES SCHOLARSHIPS

Established in 1903 by Cecil Rhodes, who dreamed of improving the world through the diffusion of leaders motivated to serve their contemporaries, trained in the contemplative life of the mind, and broadened by their acquaintance with one another and by their exposure to cultures different from their own. Mr. Rhodes hoped that his plan of bringing able students from throughout the English-speaking world and beyond to study at Oxford University would aid in the promotion of international understanding and peace. Each year, 32 U. S. citizens are among more than 90 Rhodes Scholars worldwide who take up degree courses at Oxford University.

American Rhodes Scholars are selected through a decentralized process by which regional selection committees choose 32 Scholars each year from among those nominated by selection committees in each of the fifty states. In most years, a Rhodes Scholar is selected from an institution which has not formerly supplied a successful applicant. The Rhodes Scholarships are investments in individuals rather than in project proposals.

Eligibility: 1) Literary and scholastic attainments; 2) energy to use one's talents to the full, as exemplified by fondness for and success in sports; 3) truth, courage, devotion to duty, sympathy for and protection of the weak, kindliness, unselfishness and fellowship; 4) moral force of character and instincts to lead, and to take an interest in one's fellow beings. Selection committees seek excellence in qualities of mind and in qualities of person which, in combination, offer the promise of effective service to the world.

Award: All educational costs, such as matriculation, tuition, laboratory and certain other fees, for two years of study at the University of Oxford, with the possibility of renewal for a third year. Additional maintenance allowance for necessary expenses for term-time and vacations. Necessary costs of travel to and from Oxford, and upon application, additional grants for research purposes or study-related travel

Apply by: Check your University/college for their endorsement deadline.

For more information:

Elliot F. Gerson
8229 Boone Boulevard, Suite 240   www.rhodesscholar.org/
Vienna, Virginia 22182   amsec@rhodesscholar.org

ROCKEFELLER STATE WILDLIFE SCHOLARSHIP

See Undergraduate listing.

ROCKY MOUNTAIN NATURE ASSOCIATION FELLOWSHIP

Research may range from wildlife programs to vegetation and riparian studies, fire ecology, cultural and social sciences, archeology and historic structures management. The student awarded the Fellowship will work with Rocky Mountain National Park resource managers and interpreters for a period of three to four months.

Eligibility: Currently enrolled in, or in the process of graduating from, a graduate level program at an accredited college or university.

Stipend: $5,000 + park housing, up to $3,000 for expenses related to research.

Apply by: February 1

For more information:

Rocky Mountain Field Seminars   (970) 586-3262
ATTN: Fellowship Program
Rocky Mountain Nature Association
1895 Fall River Road   sales@rmna.org
Estes Park, CO 80517   www.rmna.org

J.W. Saxe Memorial Prize

See Undergraduate listing.

Schumacher College

Schumacher College is an international center for ecological studies. based in southwest England. The college aims to explore the foundations of a more sustainable, balanced and harmonious world view. Courses are one to five weeks in length, and are led by world-renowned writers and thinkers. Subject areas of courses centre around one of the following themes: ecological economics and development issues; the links between philosophy, psychology and ecology; the new understandings emerging from recent scientific discoveries.

Applicants from the industrialized world are not eligible for scholarship larger than 50% of course fees. Applicants from Eastern Europe and the South may apply for assistance of up to 95% of course fees. The smaller the scholarship requested from the College, the greater the likelihood that it will be granted.

Eligibility: individuals who are now or are likely to become influential in their communities. Working or studying in fields of education, environmentalism, public administration, journalism/ media, community work, or green business.

For more information:

Schumacher College
The Old Postern
Dartington, Totnes
Devon TQ9 6EA, England

schumcoll@gn.apc.org
www.gn.apc.org/schumachercollege/

Albert Schweitzer Fellowship

See Health listing.

Herbert Scoville Jr. Peace Fellowship

Provides college graduates with the opportunity to gain a Washington perspective on key issues of peace and security. Twice yearly, the Fellowship's Board of Directors selects a small group of outstanding individuals to spend six months in Washington. Fellows serve as full-time project assistants at the participating organization of their choice.

Scoville Fellows, through independent projects and active participation with their chosen organization and the larger community dedicated to peace and security issues, have rich opportunities to gain experience and leadership skills and to help translate their social concerns into direct action.

Eligibility: completed baccalaureate degree by the time the Fellowship commences; experience with public-interest activism or advocacy, preferably focused on peace and security issues. Preference given to US citizens.

Stipend: $1,500 per month and health insurance, plus travel to DC.
Apply by: October 15, February 1

For more information:

Paul Revsine, Program Director

Scoville Peace Fellowship Program

110 Maryland Avenue NE, Suite 409

Washington, DC 20002

(202) 543-4100

www.clw.org/pub/clw/scoville/

SEASPACE SCHOLARSHIP PROGRAM

For students pursuing degrees in marine science fields. Approximately 75% of past awards have been to graduate students. Majors have included marine sciences, marine biology, wildlife and fisheries, environmental toxicology, biological oceanography, genetics, ocean engineering, aquaculture, and zoology with marine mammal applications.

Eligibility: junior/senior undergraduate or graduate student pursuing studies in marine biology or other related disciplines in an accredited US college or university (U.S. citizenship is not a requirement); 3.3 GPA and financial need.

Award: $500 - $3,000   # Given: 15

Apply by: February 1

For more information:

www.seaspace.org   captx@piovere.com

DAVID H. SMITH CONSERVATION RESEARCH FELLOWSHIP

Enables outstanding early-career scientists to improve and expand their research skills while directing their efforts towards problems of pressing conservation concern in the U.S. by working closely with conservation practitioners. The two year program seeks especially to encourage individuals who want to better link conservation theory and concepts with pressing policy and management applications.

Eligibility: received a doctorate within the last five years.

Award: approx. $60,000/year   # Given: 5

Apply by: January 31

For more information:

D. H. Smith Fellows Program

The Nature Conservancy

4245 N. Fairfax Drive   postdoc@tnc.org

Arlington, Virginia 22203   smithfellows.org/Smith/proposalguidelines.htm

SMITHSONIAN INSTITUTION FELLOWSHIP PROGRAM

Fellowships are offered to support research at Smithsonian facilities or field stations in a variety of disciplines for graduate, doctoral, postdoctoral research. Some of the Smithsonian institutions that offer fellowships include: National Museum of Natural History; National Zoological Park; Smithsonian Environmental Research Center; Smithsonian Tropical Research Institute; Center for Earth and Planetary Studies of the National Air and Space Museum.

Postdoctoral Fellowships

Eligibility: holds a Ph.D. or equivalent for less than seven years. Senior Fellowships are offered to scholars who have held a Ph.D. or equivalent for seven years or more. The term is 3 to 12 months.

Stipend: $30,000 per year plus allowances.

Predoctoral Fellowships

Eligibility: doctoral candidates who have completed preliminary course work and examinations, and have been advanced to candidacy. Candidates must have the approval of their universities. The term is 3 to 12 months.

Stipend: $17,000 per year plus allowances

Graduate Student Fellowships

Eligibility: students formally enrolled in a graduate program, who have completed at least one semester and have not yet been advanced to candidacy if in a Ph.D. Program. Applicants must submit a proposal for research in a discipline which is pursued at the Smithsonian. The term is 10 weeks.

Stipend: $3,700.

Apply by: January 15th for all fellowships

See listing in undergraduate section as well.

For more information:

Smithsonian Office of Fellowships	202-275-0655
PO Box 37012	siofg@si.edu
Victor Bldg, 9300, MRC 902	
Washington, DC 20013-7012	www.si.edu/ofg

SOCIAL SCIENCE RESEARCH COUNCIL

International Migration to the United States

Program fosters innovative research that will advance theoretical understanding of the origins of immigrants and refugee flows to the US, of the processes of migration and settlement, and of the outcomes for immigrants, refugees and native-born Americans.

What are the factors and processes that cause international migration and determine the types of immigrants and refugees who come to the United States? How does migration alter the gender, family, community, and other social groupings and identities of both immigrants and native-born Americans?

Eligibility: U.S. citizens, permanent residents, or international students at U.S. institutions; matriculated in social science doctoral programs.

Award: $12,000 stipend, up to $3,000 in research expenses.

Given: 7   Apply by: Mid January

For more information:

International Migration Program	(212) 377-2700 ext. 604
	migration@ssrc.org

Philanthropy and the Nonprofit Sector

Provide support for dissertation research on the history, behavior, and role of nonprofit and/or philanthropic organizations in the U.S. For graduate students in the social sciences and humanities to apply their knowledge of the theories and methods of their disciplines to issues concerning philanthropy and the nonprofit sector in the United States.

Eligibility: enrolled in a doctoral program in the U. S.; completed all requirements for the Ph.D. except the research component; conducting research on the U.S. or comparative with other countries; no citizenship requirements and applications from women and persons of color are encouraged.

Award: $18,000   # Given: up to 7

Apply by: early December

For more information: phil-np@ssrc.org

Abe Fellowships

Supports postdoctoral research on contemporary policy-relevant issues. Funds are provided by the Japan Foundation Center for Global Partnership in order to encourage international multidisciplinary research on topics of pressing global concern. The program seeks to foster the development of a new generation of researchers who are interested in policy-relevant topics of long-range importance and who are willing to become key members of a bilateral and global research network built around such topics.

Eligibility: citizens of the U.S. and Japan as well as nationals of other countries who can demonstrate strong affiliations with research communities in Japan or the U. S.; holding a Ph.D. or the terminal degree in their field, or have attained an equivalent level of professional experience.

Apply by: September 1

For more information:

Social Science Research Council
810 Seventh Avenue   www.ssrc.org web
New York NY 10019

SOIL AND WATER CONSERVATION SOCIETY

The Kenneth E. Grant Research Scholarship

Provides financial aid to members of SWCS for graduate-level research on a specific urban conservation topic that will extend the SWCS mission of fostering the science and the art of soil, water, and related natural resource management to achieve sustainability. SWCS actively promotes multi disciplinary research.

The Scholarship Committee encourages submission of research proposals to investigate the following topics: water quality of urban streams and lakes; evaluation of sediment control ordinances; urban streambank and riparian area restoration; citizen involvement in rehabilitation and ongoing care of specific areas; urban stormwater management; habitat improvement in populated areas; urban wetlands restoration and management; urban drinking water protection.

Eligibility: a member of SWCS, eligible for graduate work at an accredited institution, and financial need.

Award: $1300   Apply by: mid-February

Melville Cohee Student Leader Conservation Scholarship

For SWCS members pursuing studies in natural resource conservation such as agricultural economics, planned land use management, forestry, wildlife biology, agricultural engineering, hydrology, rural sociology, water management.

Eligibility: member of SWCS for more than one year, 3.0 GPA, first or second year graduate student at an accredited college or university.

Award: $1000   # Given: 2
Apply by: mid-February

For more information:

SWCS   www.SWCS.org/f_aboutSWCS_chrel.htm
945 SW Ankeny Road   (515)289-2331
Ankeny, Iowa 50021-9764

PAUL & DAISY SOROS FELLOWSHIPS FOR NEW AMERICANS

Provides support for up to two years of graduate study in the U.S. for continuing generations of able and accomplished New Americans to achieve leadership in their chosen fields. The Program is established in recognition of the contributions New Americans have made to American life.

Eligibility: A New American (a resident alien; i.e., holds a Green Card or has been naturalized as a U.S. citizen or is the child of two parents who are both naturalized citizens. A Green Card holder must have had more than one year of IRS filings).Must either have a bachelor's degree or be in her/his final year of undergraduate study; not be older than thirty years of age.

Award: $20,000 + 1/2 tuition grant   #Given: 30

For more information:

Ms. Carmel Geraghty   (212)547-6926
400 West 59th Street   pdsoros_fellows@sorosny.org
New York, NY 10019   www.pdsoros.org

UNIVERSITY OF SOUTHERN CALIFORNIA

Wrigley Institute for Environmental Studies

For grad students interested in environmental science, marine science, ocean engineering or marine policy. Fellowships and research stipends to pursue research interests or other professional opportunities. WIES promotes basic and applied research, as well as training in marine and environmental studies.

Apply by: end February   Renewable

See Undergraduate listing for other opportunities.

For more information:

wrigley.usc.edu/education/summer_grads.html

STANFORD UNIVERSITY CENTER FOR INTERNATIONAL SECURITY AND COOPERATION

Pre/ Postdoctoral Fellowships

The Center invites applications on a broad range of topics related to peace and international security, such as security relationships in Europe, Asia, and the Former Soviet Union; U.S.-Russian strategic relations; U.S. defense and arms control policies; proliferation of nuclear, chemical, and biological weapons; ethnic and civil conflict; peacekeeping; the prevention of deadly conflict; the commercialization of national defense technologies. Visiting fellows spend the academic year at Stanford University completing their projects.

Hamburg Fellowships

Brings outstanding young scholars from around the world to Stanford to work on issues related to preventing deadly conflict - both in the pre-conflict stage, and in the implementation phase of peace agreements. Topics might include issues of policing, judiciaries, and civil-military relations; the use of sanctions and other economic tools for the prevention of conflict; mediation processes, and other forms of third-party intervention; environmental degradation and its effect on deadly conflict; and the role of leadership in prevention.

Eligibility: For both Hamburg and Doctoral fellows, Ph.D. candidates who have made substantial progress toward the completion of their dissertation and scholars with Ph.D. or equivalent degrees in a broad range of disciplines, including anthropology, economics, history, law, political science, sociology, medicine, and the natural and physical sciences.

Stipend: $20,000 predoctoral and Hamburg fellows

$33,000 postdoctoral   Apply by: February 1

Science Fellows Program

Offers natural scientists and engineers an opportunity to explore the policy dimensions of a research topic of their choosing in an interdisciplinary environment. Past research areas have included: policy issues regarding nuclear, biological, and chemical weapons and delivery systems prospects for international control of weapons of mass destruction; nuclear-weapons safety and security; global diffusion of information technology; assessing antiballistic missile defenses; export controls on high technology defense conversion environmental security; security issues associated with energy development.

Eligibility: science and engineering post-doctoral fellows and mid-career professionals in academic and research institutions, government, and industry, from the U.S. and abroad.

Award: stipend, health insurance and funds for travel and research.

For more information:

Barbara Platt	(650) 723-9626
Center for Int'l. Security & Cooperation	barbara.platt@stanford.edu
Encina Hall	
Stanford	cisac.stanford.edu

TEMPLETON SCIENCE OF OPTIMISM AND HOPE

Awarded to a graduate student who has completed a Ph.D. dissertation on the subject of Optimism and Hope, with plans to continue research in the future.

Award: $1,000 + travel to American Psychological Ass'n. Convention.

Apply by: April 15

For more information:

Director of Communications	www.templeton.org/seligmanaward/index.htm
The John Templeton Foundation	

Five Radnor Corporate Center, Suite 100
100 Matsonford Road
Radnor, PA 19087

TINKER FIELD RESEARCH

Provides graduate students with travel funds (international and in-country) to Latin America, Spain and Portugal. Grants are awarded by university institutes/ centers for brief periods of research in areas of economic policy and governance. Targeted social science disciplines having strong public policy implications, and environmental policy studies.

Award: $10,000, $15,000   Apply by: October 1

For more information:

Tinker Field Research   (212) 421-6858
55 East 59th Street   tinker@tinker.org
New York, NY 10022   fdncenter.org/grantmaker/tinker/

TRANSPORTATION FELLOWSHIP

See Undergraduate listing.

TRIBAL LANDS ENVIRONMENTAL SCIENCE SCHOLARSHIP

This program's intent is to enable Native Americans to work for the environmental protection of tribal lands by assisting them in their pursuit of environmental science degrees. Students compete based on grade-point average, knowledge of Indian culture, commitment to environmental protection, character and leadership ability, level of study, and work experience.

Eligibility: Full-time junior, senior, and graduate students majoring in an environmental discipline are eligible to compete for the scholarships.

Apply by: June 15

For more information:

American Indian Science and Engineering Society (AISES)
1630 30th Street, Suite 301   (303) 939-0023
Boulder, CO 80301   www.aises.org

TROPICAL ECOLOGY

ICTE, Marlin Perkins Memorial & Birge Tropical Research Scholarships
Graduate research scholarship available to M.S. or Ph.D. student who is conducting research in the tropics in ecology, conservation, or systematics.

John Denver Memorial & Mallinckrodt Scholarships in Tropical Ecology
Graduate research scholarship available to M.S. or Ph.D. student who is conducting research in the tropics in ecology, conservation, or systematics.

Parker-Gentry Research Fellowship
Graduate research scholarship available to Latin American M.S. or Ph.D. student conducting field research in Bolivia, Nicaragua, Brazil, Colombia, Costa Rica, Ecuador, Guatemala, Honduras, Guyana or Peru.

Other fellowships for students from tropical countries available.

For more information:

Int'l. Center for Tropical Ecology   (314) 516-6200
University of Missouri-St. Louis   icte@umsl.edu
8001 Natural Bridge Road   www.umsl.edu/~biology/icte/
St. Louis, MO 63121

TROPICAL NON-TIMBER FOREST PRODUCTS

The Kleinhans Fellowship for Research aims to promote research into the practical means of managing and using tropical forest resources without destroying the integrity of the forest ecosystem. Research should synthesize elements of conservation and business, and must lead to the development of a product or marketing technique providing income for community-based groups living in or near tropical forest areas. Research involving any tropical forest type, in Latin America is eligible.

The results of the research should be an economically viable strategy that encourages sustainable resource extraction from tropical forests. This extraction could supply food, fiber, medicinals or other products for which there is an existing or potential domestic and/or foreign market. Research concerning products that encourage the reforestation of degraded areas is also eligible. Strategy options include using one or several forest products, building on the knowledge of native forest inhabitants (as long as this method proves useful to those same people), and adding value to forest products.

Eligibility: master's degree in forestry, ecology, environmental science, or appropriate related fields; doctoral candidates or post-doctoral researchers preferred. Relevant experience can be substituted for degrees.

Award: $15,000 per year for two years   Apply by: January 31

For more information:

Rainforest Alliance   (619) 456-2944
665 Broadway, Suite 500
New York, NY 10012

www.rainforest-alliance.org/programs/cg/kleinhans.html

UNCOMMON LEGACY FOUNDATION

See undergraduate listing.

UNITED NATIONS UNIVERSITY /SUSTAINABILITY

The Institute of Advanced Studies Fellowship provides a forum for stakeholders to discuss issues relating to global sustainability. The goals of the forums have been in keeping with a long-term perspective needed to address the many complex policy issues involved in the search for global sustainability. The Ph.D. Fellowship Program targets Ph.D. candidates from other institutions around the world who can benefit from a period of stay of up to ten months at UNU/IAS. With a view to strengthening capacity-building in developing countries, students from developing countries - particularly from developing country institutions -

are especially encouraged to apply.

Research topics should relate to sustainability and development; urban and regional development; environment; multilateralism and governance; and information technology/ virtual universities. Fellows carry out their research in Tokyo under the supervision of a UNU/IAS faculty member and/or affiliated UNU/IAS network scholars.

Eligibility: student at dissertation stage of Ph.D. with a research proposal accepted by the candidate's university, and able to make use of the UNU/IAS facilities in Tokyo to carry out their research

Award: ¥ 250,000 (that's yen.)   Apply by: May 15

For more information:

Ph.D. Fellowship Programme   813-5467-2324 fax
UNU/Institute of Advanced Studies   fellowship@ias.unu.edu
5-53-67 Gingumae   www.ias.unu.edu/fellowships/phdfellow.cfm
Shibuya-ku Tokyo 150-8304, Japan

WASTE MGM'T. EDUCATION RESEARCH CONSORTIUM

The WERC fellowship program is designed to encourage students to take environmentally focused courses while pursuing higher education. Fellowships and scholarships are available to undergraduate and graduate students who are pursuing degrees in an environmental field.

Eligibility: U.S Citizens or a permanent residents full-time students taking an environmentally related course of studies pursuing an Environmental Management Certificate or Minor.

Award: $150 to $1,000

For more information:

New Mexico State University
Environmental Fellows Program
Box 30001, Dept. 3805   (505) 646-7821
Las Cruces, NM 88003   www.werc.net/students/aid.htm

WILDERNESS SOCIETY

The Gloria Barron Wilderness Society Scholarship is awarded annually to a graduate student in natural resources management, law or policy programs. The scholarship seeks to encourage individuals who have the potential to make a significant positive difference in the long-term protection of wilderness in North America. The award is made in support of research and preparation of a paper on an aspect of wilderness establishment, protection, or management.

Award: $10,000   Apply by: March 1

For more information:

Ecology and Economics Research Department   (202) 429-3944
The Wilderness Society
1615 M Street, NW
Washington, DC 20036   www.tws.org/newsroom/barron_scholarship.htm

Wildlife Ecology scholarships

Research interests must relate to wildlife management & conservation or a closely related area including: animal behavior, biology, botany, conservation education, ecology, mammalogy, ornithology, parasitology, range science, veterinary pathology, and wildlife and fisheries sciences.

Eligibility: approved candidates for M.S. or Ph.D. degrees at U.S. colleges/universities with 3.0 GPA and GRE 1100.

Award: $1,000-$1,100 + travel allowance   Apply by: October 1

For more information:

Director   (512) 364-2643
Rob and Bessie Welder Wildlife Fdn.   welderwf@aol.com
P. O. Box 1400
Sinton, TX 78387   hometown.aol.com/welderwf/fellowship.html

Women's Law and Public Policy Fellowship Program

Enables law graduates with a special interest in women's rights to work in the nation's capital with a variety of organizations involved in legal and policy issues affecting women. Those selected for participation are placed with different entities, such as women's rights groups, civil rights groups, Congressional offices, governmental agencies, and Georgetown University Law Center (GULC) clinics working on women's issues. They are required to work exclusively on women's rights issues. They also attend regular seminars on current issues sponsored by the Program, and may audit GULC courses on gender and the law and women's legal history. Since 1993 the Fellowship Program has also administered a program for international attorneys: Leadership and Advocacy for Women in Africa Program.

For more information:

Women's Law and Public Policy Fellowship Program
The Georgetown University Law Center   (202) 662-9650
600 New Jersey Avenue, N.W. Suite 334   wlppfp@law.georgetown.edu
Washington, DC 20001   www.wlppfp.org

Woodrow Wilson International Center for Scholars

Civil Society Nonprofit Scholars Program

The Corporation for National and Community Service and the Woodrow Wilson International Center for Scholars created this program for scholars who wish to spend nine months conducting applied research that will illuminate contemporary public policy issues and increase the body of research on the intersection of civil society, the nonprofit sector, volunteerism, and public policy. Scholars will receive a stipend based on their current salary, and be located at the Corporation in Washington.

Award: up to $85,000   Apply by: early February

For more information:

civilsocietyscholars@wwic.si.edu
www.nationalservice.org/scholars
www.wilsoncenter.org/scholars

Residential Fellowships

The Center awards approximately 20-25 residential fellowships annually to individuals with outstanding project proposals in a broad range of the social sciences and humanities on national and/or international issues. Topics intersect with questions of public policy or provide the historical and/or cultural framework to illumine policy issues of contemporary importance.

Eligibility: (for both fellowships) men and women from any country with a wide variety of backgrounds (including government, the corporate world, and the professions, as well as academia). For academic participants, eligibility is limited to the post-doctoral level.

Award: up to $85,000   Apply by: October 1

For more information:

Scholar Selection and Services Office   (202)691-4170
Woodrow Wilson International Center for Scholars
One Woodrow Wilson Plaza
1300 Pennsylvania Avenue, N.W.   fellowships@wwic.si.edu
Washington, D.C. 20004-3027   wwics.si.edu

WOODROW WILSON NATIONAL FELLOWSHIPS

Wilson Public Scholarship Grants: Imagining America

Woodrow Wilson National Fellowships strive to maximize the effects of education for the public good. The Foundation seeks to further the ways in which university-based artists and humanists contribute to our civic heritage and civic future. Campus artists, humanists and community partners together will define a project that focuses on an issue of cultural or social significance at the local, regional or national level. Projects might include: documenting and interpreting the histories and cultural practices of a place; creating a performing arts piece that engages unlikely partners; or developing a public work or presentation that explores an issue of social concern such as AIDS, homelessness, aging, or environmental preservation. Preference given to projects that reach across disciplines or encourage collaboration between or among universities and colleges.

Eligibility: university-based humanists and artists with full-time appointments. Co-investigators should be teachers, artists, or other community leaders.

Award: $6,000   # Given: 5

For more information:

www.woodrow.org/imagining-america/rfp.html

Thomas R. Pickering Foreign Affairs Fellowship Program

The Graduate FAF Program provides fellowship funding to participants as they are prepared academically and professionally to enter the United States Department of State Foreign Service. Women, members of minority groups historically underrepresented in the Foreign Service, and students with financial need are encouraged to apply.

The Graduate Program develops a source of trained men and women who will represent the skill needs of the Department and who are dedicated to representing America's interests abroad. Each successful candidate is obligated to a minimum of three years service in an appointment as a Foreign Service Officer.

Eligibility:U. S. citizens with a minimum undergraduate GPA of 3.2.; applying to graduate school for a two-year full-time master's degree program (such as public policy, international affairs, public administration, or academic fields such as business, economics, political science, sociology or foreign languages).

Award: Tuition, room, board, and mandatory fees are paid for the first year and second year of graduate study, with reimbursement for books and one round-trip travel. Additional stipends during participation in one domestic summer internship between the first and second year of graduate school, and one summer overseas internship following the second year of graduate school.

Apply by: February 28

For more information:

pickeringgfaf@woodrow.org   www.woodrow.org/public-policy

Humanities at Work Practicum Grants

Support Humanities Ph.D. students who have created summer internships (May to September) for themselves that engage their scholarship in a context outside of college teaching and research. As part of the Humanities at Work initiative, Practicum Grants address three challenges: to expand the career horizons of doctoral students in the humanities; to bring the insight of the humanities to all aspects of American life; and to bring the life of the larger community into the academy.

The range of internship possibilities is unlimited. A successful applicant must demonstrate a strong relationship between the proposed internship and his/her field of study. The 2003 granting theme centers on American communities where poverty has diminished access to opportunities enabling children and adults to explore and express creative endeavors.

Eligibility: currently enrolled PhD students who are making timely progress toward completion of their degree in the humanities or humanistic social sciences. Applicants must be U.S. Citizens or Permanent Residents.

Award: up to $2,000   # Given: 20

Apply by: mid-March

For more information:

practicum@woodrow.org   www.woodrow.org/phd/Practicum/practicum.html

The Woodrow Wilson - Johnson & Johnson Dissertation Grants

Encourage original and significant research on issues related to women's health. These grants are interested in the implications of research for the understanding of women's lives and significance for public policy or treatment. Previous grants have concerned smoking, estrogen, and lung cancer; maternal and child health development; AIDS awareness and prevention; dietary determinants of morbidity and mortality; sex and violence in everyday life; and new reproductive technologies.

Eligibility: Students in doctoral programs such as nursing, public health, anthropology, history, sociology, psychology, and social work, at U.S. schools.

Awards: $5,000   # Given: 10

Apply by: early November

For more information:

www.woodrow.org/womens-studies/health/purpose.html

Charlotte W. Newcombe Doctoral Dissertation Fellowships

Designed to encourage original and significant study of ethical or religious values in all fields of the humanities and social sciences. In addition to topics in religious studies or in ethics (philosophical or religious), dissertations might consider the ethical implications of foreign policy, the values influencing political decisions, the moral codes of other cultures, and religious or ethical issues reflected in history or literature.

Eligibility: candidates for Ph.D. or Th.D. degrees in doctoral programs at graduate schools in the U.S., in the writing stage of the dissertation.

Award: $17,000   # Given: 33

Apply by: early December

For more information

www.woodrow.org/newcombe/newcombe_purpose.html

The Woodrow Wilson Dissertation Grants in Women's Studies

Encourage original and significant research about women that crosses disciplinary, regional, or cultural boundaries. Recent winning topics include Women, Law, and the Victorian Novel; Middle East Feminists, Gender and Computer Communication; African American Women in Slave Revolts; and Women, Violence, and Visual Representation in South Africa.

Eligibility: Students in doctoral programs who have completed all pre-dissertation requirements in any field of study at graduate schools in the U.S.

Awards: $3,000   # Given: up to 15

Apply by: early November

For more information:

www.woodrow.org/womens-studies/purpose.html

Woodrow Wilson National. Fellowship Foundation

CN 5281   www.woodrow.org

Princeton NJ 08543-5281   (609) 452-7007

WORCESTER COUNTY HORTICULTURAL SCHOLARSHIP

See undergraduate listings.

WORLD WITHOUT WAR COUNCIL

Americans and World Affairs Fellows Program

A jointly sponsored career development project serving Bay Area non-governmental organizations with a range of political perspectives and work strategies. Program is intended to develop leaders capable of contributing to progress toward the non-violent resolution of international conflict and the well-being of democratic societies. Provides fellows with work experience; seminars that study competing goals, assumptions; and ethical perspectives which shape differing positions on international issues; and encounters with key organizational leaders.

For more information:

World Without War Council   (510) 845-1992

YALE

Summer Public Interest Funding/Law

Yale students working in public interest, government, & nonprofit organizations.

Eligibility: Yale law students; financial need.

Award: $294 per week up to 12 weeks   # Given: 100+

For more information:

www.law.yale.edu/outside/html/financial_aid/fa-summer.htm

President's Public Service Fellowship

The President's Public Service Fellowship provides support 8 weeks of summer work in New Haven nonprofit and municipal agencies.

Eligibility: Yale undergraduate, graduate, and professional students.

Award: $3,600 - $6,000   # Given:30-40

Apply by: end January

For more information:

Yale Office of New Haven Affairs   www.yale.edu/ppsf/index.html

433 Temple St.

New Haven, CT 06520

Cover/Lowenstein Fellowship

A two-year position designed for lawyers with international human rights or other relevant experience who are interested in preparing for a career in human rights practice or human rights teaching. The Fellow will help supervise the Allard K. Lowenstein International Human Rights Clinic and coordinate activities of the Orville H. Schell, Jr. Center for International Human Rights.

Eligibilty: an American J.D. degree; Bar membership in a state/ jurisdiction of the U.S.

Stipend: $40,000/year + health benefits   Apply by: March 1

For more information:

Orville H. Schell, Jr. Center for International Human Rights

P.O. Box 208215

New Haven, CT 06520-8215

schell.law@yale.edu

INDEX

UnderGrad Scholarships

Amer. Geological Inst. Minority Geoscience
American Geological Institute
American Humanics Association
American Meteorological Society
American Occupational Therapy
American Planning Association
Arizona Hydrological Society
Arkansas Environmental Association
Association of California Water Agencies
Association of State Dam Safety Officials
Bat Conservation International
Blinks Research Fellowship Program
CA Adolescent Nutrition & Fitness
CA Ass'n. of Black Social Workers
CA Congress of Parents & Teachers
Cabell Brand Fellowships
California Sea Grant
California Teachers Association
California Water Environment Association
Center for Environmental Citizenship
Congressional Hispanic Caucus Institute
Connecticut Forest and Park Association
Conservation Federation of Missouri
Council on Int'l. Educational Exchange
CT Ass'n. of Latin Americans in Higher Ed
Darling Marine Center
Demonstration of Energy-Efficient Dev'ts
Entomological Society of America
Financial Women's Assoc. of San Francisco
FIRST Scholarship
Florida Excellence in Service Awards
Forest Landowners Foundation
Freehold Soil Conservation District
Garden Club of America
Gates Millennium Scholars
Glamour's Top Ten College Women
Golden Apple Scholars of Illinois
Hawaii Community Foundation
Hawkinson Foundation for Peace and Justice
Hearst Minority/Philanthropic/Non-Profit
Hewitt Memorial Scholarship
Hudson River Foundation
Indiana Wildlife Federation
Institute for International Public Policy
Kentucky Environmental Protection
Kettle Range Conservation Group
Key Club International
Leaders of Tomorrow Scholarship Program
Louisiana Water Environment Association
Maine Community Foundation

Maine Mitchell Scholars
MANA Raquel Marquez Frankel Scholarship
Marine Summer Science
McDonald's "Serve Your Community"
Scholarship
Mellon Minority Fellowship for Ecology
Migrant Scholarships
Mote Marine Laboratory
Nat'l. Council of State Garden Clubs
Nation Institute
National Network for Environmental
Management Studies Fellowships
National Pathfinders Scholarship
National Security Education Program
New Education Foundation College Grants
NYC Government Scholars Program
NSF Research Experience for Undergraduate
NY Water Environment Association
OTS Minority Scholars Program
Park People
Posse Foundation
Public Service Scholarship
Resource Conservation/ San Diego
Rhode Island Foundation
Rockefeller State Wildlife Scholarship, LA
Rocky Mountain Elk Foundation
Saw Mill River Audubon, NY
Saxe Memorial Public Service
Smithsonian Institute
Soil & Water Conservation Society
Student Environmental Associate Program
and Diversity Initiative
Telacu Educational Foundation
Toad Suck Daze Scholarships
Transportation Fellowship
Tribal Lands Environmental Science
Uncommon Legacy Foundation
United Negro College Fund
Waste Mgm't. Ed. Research Consortium
Water Environment Federation
Woodrow Wilson Fellowship Program
Young Feminist Scholarship

College & University Based Scholarships

Allegheny College
AmeriCorps Matching Scholarships
Antioch College
Arizona State University
Augsburg College
Bates College
Bonner Scholar Program
Brevard Community College
Brown University
Cansius College
Center for Global Education
Chatham College
Clemson University
Colorado State University
Cornell University
Cumberland College
Defiance College
DePauw College
Duke University
Earlham College
Eckerd College
Emory & Henry College
Evergreen State College
Florida State University
Fresno/ CA State
Green Mountain College
Hiroki Kaku Memorial
Hood College
Hunter College
Indiana-Purdue U Indianapolis
Lansing Community College
Lasell College
Lesley College
Loras College
Manchester College
Marquette U
Maryville College
McKendree College
Millikin University
Missouri Valley College
Monterey Institute
New College Florida Heritage Award
New England College
North Carolina State University
Northern Arizona University
Norwich University

Notre Dame University
Oberlin College
Ohio Wesleyan U
Olivet College
Otterbein College
Pitzer College
Plattsburgh
Portland State University
Providence College
Purdue University
Sam Houston State
Seattle University
Smith College
Sonoma State University
Southwest Missouri State
St. John Fisher College
Stanford University
Sterling College
Strauss Scholarship
Swarthmore College
University of Maryland/ Shriver Center
University of Massachusetts
University of Michigan-Flint
University of Minnesota
University of New Hampshire
University of Puget Sound
University of San Francisco
University of Southern California
University of Washington
University of Wisconsin-Madison
Vanderbilt
Virginia Tech University
Wabash College
Warren Wilson College
Washington State University
Wesleyan University
Western Washington University
Wheaton College
Wilson College
Xavier University
Yale

HEALTH

ACOG/Ortho-McNeil History Fellowship
AMBUCS Scholarships for Therapists
American College of Nurse-Midwives
American Dental Hygienists
Betty Ford Center
Critical Care Nurses
Georgia Country Doctor
Harvard Minority Health Policy
Indian Health Service
Michigan Osteopathic Scholarships
Migrant Health Care
N.C. Health, Science, & Math Loan
National Health Service Corps
National Medical Fellowships
National Student Nurses' Association
Native Hawaiian Health Professions
NC Health, Science and Math
NY State Primary Care Service Corps
NY State Regents Medicine and Dentistry
RMHC/UNCF Health/Medical Scholars
Schweitzer Fellows Program
Utah Rural Physician Scholarship
WA Rural Physician/Midwife

GRADUATE AND POST-GRADUATE FELLOWSHIPS (INCLUDING NON-PROFIT & COMMUNITY BASED)

AEF Summer Fellowships
Air & Waste Management
Amer. Ass'n. for Advancement of Science
Amer. Geological Inst. Minority Geoscience
American Ass'n. of University Women
American Bar Association (ABA) Legal Opportunity Scholarship Fund
American Geological Institute
American Meteorological Society
American Museum of Natural History
American Occupational Therapy
American Planning Association
American Sociological Association
American Water Works Association
Arizona Hydrological Society

Arkansas Environmental Association
Asian-Pacific Amer. Inst.
Association to Unite the Democracies
Atlantic Fellowships in Public Policy
Atlantic Salmon
Axford Fellowships in Public Policy
Bat Conservation International
Blackmun Law
Blinks Research Fellowship Program
Boston Consortium on Gender, Security and Human Rights Fellows Program
CA Ass'n. of Black Social Workers
California Teachers Association
California Water Environment Association
Carnegie Endowment for Int'l Peace
Central States Water Association
Churchill Scholarship
Colorado Trust Fellows
Concern America
Congressional Fellowships on Women and Public Policy
Congressional Hispanic Caucus Institute
Connecticut Forest and Park Association
Conservation Federation of Missouri
DISL Graduate Fellowships
Dolan, IV Conservation Fellowship
Douglass African/African-American
Du Bois-Mandela-Rodney Fellowship
Ducks Unlimited's Institute
Duke Conservation Fellowship Program
East-West Center,
Easthjustice Legal Defense
Eisenhower/Clifford Roberts
El Pomar Fellowship
Entomological Society of America
Environmental Fellowship & Leadership
Environmental Law Essay
Environmental Management
Environmental Protection Agency
Equal Justice Works
ETS
Financial Women's Assoc. of San Francisco
Fulbright
Garden Club of America

Gardner Fellowship

Gender and Globalization in Asia/ Pacific

Global Public Service Law Project

Hanke - Community Associations

Harvard Public Interest Law

Hawaii Community Foundation

Hawkinson Foundation for Peace and Justice

Hearst Minority/Philanthropic/Non-Profit

Heller School for Social Policy

Institute for Women's Policy Research

International Peace Scholarship Fund

Joint Japan/ World Bank

Kentucky Environmental Protection

Krauss Fellowship Competition

Land Economics

Land Stewardship for Conservation Prof's

Levy Fellowships

Link Foundation Energy Fellowship

Louisiana Water Environment Association

MacArthur Consortium Int'l. Peace

MacArthur Fellowship

Marsh Conservation Fellowship

McNamara Fellowship

Mellon Fellowships in Humanistic Studies

Mexican Amer. Legal Defense/Ed. League

Missouri Botanical Garden

Nat'l. Council of State Garden Clubs

Nation Institute

National Estuarine Research Reserve

National Network for Environmental Management Studies Fellowships

National Pathfinders Scholarship

National Sea Grant Federal Fellows

National Security Education Program

National Urban Fellows

National Wildlife Federation Environmental Conservation Fellowship

Native American Economic Development

NJ School of Conservation

Nonprofit Sector Research

Northern Arizona University

NYC Government Fellows Program

NYC Urban Fellows Program

Park People

Peace Scholar Dissertation

Population Fellows, U Michigan

Public Interest Law Fellows Program

Public Interest Pioneers

Public Service Scholarship

Radcliffe Institute

Rhodes Scholar

Rockefeller State Wildlife Scholarship, LA

Rocky Mountain Nature Association

Saxe Memorial Public Service

Schumacher College

Scoville Peace Fellowship

Seaspace

Smith Conservation Research Fellowship

Smithsonian Institute

Social Science Research Council

Soil & Water Conservation Society

Soros Fellowships for New Americans

Soros Justice Fellowships

Stanford University

Templeton Science of Optimism & Hope

Teresa Heinz Environmental Research

Tinker Field Research

Transportation Fellowship

Tribal Lands Environmental Science

Tropical Ecology

Tropical Non-Timber Forest

Uncommon Legacy Foundation

United Nations University/ Sustainability

University of Peace

University of Southern California

Waste Mgm't. Ed. Research Consortium

Wilderness Society

Wildlife Ecology

Women's Law and Public Policy Fellowship

Woodrow Wilson Fellowship Program

Woodrow Wilson International Center for Scholars

World Without War

Yale

ORDER FORM

Please send me ___ copy (ies) of
    ❑ Making A Difference College & Graduate Guide
Enclose $18.50 per copy, plus $4.50 for shipping for first copy,
$2.00 shipping for each additional book.

Please send me ___ copy (ies) of
    ❑ Making A Difference Scholarships
      For A Better World
Enclose $14 per copy, plus $4.50 for shipping for first copy,
$2.00 shipping for each additional book.

❑ Please bill my Mastercard/Visa account # _____

Signature_____ Exp. Date_____

Name_____ PO#_____

Address_____

City, State, Zip _____

Telephone_____

Please send the person named below information about your books.

Name_____

Address_____

City, State, Zip _____

Make checks payable to:
SageWorks Press
P.O. Box 441
Fairfax, CA 94978-0441

or call (800) 218-GAIA

info@sageworks.net
www.making-a-difference.com